W9-DEC-573

*Barth does say everything that has to be said
here, but he says too much else beforehand.*

Dietrich Bonhoeffer,
Act and Being, 1930

*Dear Mr Bonhoeffer!
What a pickle to be in!*

Charlotte von Kirschbaum,
letter to Bonhoeffer
dated 17 May 1942

*Karl's cigar is on the table in front of me,
and what an unimaginable reality that is.*

Dietrich Bonhoeffer,
letter to Eberhard Bethge
dated 26 November 1943

Bluml
5/00

KARL BARTH
in the Theology of
DIETRICH BONHOEFFER

Andreas Pangritz

Translated by

Barbara and Martin Rumscheidt

WILLIAM B. EERDMANS PUBLISHING COMPANY

GRAND RAPIDS, MICHIGAN / CAMBRIDGE, U.K.

Originally published in German as
Karl Barth in der Theologie Dietrich Bonhoeffers: eine notwendige Klarstellung
© 1989 Alektor Verlag, Westberlin, Germany

This English translation © 2000 by Wm. B. Eerdmans Publishing Co.
255 Jefferson Ave. S.E., Grand Rapids, Michigan 49503 /
P.O. Box 163, Cambridge CB3 9PU U.K.
All rights reserved

Printed in the United States of America

05 04 03 02 01 00   7 6 5 4 3 2 1

ISBN 0-8028-4281-X

For Eberhard Bethge

Contents

Foreword   ix

Abbreviations   xi

Introduction: Bonhoeffer as Prophet of the
  "Post-Barthian Period"?   1

I. **The Problem**   5

  1. Bonhoeffer's "Arcane Discipline" and Barth's
  "Positivism of Revelation"   5

  2. Lutheran or Reformed? The Search for the
  "Point of Difference"   7

  3. A Critical Movement within the Barthian Movement   11

II. **Karl Barth in Bonhoeffer's Theological Development**   15

  1. The Discovery of Dialectical Theology   15

  2. In the Undertow of the Luther Renaissance   18

  3. The Critical Academic Discussion with Barth   22

  4. As a "Barthian" in the United States of America 31

  5. The Meeting in Bonn and Its Consequences   34

CONTENTS

6. The Question of Ethical Concreteness   39

7. The "Aryan Clause" as *Casus Confessionis*   47

8. An "Ongoing, Silent Discussion"   51

9. Bonhoeffer's Swiss Visits and the *Ethics*   60

10. An Interim Summation   69

III. Once Again: What Is "Positivism of Revelation"?   71

1. "Positivism of Revelation" in Luther   71

2. "Positivism of Revelation" in the Confessing Church   76

3. Once More: "Positivism of Revelation" in Karl Barth?   82

4. Critique of Religion and "Nonreligious" Christianity   87

5. "Prayer and Righteous Action"   94

6. A Difference in Method?   97

7. "Virgin Birth, Trinity, or Anything Else"   99

IV. Proceeding on Barth's and Bonhoeffer's Way   115

1. Merely a Misunderstanding?   115

2. "Arcane Discipline" and "Double Predestination"   118

3. Barth's "Doctrine of Lights" as a Correction of
"Positivism of Revelation"?   132

Conclusion: Theological Liberalism Recycled?   143

Bibliography   149

Index   161

Foreword

Scholarly research and publication in the humanities follow a fairly consistent pattern. Someone's thought and writing evoke response and discussion, which, in turn, elicits rejoinder and critique in both informal and formal publication. Over time, articles in journals give way to monographs, the fertile ground on which grow dissertations in graduate studies research. The significance of this penultimate phase lies in that it provides a broad overview of the preceding discussion and establishes initial summary conclusions. The final phase is the encyclopedic entry on the subject matter, which includes the initial work of the thinker involved and the subsequent engagement of that work. But the pattern does not come to a halt in this final phase. The encyclopedia article itself initiates a new and similar pattern of response, discussion, rejoinder, and publication, and so on.

Andreas Pangritz's book competently depicts this pattern. His thorough knowledge of the primary materials, the works of Karl Barth and Dietrich Bonhoeffer, and much of the rather extensive secondary literature on these two seminal theological minds, his own authoritative dissertation on Bonhoeffer's concept of arcane (or secret) discipline, and, finally, his critical engagement of the full presentation in the newest edition of *Theologische Realenzyklopädie* of Dietrich Bonhoeffer's life and work and their reception in church and theology are all very much present in this book. He opens a new round of discussion with his well-argued, ground-breaking, and provocative thesis.

The original German edition has for its subtitle these words: *eine notwendige Klarstellung,* "a necessary rectification." To combine "necessary" and "rectificaidt" is tantamount to throwing down the glove in the arena of theological scholars. A generation's interpretation of Bonhoeffer's charge that Barth had lapsed, so to speak, into the error of positivism of revelation is said to be in need of "rectification." One may confidently anticipate rejoinders to Pangritz's "rectification" and critique of the diverse aspects of Bonhoeffer's own understanding of Barth's theology and of the subsequent interpretation of Bonhoeffer that he addresses in this book. His own depiction of positivism of revelation, benefiting from a discussion that has been in process for well over three decades, will itself result in new approaches to both theologians on whom this book focuses.

Andreas Pangritz's participation in the International Bonhoeffer Society for Archive and Research, in both its English- and German-language sections, has helped him to link fruitfully the study of Bonhoeffer on both sides of the Atlantic. His attentiveness to North American scholarship in this area has met with appreciation here. As a result, this book will be welcomed as a conversation *entre nous* even though his challenge very much addresses the study of Dietrich Bonhoeffer (and, one would add, of Karl Barth) in the United States and Canada. Yet, the value of this work extends to English-language research on Bonhoeffer beyond the boundaries of this subcontinent inasmuch as Pangritz adds to the knowledge of not only what contributed to the *development* of Bonhoeffer's theology but also, and in particular, of how the person and work of Karl Barth *impacted* Bonhoeffer over the course of more than twenty years.

The publication of this extensively revised and expanded translation of the German version almost coincides with the ninetieth birthday of Eberhard Bethge and is dedicated to him. Andreas Pangritz's book is a strong tribute to this respected nonagenarian and to his life's work. This study listens to Bethge attentively and appreciatively and then does what amounts to the highest honor a student can pay to the teacher: it goes *with* him *beyond* him. In advancing Bethge's work, now at rest, may this book continue it by keeping Dietrich Bonhoeffer's witness close to theology and church.

MARTIN RUMSCHEIDT
Halifax, Nova Scotia
October 1999

Abbreviations

AB	Dietrich Bonhoeffer, *Act and Being*
CC	Dietrich Bonhoeffer, *Christ the Center* (U.K. edition: *Christology*)
CD	Karl Barth, *Church Dogmatics*
CF	Dietrich Bonhoeffer, *Creation and Fall*
CoD	Dietrich Bonhoeffer, *The Cost of Discipleship*
DB	Eberhard Bethge, *Dietrich Bonhoeffer. Theologe, Christ, Zeitgenosse*
DBE	Eberhard Bethge, *Dietrich Bonhoeffer: Man of Vision, Man of Courage*
DBW	*Dietrich Bonhoeffer Werke* (New German Critical Edition)
DBWE	*Dietrich Bonhoeffer Works in English* (New English Critical Edition)
E	Dietrich Bonhoeffer, *Ethics*
ET	English translation
GS	Dietrich Bonhoeffer, *Gesammelte Schriften*
LPP	Dietrich Bonhoeffer, *Letters and Papers from Prison*
MBBC	John Godsey, ed., *More Bonhoeffer-Barth Correspondence*
NEB	New English Bible
NRS	Dietrich Bonhoeffer, *No Rusty Swords*
NRSV	New Revised Standard Version of the Bible
Romans	Karl Barth, *The Epistle to the Romans*
SC	Dietrich Bonhoeffer, *Sanctorum Communio*

T.a.	Translation altered by the translators
TF	Dietrich Bonhoeffer, *A Testament to Freedom*
TP	Dietrich Bonhoeffer, *True Patriotism*
WCA	Ronald Gregor Smith, ed., *World Come of Age*
WF	Dietrich Bonhoeffer, *The Way to Freedom*
WGWM	Karl Barth, *The Word of God and the Word of Man*

Bonhoeffer as Prophet of the "Post-Barthian Period"?

It was Hendrikus Berkhof who declared that when Dietrich Bonhoeffer chided Karl Barth for his "positivism of revelation," he rang in the "post-Barthian period."[1] Wolfhart Pannenberg assures us that "a view of theology based on the positive nature of revelation is untenable."[2] He notes that "the positivity of revelation which Dietrich Bonhoeffer detected in Karl Barth, . . . is the fact of the word of God or of his revelation in Christ. Barth took this as the basis of all his arguments without considering what grounds he had for such an assumption."[3] If this comprises the "positivism of revelation" that, according to Pannenberg, Bonhoeffer perceived in Barth, then one must indeed conclude that in his rebuke

1. See Hendrikus Berkhof, *Two Hundred Years of Theology: Report of a Personal Journey,* trans. John Vriend (Grand Rapids: Eerdmans, 1989), 209: "But when in prison Bonhoeffer saw 'the religionless age' approach, this discovery brought with it as its counterpart a farewell to Barth's theology. Although he expressed himself — probably on purpose — only incidentally about this consequence, which was also painful to him, his words about Barth's 'positivism of revelation' ('Take it or leave it') . . . struck like a bomb. These words were exceedingly painful to Barth. One can say that the post-Barthian period really starts with the publication of this position of Bonhoeffer."

2. Wolfhart Pannenberg, *Theology and the Philosophy of Science,* trans. Francis McDonagh (Philadelphia: Westminster, 1976), 275-76.

3. Pannenberg, 29.

1

Bonhoeffer sought to call attention to the untenability of Barth's theological approach.

Given the impression from Berkhof's and Pannenberg's comments that on account of his "positivism of revelation" Barth has been overtaken by history of theology, if not even untenable from the perspective of philosophy of science, is it not surprising that certain theologians maintain that one may still derive much from this "church father of the twentieth century"? What is even more surprising is that a sharp-eyed theologian like Dietrich Bonhoeffer was taken in for so long by the bogus, for there can be no doubt that Karl Barth — next to Martin Luther perhaps — exercised the most sustained influence on Bonhoeffer's theological development.[4]

Eberhard Bethge's observation is surely true that "whoever had grown tired of Karl Barth found ample ammunition in the slogan of 'positivism of revelation.'"[5] But would this observation not also have to be applied to Bonhoeffer himself? It was not he who had invented the slogan; most probably, he encountered it in the theological faculty of Berlin where, most interestingly, it was used in an affirmative manner to depict nothing less than Luther's theological approach and in particular his attacks on "the whore reason."[6] In light of this, it seems to make sense that Bonhoeffer, in face of the "destruction of reason,"[7] in which process German theology had played no small role, finally had to reject this "positivism of revelation." It is nonetheless astonishing that he made his diagnosis of it in Karl Barth, of all people, and in relation to him in particular. Or did he say Barth while meaning Luther?

The case appears to be more complicated than what Berkhof's declaration suggests about "the post-Barthian period" or Pannenberg's judgment concerning the untenableness of Barth's theological approach. One could well let the matter rest had the rebuke not become a political weapon. One can no longer reject offhand the contention that the slogan "positivism of revelation" is used to play off the middle-class, liberal Bonhoeffer, whose theology seems to be made believable on account of

4. See below, 15ff.
5. Eberhard Bethge, *Dietrich Bonhoeffer. Theologe — Christ — Zeitgenosse* (Munich: Chr. Kaiser Verlag, 1967), 999. [This section has not been included in the English version of Bethge's biography of Bonhoeffer. Trans.]
6. See below, 71ff.
7. Cf. Georg Lukács, *The Destruction of Reason,* trans. Peter Palmer (London: Merlin, 1980).

his death as a "martyr," against the Swiss democrat Barth, in particular his socialist leanings. Resistance against the Nazis — yes! as long as it remains within the domain of the middle class and as long as the military plays a decisive part in maintaining security; no! as soon as it tends toward a socialist revolutionizing of the order of society: this is how the message goes. That Bonhoeffer himself condemned such rotten games bothers no one — after all, he is dead. We have a new state-theologian to whom even the country's defense forces can appeal.[8]

If one lays aside the misuse of this concept as a political and theological club with which one seeks to get rid of an opponent, then Bonhoeffer's contending with Barth, seen against the background of his own theological development, is still somewhat surprising but by no means simply without sense. This altercation signals, rather, a problematic internal to Barth's *and* Bonhoeffer's theology that is related to the political significance and the societal meaning of the "christological concentration" as expressed in exemplary fashion in the first thesis of the Barmen Declaration: "Jesus Christ, as he is attested to us in Holy Scripture, is the one Word of God which we have to hear, and which we have to trust and obey in life and in death." But what does that mean in relation to the many other words that the world utters for our hearing and that demand our attention? Were Christians to ignore them in "christomonistic" exclusivity and in an alleged fidelity toward the Barmen Declaration of 1934, then Christians would see themselves as "from a religious point of view . . . specially favoured"; Christ would then be "an object of religion" and not "really the lord of the world" (*LPP*, 281). The world would then be "left to its own devices." For Bonhoeffer, this would be a "mistake" (*LPP*, 286), and he refers to it as "positivism of revelation."

On the other hand, it was the first thesis of Barmen which rejected "the false teaching . . . as if the Church could and should recognize as a source of its proclamation, beyond and besides this Word of God [scil., Jesus Christ, A.P.], yet other events, powers, historical figures, and truths as God's revelation." Even in prison Bonhoeffer did not want to turn away from that decision. But how would he himself escape from the "positivism of revelation" which, according to Pannenberg, consists in that

---

8. The reference is to the speech the West German minister of defense delivered on the fortieth anniversary of the death of Bonhoeffer, 9 April 1985, at the site of the former concentration camp at Flossenbürg.

"the givenness of God's Word or of God's revelation in Christ" is presupposed at every turn but never tested? The problem may be solved most easily when one does not seek to avoid the labor of understanding the charge of "positivism of revelation" in the context of the prison correspondence in which it had been formulated. But part of that labor is to determine what meaning Karl Barth had had before then in the development of Bonhoeffer's theology.

We begin with a chapter on the theological conception found in the fragmentary statements of Bonhoeffer's prison letters. In the second chapter we shall look at Barth's significance for Bonhoeffer's theological development in the time before his imprisonment. In the third chapter we return — in light of this biographical recollection — to the opening question concerning the meaning of "positivism of revelation" in order to establish a perspective on questions that Barth and Bonhoeffer raise for us.

CHAPTER I

The Problem

1. Bonhoeffer's "Arcane Discipline" and Barth's "Positivism of Revelation"

It should be noted that the first two times Barth's "positivism of revelation" is raised in the prison letters, the contention with Barth is connected with Bonhoeffer's own central theological call for a "secret discipline," a commitment to safeguarding the mystery. The demand that a "secret or arcane discipline" must be restored "whereby the *mysteries* of the Christian faith are protected against profanation" (*LPP,* 286) has to be regarded as the *"cantus firmus"* of the prison letters.[1] The interpretation of Bonhoeffer's theology stands or falls with the proper discernment of this *cantus firmus.* There is little doubt that "the concept of 'arcane' undergoes a change in Bonhoeffer in comparison to its meaning in the ancient church."[2] It is not enough simply to take over the dictionary definition of "arcane"; rather, attention has to be paid to the contrapuntal context in which the *"cantus firmus"* rings out.[3]

1. Cf. the article by Reinhart Staats, "Adolf von Harnack im Leben Dietrich Bonhoeffers," *Theologische Zeitschrift* 37 (1981): 121 n. 87.
2. Hanfried Müller, *Von der Kirche zur Welt* (Leipzig: Koehler & Amelang, 1961), 393; on the meaning of secret discipline in the ancient church, see Douglas Powell, "Arkandisziplin," in *Theologische Realenzyklopädie,* IV (1979), 1ff.
3. Cf. my *Dietrich Bonhoeffers Forderung einer Arkandisziplin — eine unerledigte Anfrage an Kirche und Theologie* (Cologne: Pahl-Rugenstein Verlag, 1988). The present study represents in a certain sense an offshoot of my study of "arcane discipline."

Bonhoeffer's rebuke of Barth's "positivism of revelation" doubtlessly belongs to the contrapuntal surroundings of the call for a "secret discipline" along with the call for a "non-religious interpretation of biblical concepts."

In the first "theological" letter, dated 30 April 1944, we read that Barth was "the only one to have started along this line of thought" of what being a religionless-worldly Christian would mean. However, he "did not carry it to completion, but arrived at a positivism of revelation, which in the last analysis is essentially a restoration." In connection with his own concern for a "Christian life in a religionless world," in which Christ "is no longer an object of religion but . . . really the Lord of the world," Bonhoeffer continues: "But what does that mean? What is the place of worship and prayer in a religionless situation? Does the secret discipline, or alternatively the difference . . . between penultimate and ultimate, take on a new importance here?" (*LPP,* 280-81). On account of its textual proximity to the polemics against Barth's "positivism of revelation," Bonhoeffer's question about the significance of the "arcane discipline" manifests itself at the same time as a question to Barth and has to be understood against this background.

It appears, in addition, that "the basic structure of the ancient church's arcane discipline is taken up here in its relation to the mystery and its gradated mediation of knowledge,"[4] for we read in the next letter, dated 5 May 1944, that in the place of religion Barth had put "a positivist doctrine of revelation which says, in effect, 'Take it or leave it': virgin birth, Trinity, or anything else; each is an equally significant and necessary part of the whole, which must simply be swallowed as a whole or not at all" (*LPP,* 286). But that is "unbiblical," for there are "degrees of knowledge and degrees of significance; that means that a secret discipline must be restored whereby the *mysteries* of the Christian faith are protected against profanation. The positivism of revelation makes it too easy for itself . . ." (*LPP,* 286).[5] One may indeed note here a "genuine connection with the ancient church's arcane discipline." But, on account of its orientation toward the "religionless world" — the world that must not be left to its own devices,

4. Müller, 393.

5. In the third letter in which Bonhoeffer discusses Barth's "positivism of revelation" (8 June 1944; *LPP,* 324f.), the *cantus firmus* "secret discipline" is not explicitly mentioned. One may imply, nevertheless, that it is there, for example, when Bonhoeffer says "mythology (resurrection etc.) is the thing itself" (329), but that it is in need of nonreligious interpretation.

which is precisely what "positivism of revelation" does — "arcane discipline" obtains a "dialectical character"[6] which blocks it from being understood simply in relation to the tradition of the ancient church.

Unfortunately, research to date has had to find its way in heavy fog as much in relation to the meaning of "positivism of revelation" as in relation to that of "arcane discipline." Worse than that is the claim that everybody knows what Bonhoeffer meant to chide Karl Barth for, namely, the "Old Testament, prophetic" (*LPP*, 317), the authoritarian gesture "vertically from above" that does not sit well with the interpreters. "Whoever had grown tired of Karl Barth found ample ammunition in the slogan of 'positivism of revelation,'" Eberhard Bethge said. But such false certainty in relation to the point of Bonhoeffer's polemics does not match well the admiration the imprisoned Bonhoeffer still held even then for Barth's "really great merit," namely, to have been "the first theologian to begin the criticism of religion" (*LPP*, 286). Barth's confused and resigned response to Bonhoeffer's rebuke may therefore appear very understandable: "Now he has left us alone with the enigmatic utterances of his letters — at more than one point clearly showing that he sensed, without really knowing, how the story should continue — for example, what exactly he meant by the 'positivism of revelation' he found in me, and especially how the programme of an unreligious speech was to be realized" (*WCA*, 90). Yet, it would be too simple to follow Barth's advice, namely, to rest content in "remaining behind, somewhat confused," in order "to take the best" of Bonhoeffer (*WCA*, 91). Perhaps it is possible after all to say more clearly somehow what Bonhoeffer "sensed" when one has traced in detail the development of his theological relationship to Barth. But in that undertaking one must heed from the outset the warning against too hasty conclusions and apparent solutions.

2. Lutheran or Reformed?
The Search for the "Point of Difference"

Behind Bonhoeffer's polemics against Barth's "positivism of revelation" and Barth's puzzlement with that "enigmatic utterance," there lies indeed a theological relationship of many years. Regin Prenter, the Danish Lu-

6. Müller, 394.

theran, thought he could even demonstrate that from Bonhoeffer's early questions about Barth's doctrine of revelation, as expounded, for example, in the second edition of *The Epistle to the Romans* (1922; ET, 1933), there is

> a straight line . . . to the criticism of Barth's positivism of revelation. . . . For Barth, the dialectics of the theology of revelation must increasingly search for that constant point in universalism, in God's eternal decision, because for him cognition is above being. . . . Thus cognition will necessarily dare to enter into God's supralapsarian eternity in order to search his unity. Thus all theological inquiry will seek to comprehend his inner-trinitarian love and his supralapsarian predestination . . . [and make this] the focal point of the understanding of faith. The supralapsarian speculation, which is developed in the *Church Dogmatics . . .* , is however *quite* far removed from the passion for this world, which became so significant for Bonhoeffer, especially in the last years of his life. (*WCA*, 125-26)[7]

With Barth "everything points to eternity" while Bonhoeffer's road led in "another direction," namely, "into temporality, away from eternity towards the religionless human being, to the godless human being for whom the church must be present with God in Christ in order to be truly the church" (*WCA*, 128).

This thesis must be judged as a gross simplification, even though Prenter can cite some evidence for his view concerning the "direct" line from Bonhoeffer's early questioning of Barth's dialectics to the later polemics against his "positivism of revelation." Prenter's thesis ignores Bonhoeffer's descriptions of the changes in Barth's theological development[8] just as much as Bonhoeffer's several corrections of his own view of Barth, the last of which is in the prison correspondence itself.[9] After all, if

7. One searches in vain in Bonhoeffer's prison letters for an explicit critique of Barth's "purified Supralapsarian theory" (*CD* II/2, 142) which had still come to Bonhoeffer's attention during his imprisonment.

8. In his "analysis of Barth's concept of revelation," Prenter refers almost exclusively to the second edition of Barth's *Epistle to the Romans*. He assumes that the understanding of revelation found there is maintained in its basic features (actualism, analogism, and universalism) also in the *Church Dogmatics* (*WCA*, 106).

9. See *LPP*, 328, "It was not in ethics, as is often said, that he subsequently failed," which Bonhoeffer himself had said earlier.

there is a line from Bonhoeffer's early questions about Barth to the late charge, it is more likely a winding path. An examination of this line would have to trace in detail its various twists and turns.

But Prenter's thesis is obviously meant to be quite fundamental. If the point of difference between them, signaled by "positivism of revelation," can be made plain in terms of how the two men relate to the baptism of children, as Prenter maintains, then an old dispute within the theology of the Reformation — if not the history of theology as such — is the issue. Since Barth interprets baptism in relation to "cognition," the baptism of children needs to be eliminated. And "nothing is more typical of Barth's thought than his criticism of infant baptism." In Bonhoeffer, on the contrary, "the main line of his intentions leads to an ontic interpretation of the history of revelation," toward a "being . . . which encompasses all comprehension," for which reason he, unlike Barth, can find a meaning for infant baptism (*WCA*, 128-29).

One may well ask again whether the difference between the two theologians' understanding of baptism is really as unambiguous as that.[10] What is important to acknowledge in this context is that Prenter seeks to trace the difference between them back to the old interdenominational controversy between Lutheran and Reformed — more accurately: Zwinglian or Anabaptist — sacramental theology.

This suspicion was expressed more clearly than in Prenter by the American theologian James H. Burtness. He stated that "the two do divide on the capax/non capax question along classical Lutheran/Reformed lines."[11] Burtness is able to call on the witness of Eberhard Bethge, who noted in a lecture delivered in 1961 that "Bonhoeffer vigorously protests with Luther against this [*finitum incapax infiniti*] all his life. . . . In order to save the majesty of God [Barth] started pushing God away; Bonhoeffer

---

10. See Bonhoeffer's early doubts about the justification of infant baptism when a congregation no longer seriously thinks of "carrying" the child (*SC*, 241). In addition, see his "On the Question of Baptism" of 1942: "A misuse of infant baptism (and such a misuse can without doubt be established in the past history of our Church) will therefore inevitably lead the community to an appropriate limitation of its use and to a new evaluation of adult baptism" (*TP*, 159). Karl Barth expressed himself in 1943 in a similarly restrained way in his critique of infant baptism; see his work *The Teaching of the Church regarding Baptism*, trans. Ernest A. Payne (London: SCM, 1948).

11. James H. Burtness, "As though God Were Not Given: Barth, Bonhoeffer and the *Finitum Capax Infiniti*," *Dialog* 19, no. 4 (fall 1980): 250.

started by drawing him in — in order to save the same majesty of God."[12] Thus the difference between the two can be adequately understood against the background of their common concern to protect the majesty of God in its condescension.

Paul Lehmann similarly related the difference to a mutually shared concern, namely, their search for the concreteness of revelation. "For Barth, the *incapax* protected the concreteness of *God* in his revelation, as it were, on the giving end of the stick. For Bonhoeffer, the *capax* protected the *concreteness* of the *revelation* of God, as it were, on the receiving end of the stick, that is, in the reality of faith. For both, the major question of theology was the question of concreteness."[13] In relation to this view of the difference, Burtness correctly refers to the critique of Barth in Bonhoeffer's second dissertation, *Act and Being*. "God is free not from human beings but for them. . . . God *is* present, that is, not in eternal nonobjectivity but — to put it quite provisionally for now — 'haveable,' graspable in the Word within the church" (*AB,* 90-91).[14]

In commenting on this early critique of Barth by Bonhoeffer, Eberhard Bethge writes: "To Bonhoeffer the old extra Calvinisticum is a troubling contestation . . ." (*DBE,* 90). But the question is whether this difference still governs Bonhoeffer's polemics against Barth in the context of the prison letters.[15] Yet Burtness neglects this question in commenting on Bonhoeffer's statement that we must "live before and with God . . . without God" (*LPP,* 360) as follows: "If the finite is not capable of bearing the infinite, that kind of talk makes no sense. At best it is 'enigmatic' [Barth]."[16] Such co-opting of Bonhoeffer for the Lutheran party against Barth with the assistance of the "positivism of revelation" charge seems hasty, to say the least. Later on, Bonhoeffer did not explicitly take up the

12. Bethge's address was entitled "The Challenge of Dietrich Bonhoeffer's Life and Theology"; Burtness cites it in his article on p. 250.

13. Paul Lehmann, "The Concreteness of Theology: Reflections on the Conversation between Barth and Bonhoeffer," in *Footnotes to a Theology: The Karl Barth Colloquium of 1972,* ed. Martin Rumscheidt (Waterloo, Ontario: Canadian Corporation for Studies in Religion, 1974); cited in Burtness, 251.

14. Cited in Burtness, 252.

15. In his Bonhoeffer biography, Bethge is more circumspect than in the 1961 Chicago address that Burtness cites. Bethge refers here only to Bonhoeffer's habilitation dissertation and leaves open the question whether this difference with Barth stood up for the rest of Bonhoeffer's life.

16. Burtness, 254.

Lutheran argument against Barth from the habilitation dissertation. Other polemical questions had become more important to him. In the Christology lectures of 1933, he spoke of the Lutheran *"capax"* only in terms of what sounds like a Reformed proviso: *Finitum* capax *infiniti, non per se sed per infinitum!* — "The finite can hold the infinite, not by itself, but it can by the aid of the infinite!"[17] Barth could have put the matter that way.[18] Finally, Bonhoeffer approached Barth in 1936 requesting that "the questions of substance which divide Lutherans and Reformed could be brought into the open and discussed" by Barth, since "Sasse's arguments are always completely formal and so too are all our counterstatements" (*WF,* 118). In 1933 Bonhoeffer had tried in vain together with Sasse to compose a Lutheran confessional statement. Would Bonhoeffer have placed himself into a common theological front with Barth against the Lutherans in such a way if he had upheld without change his earlier concerns with the *extra Calvinisticum?* It seems, rather, as if the Lutherans' church-political retreat from the common confessional front the Reformed and United Church had formed in Germany had discredited the Lutheran arguments theologically as well. John D. Godsey appears to be right when he tries not to overemphasize the denominational differences between Barth and Bonhoeffer: "although the confessional differences are important, they are not decisive."[19]

3. A Critical Movement within the Barthian Movement

Eberhard Bethge rightly stresses that Bonhoeffer's "early and later criticisms of Barth" in all phases of this change-filled relationship are to be understood "as a movement within rather than outside the Barthian movement itself" (*DBE,* 134). Helmut Gollwitzer even asserted that the later charge of "positivism of revelation" against Barth does not touch Barth at all. It touches "instead [Bonhoeffer's] own earlier period, namely what he understood and incorporated in the thirties as the anti-liberal

17. *DBW,* 12:332; ET, *Christ the Center* (New York: Harper & Row, 1978), 93.

18. See Barth's relativization of the contrast in *CD* I/1, 406f. (1975 ed.), *465f.* (1936 ed). [The pagination of these two different translations of *CD* I/1 will be signaled in the text by printing the older version's page number in italics. Trans.]

19. John D. Godsey, "Barth and Bonhoeffer: The Basic Difference," *Quarterly Review: A Scholarly Journal for Reflection of Ministry* 7, no. 1 (spring 1987): 18.

orientation of Barth's theology" and what caused Bonhoeffer to give fundamentalistic interpretations of the First Testament in disregard of historical-critical studies.[20] Repeatedly in the prison letters Bonhoeffer indeed retracts earlier positions,[21] for which reason Gollwitzer's surmise is not easily dismissed. Still, an attempt like that to solve the problem looks too easy, particularly because of the suspicion that Gollwitzer here actually projects his own theological reservations about Bonhoeffer's temporary "positivism of the church" of the thirties into Bonhoeffer's late critique of Barth.[22] But with the charge of "positivism of revelation," Bonhoeffer clearly seeks to confront also Barth himself and certainly how Barth was received in the Confessing Church, even if that affected Bonhoeffer's earlier position also.

John D. Godsey believes that he has found the "clue" to the problem in Bonhoeffer's parenthetical remark about Barth in the letter of 8 June 1944. Asking how liberal theology might be overcome, Bonhoeffer writes that Barth "is still influenced by it, though negatively" (*LPP,* 329). Godsey asks: "Can it be that the basic difference between Bonhoeffer and Barth has to do with their assessment of liberal theology and how it was to be overcome?"[23] He concludes that Barth and Bonhoeffer, "holding common ground, . . . diverged because they perceived different dangers for the church. One difference involves the church's relationship to the world. . . . Another difference is christological" in nature. So one might say "that their deepest theological differences come at the point where they are most closely bound together. Both accepted the general guidelines of Chalcedon that in Jesus Christ there is united both true divinity and true humanity. But Barth tended to emphasize the divinity. . . . Bonhoeffer, on the other hand, stressed the hiddenness of divinity in the humiliated One. . . ."[24] Finally, "Barth's theology tends toward a *theologia gloriae* in order to assure the *graceousness* [*sic*] of God's action in

---

20. Helmut Gollwitzer, "Weg des Gehorsams," in *Begegnungen mit Dietrich Bonhoeffer,* ed. Wolf-Dieter Zimmermann (Munich: Chr. Kaiser Verlag, 1969), 132.

21. See, e.g., *LPP,* 192f., in relation to the "doctrine of the mandates" of *Ethics,* and next to that, *LPP,* 157 and 369, in relation to *Discipleship.*

22. Cf. Helmut Gollwitzer, "Comments on Bonhoeffer's Article," in *WF,* 101: "The Confession of the church is not the Word of God but the church's testimony of the Word of God."

23. Godsey, 24.

24. Godsey, 26.

Christ. . . . In contrast, Bonhoeffer's theology is a *theologia crucis* in order to assure the *costliness* of God's grace in Christ." Yet all these differences notwithstanding, Godsey does not play off Barth and Bonhoeffer against each other. "Barth and Bonhoeffer, Bonhoeffer and Barth. They make quite a team! It would be tragic, in my judgement, if Barth were listened to only by the conservative evangelicals and Bonhoeffer only by the liberation theologians."[25] Despite its carefully weighed argumentation, Godsey's attempt to explain the differences is nonetheless in danger of bringing about precisely what he seeks to avoid, namely, that Barth and Bonhoeffer *are* played off against each other. For, if one follows Godsey, did Bonhoeffer not raise the more relevant questions in which the advantage of greater actuality would accrue to him today?

In light of this, it seems important to note a comment by Eberhard Bethge in which he speaks of a "shift of interest" in Barth and Bonhoeffer that occurred at different times. "For all their mutual sympathy, they differed in the phases of their development. The one arrived where the other was just saying good-bye, or had left a place toward which the other was striving" (*DBE,* 135). Because Bonhoeffer's interests were initially shaped by a "positivism of the church" and by ethics, he raised questions about the ecclesial and ethical concreteness of Barth's dialectics. Having been politicized very differently by his participation in the conspiracy against Hitler, Bonhoeffer raises critical questions in his prison letters. In the name of the nonreligious world, he addresses his questions to Barth's *Dogmatics,* which, in correspondence with Bonhoeffer's earlier concerns, seems "ecclesially" qualified. Before the charge of "positivism of revelation" can be examined once again for its theological substance, one needs to look in detail at the "phases" of the difficult theological relationship between Bonhoeffer and Barth.

25. Godsey, 27.

CHAPTER II

Karl Barth in Bonhoeffer's Theological Development

1. The Discovery of Dialectical Theology

Bonhoeffer's first encounter with the theology of Karl Barth took place in the winter of 1924/25 when he read the first volume of Barth's essays *Das Wort Gottes und die Theologie* (ET: *The Word of God and the Word of Man*). Bonhoeffer quickly made himself the "propagandist for this book" and arranged to have the lecture notes of Barth's first course on dogmatics sent from Göttingen (*DBE,* 51). According to Eberhard Bethge, the discovery of dialectical theology came upon the Berlin student of Adolf von Harnack "like a liberation" (*DBE,* 52). Although Bethge remarks that Bonhoeffer had critical objections right from the start, especially where "Barth's assertion of the inaccessibility and free majesty of God threatened and volatilized earthly concreteness and affectedness" (*DBE,* 53), the Lutheran reservation against the *extra Calvinisticum* is not applicable to the period of Bonhoeffer's very first encounter with Barth's theology. On the contrary, in the seminars of 1925 and 1926 Bonhoeffer shows himself very much a "Barthian," much to the displeasure of his teacher Reinhold Seeberg.[1] This is made evident in Bonhoeffer's acceptance of Barth's interpretation of Israel and church from the second edition of *The Epistle to the*

---

1. Cf. *DBE,* 56: ". . . the whole thing was a disturbing exercise in Barthianism."

15

Romans,[2] and even more so in his continual repetition of the statement "things can be known only by their like" (*DBE,* 57) as a way of expressing the Calvinian *incapax.*[3] Hans Pfeifer notes, therefore, that there are "almost no critical reservations whatever" against Barth in Bonhoeffer's writings preceding his dissertation; Bonhoeffer merely raised certain objections against Barth's concept of the canon.[4]

However, according to Bethge, there are "signs that he feared that the dogmatics being developed by Barth might represent a regression in comparison with *The Epistle to the Romans*" (*DBE,* 53). But this expresses the concerns of a biblical theologian of liberal orientation about the structural constraints of theological orthodoxy, concerns which certainly cannot be reduced to the Lutheran reservations about the *extra Calvinisticum.* Barth's statement, "I prefer erring with the fathers of Chalcedon to painting a portrait of Jesus from the New Testament on my own account" (*DBE,* 54), seems to have sounded in Bonhoeffer's ears suspiciously like fits of neo-orthodoxy on the part of the dialectician from Göttingen.[5] A letter of Rich-

2. Karl Barth, *The Epistle to the Romans,* 2nd rev. German ed. of 1922 translated by Edwyn C. Hoskyns (London: Oxford University Press, 1933), 330; when Bonhoeffer showed his agreement with Barth, Seeberg marked the section of the seminar paper with a question mark. Cf. "Lässt sich eine historische und pneumatische Auslegung der Schrift unterscheiden und wie stellt sich die Dogmatik dazu?" (Are historical and pneumatic interpretations of Scripture distinguishable and how does dogmatics respond to that?), in *DBW,* 9:305ff. (cf. H. Pfeifer, "Das Kirchenverständnis Dietrich Bonhoeffers" [diss., Heidelberg, 1963], 77).

3. Cf. "Luthers Anschauungen vom Heiligen Geist" (Luther's understandings of the Holy Spirit), a presentation in Karl Holl's seminar, 1926. *DBW,* 9:355ff. H. Pfeifer refers in addition to the study on historical and pneumatic interpretation of Scripture as well as to "Franks Anschauungen vom Geist und von der Gnade" (Frank's understandings of the Spirit and of grace), both for Seeberg. In the latter, Bonhoeffer writes: "But *finitum incapax infiniti,* like is known only through like, God only through God's Spirit." (Cf. Pfeifer, 77f., esp. 78 n. 1.)

4. In contrast to "Calvin's Reformed principle of Scripture and its repristination by Karl Barth," Bonhoeffer wants to uphold "what makes Christ known" as "the measure for the understanding of Scripture." (Cf. Pfeifer, 78 n. 2.)

5. However, see Barth's own skepticism about what he intended to do as expressed in a letter of 28 May 1924 to Eduard Thurneysen. "Even though I still see some advantages in doing so, it would be advisable to sleep some more on it before we confront the astonished Central Europe with a new Nicene Creed. But my poor students have to let all this rush over them like a mountain brook; they write or take down in shorthand everything including the polemical observations that I insert not infrequently. Who knows where they will go with all of this?" (Karl Barth and Eduard Thurneysen, *Briefwechsel* Band 2 *1921-1930* [Zürich: TVZ, 1974], 254). Some took it to Berlin.

ard Widmann to Bonhoeffer, written in February 1926, confirms "how great must have been Bonhoeffer's fears of 'reactionary gestures' on the part of the new master" (*DBE*, 54). Enrolled in Barth's courses at Göttingen, Widmann expresses first of all how pleased he is that in the dogmatic lectures "something is being said better and more precisely than in *The Epistle to the Romans*." Barth's systematic progression lets "the problems emerge in clearer contours and more carefully defined. . . . There is much that is sensational and journalistic in *Romans*, whereas the dogmatics is more objective" (*DB*, 106). And even though Bonhoeffer once objected that he "deplored the servitude into which Barth has relapsed in these dogmatics — that he takes anxious care (yes, just that) to follow in the footsteps of the dogmaticians of ancient times . . . this reactionary gesture" ought not be seen "as being wrong." For the issue at that time was foremost "to establish a link with the past." At the same time, "we equally need . . . a dogmatics that manages without these reactionary crutches and looks *forward* for links. Certainly *The Epistle to the Romans* is much less reactionary in its formulations," for which reason one could see the dogmatics as "a step backwards. Perhaps next time, when his dogmatics have fulfilled their 'tactical purpose' — his reliance on the ancients will not have amounted to more than that — he will take *two* steps forward" (*DBE*, 54).[6]

Eberhard Bethge wonders whether this promotes understanding of the prison letters where Bonhoeffer states that Barth alone was correct in *starting* to think along the line of critique of religion. However, Bonhoeffer sees Barth as having failed to carry it "to completion," landing instead in a "positivism of revelation" which "in the last analysis is essentially a restoration" (*DBE*, 54; see *LPP*, 280). Benkt-Erik Benktson has shown that, indeed, there are sentences in Barth's first volume of essays that come very close to Bonhoeffer's language in the prison letters about

---

6. Richard Widmann to Bonhoeffer, cited in *DBE*, 54. In its terminology, the letter is peculiarly reminiscent of Lenin's writing of April 1918, "The Coming Tasks of Soviet Power." Referring to the use of "bourgeois resources" (such as remunerating specialists) by the proletarian state, Lenin writes: "It is obvious that such a measure represents not only an interruption of the offensive against capital but also *a step backwards* for our socialist Soviet state-power." But such an interruption is "necessary in the interest of the total victory." "So that the *further* offensive may succeed, the offensive *now* is to be halted." Cited from W. I. Lenin, *Ausgewählte Werke* (Moscow: Verlag Progress, 1981), 444-45.

"non-religious Christianity."[7] For example, Barth says that "Biblical piety is not really pious; one must rather characterize it as a well-considered, qualified worldliness" (*WGWM,* 66, T.a.). In light of such remarks, the tendency toward "churchiness" manifest already in Barth's first course of lectures on dogmatics would strike a Harnack pupil from Berlin as a "reactionary gesture."

2. In the Undertow of the Luther Renaissance

The next phase of Bonhoeffer's engagement with Karl Barth's theology is depicted in his doctoral dissertation, *Sanctorum Communio,* and the habilitation dissertation *Act and Being.* Contrary to the early seminar papers, these works actually contain specifically Lutheran criticism of Barth's insistence on God's being utterly beyond human disposition. It is useful, therefore, to diverge for a moment and to depict Bonhoeffer's "Lutheranism," particularly as it was represented by Karl Holl, his teacher in Berlin.

It was from Holl that Bonhoeffer could learn what at that time was the "most modern" form of Lutheranism, also known as the "Luther renaissance." "Bonhoeffer eagerly immersed himself in Holl's interpretation of Luther's doctrine of justification. Holl irrevocably implanted in him the doctrine of 'by grace alone' as the one *articulus stantis et cadentis ecclesiae.* . . . As against what had become a vague cultural Protestantism, he liked Holl's epoch-making advance into the centre of Luther's doctrine of justification" (*DBE,* 46).

It is not unlikely that Bonhoeffer's own perception of Luther was shaped, among other things, by Holl's interpretation of justification as a genuine process of being rendered just, as outlined in his major volume of Luther studies. "The purpose God seeks to accomplish in 'justification' is reached only when human beings have been rendered genuinely just. In sub-

7. B.-E. Benktson, *Kristus och den myndigvordna världen. En studie i Dietrich Bonhoeffers teologie* (1964), cited in *DBE,* 54; cf. also Benktson's *Christus und die Religion. Der Religionsbegriff bei Barth, Bonhoeffer und Tillich* (Stuttgart: Calwer Verlag, 1967). In his *Theology of Dietrich Bonhoeffer,* trans. H. Martin Rumscheidt (Philadelphia: Fortress, 1985), Ernst Feil rejects Benktson's view that "presuppositions of Bonhoeffer . . . are to be traced back" to Barth because "Bonhoeffer had a thoroughly different understanding of worldliness . . . than Barth" (233 n. 159). This view will be examined later.

stance, justification and being rendered just belong together. They are related as means are to ends. It is the one and the same will of God that embraces the totality of God's action upon human beings."[8] Melanchthon had distorted this teaching, in that he was unable "to comprehend the whole of new life as an integrated action of God, as the goal toward which God moves in the work of justification."[9] Luther's understanding of justification as a process rendering human beings just was simply a reinstating of Paul's doctrine of justification which, next to the well-known declaration of *sola gratia,* also included the assertion that "for God it is not they who hear the law that shall be just, but they who do it."[10] Seen in this light, even monasticism had been "no obstacle but a furtherance on Luther's way. He appropriated into his new consciousness the best of what monasticism — in contrast to the church — had received as an inheritance from the early church."[11] According to Holl, Luther's ecclesiology as well as his ethics was influenced by this. Thus, Luther's doctrine of justification "translated itself directly into an understanding of the church," which itself owes "important impulses" to monasticism, "only at this point it is monasticism itself that drives him beyond monasticism." Holl refers in this context to the understanding of the "monastic community" of Basil the Great as a "covenant of brothers, an understanding that Luther took up and applied to the whole of the church."[12]

8. Karl Holl, "Die Rechtfertigungslehre in Luthers Vorlesung über den Römerbrief mit besonderer Rücksicht auf die Frage der Heilsgewißheit" (1910), in *Gesammelte Aufsätze zur Kirchengeschichte I: Luther,* 4th/5th ed. (Tübingen: J. C. B. Mohr, 1927), 123 (cited as *Luther*).

9. Holl, *Luther,* 128.

10. Holl, *Luther,* 117; cf. Rom. 2:13.

11. Karl Holl, "Der Neubau der Sittlichkeit" (1919), in *Luther,* 203. This view of Luther's monasticism may well have contributed to Bonhoeffer's assessment of Luther's "road through the monastery" in *The Cost of Discipleship* and *Ethics,* as well as the "monastic" experiment in Finkenwalde. Cf. my *Dietrich Bonhoeffers Forderung einer Arkandisziplin — eine unerledigte Anfrage an Kirche und Theologie* (Cologne: Pahl-Rugenstein, 1988), 272ff. and 300.

12. Karl Holl, "Die Entstehung von Luthers Kirchenbegriff" (1915), in *Luther,* 300f.: "It might be said that Luther took up again and brought to its completion the idea of Basil the Great. Basil founded his monks' community to reconstitute the first Christian congregation, to be a covenant of brothers who in mutuality would spiritually advance and support one another. This is how Luther viewed the church. . . . If such interiorized community was the form of bondedness that God desires and that is alone appropriate to Christianity, then it could not be restricted to a small, secluded circle; it had to embrace the totality of Christians."

Holl insists that Luther strove for the territorial rulers' governance in a church comprising the whole populace. However, what is characteristic of Luther is that the other side was given equal emphasis: "Luther desired both, a church comprising the whole populace and a voluntary church *(Volkskirche und Freiwilligkeitskirche)*. . . . Both are rooted equally in his basic reformatory ideas: the church of the populace is rooted in his certainty of the victorious power of the Word, and the voluntary church in his call for personal conscientiousness."[13] In a number of statements Luther came close "even to the idea of a confessional church *(Bekenntniskirche)*."[14]

In relation to "rebuilding morality," justification as a process of rendering human beings just means for Luther that "the time would come when there were no more poor people in town or among the populace."[15] On this plane, a neat separation of the two kingdoms became increasingly untenable for Luther, because "the general priesthood and the understanding of the congregation as a covenant of brothers" had to prove itself true, especially in the realm of economics.[16] Luther had tried "also to lay hold of the evil at the root of capitalism itself by subjecting the forms of prevailing commerce and exchange of money to a purification according to Christian principles."[17] Luther stressed in this context "that those words in the Sermon on the Mount are not simply 'counsels' but strict commandments. For him this really meant that Christians who are in a position of having something more than what their own needs and those of their family require are obligated to lend this surplus without interest to the needy or, better still, to give it to

13. Karl Holl, "Luther und das landesherrliche Kirchenregiment" (1911), in *Luther,* 359. There is an echo of this characterization in Bonhoeffer's dissertation *Sanctorum Communio,* particularly in the section (deleted from the 1930 publication of *SC*) on "national churches" and "gathered churches," *Volkskirche und Freiwilligkeitskirche, SC,* 269-71 n. 429. Cf. *SC,* 219-20, 258-59 n. 130, and 267ff.

14. Holl, *Luther,* 358f.

15. Holl, *Luther,* 275. "Care of the poor, as it had been administered hitherto partly by the church and partly by the towns, did not match Luther's understanding of loving the neighbor. . . . The simple thing that had been everywhere forgotten was the very first thing Luther brought to the fore, namely, that support meant truly to help the poor rather than dropping alms on them" (275).

16. Holl, *Luther,* 276.

17. Holl, *Luther,* 277. Cf. F.-W. Marquardt, "Gott *oder* Mammon aber: Theologie *und* Oekonomie bei Martin Luther," in *Einwürfe,* ed. Marquardt et al. (Munich: Chr. Kaiser Verlag, 1983), 167ff.

them outright."[18] As in the case of the church's order, Luther appealed first to the rulers in the matter of limiting the taking of interest; later he urged that they "intervene directly and tear up the letters of the loan-sharks and break their seals." But since he had finally to acknowledge how badly the state failed in the domain of economics, he turned to the church, calling upon it to address the issue "by declaring it a matter of pastors' obligation to oppose the money-lenders with the strongest spiritual means, including refusing to administer the sacraments and to give burial to them."[19]

Holl's understanding of justification as the process of rendering human beings just and sanctified is, indeed, echoed a number of times in Bonhoeffer's work. Still, he found this "epochal advance into the centre of Luther's doctrine of justification . . . to be too weakly anchored in Luther's Christology." In his view "Holl's interpretation of Luther's faith as a religion of conscience" stunted the teaching of the Reformation (*DBE*, 46).[20] Accordingly, it was a "liberation" for Bonhoeffer to find in Barth, in contrast to Holl, that the "certainty for which he strove was anchored, not in the human being, but in the majesty of God, with the result that it was not a theme in itself apart from God" (*DBE*, 52). Still, Holl's por-

18. Holl, *Luther,* 279. Cf. Bonhoeffer's comment at the end of his "Die systematische Theologie des 20. Jh.s" (winter term 1931/32) in the stenographic version of an auditor: "Luther could compose his *De servo arbitrio* and his pamphlet on tribute money at the same time. Why can we do so no more? Who will show us Luther?" (*DBW,* 11:213).

19. Holl, *Luther,* 281. Cf. Bonhoeffer's call for a boycott on funeral services in response to the installation of a state commissar in the Prussian church at the end of June 1933 (*DBE,* 223f.).

20. Cf. Bonhoeffer's inaugural lecture at the Berlin faculty on 31 July 1930 on the question of the human in contemporary philosophy and theology. "Holl named Luther's religion a religion of conscience. This went hand in hand with a remarkably low assessment of Luther's Christology" (*DBW,* 10:370). Cf. also the course on the history of systematic theology in the twentieth century, *DBW,* 11:139ff. Karl Holl "sees the themes of theology to reside in justification. God is utterly just and utterly gracious. Holl, Ritschl and Cremer did not resolve this paradox, for in them God speaks only as the just one. An act of arbitrariness. Humans must be just in God's eyes, they are not sanctified in the world but eschatologically. The doctrines of justification and sanctification are conceived of together. Justification is an analytical judgment. Christ is not the foundation of justification, but the First Commandment which validates itself in my conscience. Conscience is the final instance of certainty and, thus, Holl describes Luther's ethics as an ethics of conscience" (*DBW,* 11:184f.).

trayal of Luther "enabled him to meet the powerful onslaught of Barth's theology with critical acumen" (*DBE,* 48, T.a.). Thus, wherever Barth's assertion of God's free majesty, or his insistence that God is at no one's disposal, threatened and volatilized a due emphasis on the earthly concreteness and affectedness (*DBE,* 53), Bonhoeffer raised critical "questions." In other words, Bonhoeffer protested wherever he thought Barth too was neglecting Christology. This holds true particularly for Bonhoeffer's academic studies, his doctoral and habilitation dissertations, to which we now turn.

3. The Critical Academic Discussion with Barth

In contrast to the "Barthianism" of the seminar studies from Berlin that have already been mentioned, there are in Bonhoeffer's two dissertations critical observations, originating in Lutheran thought, against Barth's theology.[21] "In 1927 and 1929 Bonhoeffer, in excited and grateful acceptance of the Barthian message, raises a number of theological-epistemological questions directed at Barth while holding fast to the principle of *finitum capax infiniti*" (*DBE,* 134, T.a.).

This discussion is more peripheral in *Sanctorum Communio.* On the one hand, there is basic agreement with the theological insight that "the Christian church is the church of the Word, that is, of faith," an insight that at one and the same time has "been brought home to us by modern Luther research," that is, by Karl Holl, "as well as the most recent change of direction in theology," that is, by Karl Barth (*SC,* 212-13).[22] On the other hand, Bonhoeffer states that the concept of the church as one of

---

21. One may ask indeed whether this shift in accent is not in part a concession to his thesis director, R. Seeberg, who had found fault with the "Barthianism" of the seminar studies.

22. Cf. the section "Authority and Freedom in the Empirical Church" that was added for the published version of *SC.* The first sentence of that section refers explicitly to Barth's 1927 *Dogmatics.* "The church rests upon the Word" (*SC,* 250). Cf. Karl Barth, *Die christliche Dogmatik im Entwurf,* vol. 1, *Die Lehre vom Worte Gottes. Prolegomena zur christlichen Dogmatik* (Munich: Chr. Kaiser Verlag, 1927), secs. 21 and 22. On the substitution of the section "Church and Proletariat" by that of "Authority and Freedom," see my "Eine Entdeckung — und eine verpasste Chance," *Weissenseer Blätter* (Berlin), no. 3 (1986): 45ff.

person and of community cannot be "understood theologically 'in itself,' but only within a real historical dialectic — not a dialectic of concepts" (*SC,* 62).[23] That this comment is in reference to "the most recent trend in theology" is demonstrated by the ninth of Bonhoeffer's theses for the doctoral examinations (17 December 1927). "The dialectic of so-called dialectic theology has logical and not real character, and thus runs the risk of neglecting the historicity of Jesus" (*NRS,* 29). In addition, there is in the doctoral dissertation an explicit discussion of the ethics and ecclesiology of Barth's *Epistle to the Romans* (2nd ed.). Bonhoeffer "cannot agree with the way in which in that commentary Barth interprets the command to love, or with the idea of community that he deduces from it." One may well say with Barth that "in . . . our contemporaries the problem of God is . . . formulated concretely and in such a manner as to demand a concrete answer" (*Romans,* 452). But one must then also concede "that love really loves the other human being, and not the One in the other," as Barth maintains.[24] "Who gives Barth the right to say that the other is 'as such infinitely unimportant' (452), when God commands us to love precisely that person? . . . Should I after all ultimately be alone with God in the world?" (*SC,* 170).[25] In the final analysis, Barth's understanding of oneness, "where there is only love of the One in the other,"[26] ends up in "ro-

23. The Primal State and the Problem of Community. A. Methodological Problems (*SC,* 58ff.).

24. Cf. Karl Barth, *Romans,* 454: "Love is without dissimulation when . . . it seeks the *one* in the *other,* serves the *one,* means the *one.*" See also 480f.

25. Cf. *Romans,* 452: "Worship . . . *represents* love towards God . . . in so far as it is *significantly engaged* in the doing of what corresponds to God's love to one's fellow humans who, as such, are infinitely unimportant" (T.a.). Bonhoeffer counters: "God has made 'the neighbors as such' infinitely important, and there isn't any other 'neighbor as such' for us . . . ; rather, the other is infinitely important as such, precisely because God takes the other person seriously" (*SC,* 170). Cf. on this matter T. R. Peters, "Der andere ist unendlich wichtig. Impulse aus Bonhoeffers Ekklesiologie für die Gegenwart," *Weissenseer Blätter* 1 (1986): 8ff.

26. Cf. *Romans,* 494-95: "We have no other option but to acknowledge the *oneness* that is beyond our thinking of our most questionable 'I' with the 'You' by which we are confronted. . . . In Christ, . . . I am not only one with God, but, because 'with God,' one also with the neighbor" (T.a.). Bonhoeffer counters: " 'To be one' with God and with the neighbor is something entirely different from being in community with them. Barth, however, uses both expressions synonymously. But where only the one is loved in the other no communio is possible, and there is the danger of romanticism" (*SC,* 170).

manticism" (*SC,* 170). But "The person who loves God must, by God's will, really love the neighbor" (*SC,* 169).[27]

While serving a German congregation in Barcelona in 1928, Bonhoeffer continued his engagement with Barth's work. He studied the "Prolegomena" of the *Christian Dogmatics* of 1927 anew, and found reading that volume very worthwhile.[28] It would appear, however, that, in the context of Bonhoeffer's experiences in Spain, this rereading of Barth tended to strengthen Bonhoeffer's reservations. "I have come to question whether Barth could have written at all in Spain, whether he ever had eyes for conditions outside Germany. Given the way things are here, the ecclesiastical and political conditions, one is inclined at least to examine his theology from its very beginning."[29]

A few weeks later, Bonhoeffer expresses himself more clearly. In the letter to W. Dress, undated but postmarked 20 April 1928, he writes that he is reading the novel *Leben Jesu in Palästina, Schlesien und anderswo* (The life of Jesus in Palestine, Silesia, and elsewhere) by the Catholic theologian Joseph Wittig, published in 1927, and admits that, in face of the "grave conditions" that one "encounters again and again" in the congregational life in Barcelona, this man's "great piety" does indeed affect him — despite the fact that the novel is close to "mystical literature and

27. It is interesting that Bonhoeffer relies on Bultmann in this context; *Jesus and the Word,* 115: "Whatever of kindness, pity, mercy, I show my neighbour is not something that I do for God; . . . the neighbour is not a sort of tool, by means of which I practice the love of God," cited in *SC,* 170, while behind Barth's realization of the commandment to love the neighbor there lurks "Luther's utterly insightful discussion about 'cursing as a work of the Holy Spirit'" (*Romans,* 453, T.a.). "(In view of the double nature of predestination and in recalling that God is *free* before even the greatest love shown to God!,)" there remains for Barth "the possibility, which no absolute love-ethic can eradicate and which has to be considered in fear and trembling, that worship of God can also be engaged in significantly in an *other* palpable activity namely as *love* of the neighbour" (*Romans,* 452f., T.a.). Here Barth is more "Lutheran" than the Lutheran Bonhoeffer!

28. Dietrich Bonhoeffer in a letter to Walter Dress, dated 13 March 1928; cf. "Dietrich Bonhoeffers Abschied von der Berliner 'Wintertheologie' — Neue Funde aus seiner Spanienkorrespondenz 1928," ed. R. Staats and M. Wünsche, *Zeitschrift für Neuere Theologiegeschichte/Journal for the History of Modern Theology* 1 (1994): 188: "I am reading Barth's *Dogmatics* again. It is very much worth the effort." In light of this comment, the editors' statement that Bonhoeffer realized "how utterly apart from Barth" he was appears, to say the least, somewhat exaggerated.

29. Staats and Wünsche, 188.

how theologically uninhibited that literature is." Bonhoeffer admits that "Barth had immunized me against that sort of thing for some years," and that he had virtually "become personally dangerous." Bonhoeffer now perceives theology, generally speaking, "in constant danger of imposing norms on piety, of forcing it into specific rules and regulations and limiting it." That is "surely an advantage," but it can become "fruitful" only "when there is an overabundance that has to be kept in check lest it become dangerous."[30]

The danger of regulating piety theologically became clear to Bonhoeffer particularly in connection with the "naïveté and piety" of an "otherwise rather wild young man."[31] Writing to W. Dress on 14 June 1928, Bonhoeffer ponders the idea of writing his habilitation dissertation on the topic of "the child and theology."[32] But even where he feels that he has to oppose him, Barth remains the standard by which he measures his work. Bonhoeffer is searching for a way of making the doctrine of the "sinlessness" of Christ fruitful for pastoral care, "so that one no longer looks to one's sin but only to Christ and that conscience ceases to be seen as the voice of God but as that of the tempter who only wants to fasten attention to the past instead of the present and what is to come. I find these ideas quite redeeming and liberating, however unBarthian they are."[33]

We draw the following preliminary conclusion: the naive piety that Bonhoeffer encountered among pietistic members of his congregation, in the uninhibitedness of Catholic "literary mysticism," but above all in the faith of children, seems to him to be addressed far too little in academic theology as a whole and particularly in Barth.

This critique of Barth is given its epistemological supports in Bonhoeffer's habilitation dissertation, *Act and Being*, in terms of the Lutheran dictum *finitum capax infiniti*. In this study, it is Barth who deci-

---

30. Staats and Wünsche, 189f.

31. Staats and Wünsche, 196; this letter is dated 1 September 1928.

32. Staats and Wünsche, 193. The dissertation Bonhoeffer wrote for his habilitation, *Act and Being*, in fact concludes with a section entitled "The Definition of Being in Christ by Means of the Future: The Child" (*AB*, 157-61).

33. The picture of Barth that emerges in this "eudaemonistic" reflection of Bonhoeffer's on the doctrine of sin is rather odd. It was Barth, of all people, who was later accused, especially by Lutherans, of not taking sin seriously enough in his doctrine of the "nihil."

sively shapes the argument next to, or more precisely, as the antipode to, Heidegger. In commenting on this work, Eberhard Bethge remarks pertinently that "to Bonhoeffer the old *Extra Calvinisticum* is a troubling contestation when it ends up by preventing the complete entry into this world of the majesty of God, and he surmises that it is at work when he sees Barth establishing the majesty of God by the methods of Kantian transcendentalism" (*DBE*, 98, T.a.). Yet, in *Act and Being* Bonhoeffer relativizes his summary of the formally logical character of Barth's dialectics when he notes that "the proviso made by dialectical theology is not a logical one that might be cancelled by the opposite but, in view of predestination, a real one in each case" (*AB*, 86). Nonetheless, he senses in Barth's corresponding "attempt of unsystematic thought" (*AB*, 87)[34] the danger that "the contingent positivity" of "the occurrence of salvation" be formalized and rationalized (*AB*, 124) in that God is "understood as pure act" (*AB*, 83).[35] Bonhoeffer retorts:

> In revelation it is not so much a question of the freedom of God — eternally remaining within the divine self, aseity — on the other side of revelation, as it is of God's coming out of God's own self in revelation. It is a matter of God's *given* Word, the covenant in which God is bound by God's own action. . . . God is free not from human beings but for them. Christ is the word of God's freedom. God *is* present, that is, not in eternal nonobjectivity but — to put it quite provisionally for now —

34. Here Bonhoeffer renders Barth's reasons for this "attempt of unsystematic thought" according to the essay "Fate and Idea in Theology" (1929), in *The Way of Theology in Karl Barth: Essays and Comments*, ed. H. Martin Rumscheidt, trans. George Hunsinger (Allison Park, Pa.: Pickwick, 1986), 25-61. "No theological idea can as such ever comprehend God, it remains 'strictly speaking . . . a witness to the devil.' . . . Of this Barth himself is conscious: even dialectical thinking is no way to capture God. How could it be otherwise, we might ask, since before all thought there stands unfathomable predestination?" (*AB*, 86-87).

35. Not only is God understood by Barth "as pure act," but God's revelation "is interpreted purely in terms of act," as "an event that happens to someone who listens, free to suspend the relation at any moment. How could it be otherwise, since it is the 'majestically free favor of God' [Barth] which establishes the relation and remains its lord?" (*AB*, 83). Bonhoeffer refers here to Barth's 1927 *Dogmatics* (p. 295; new critical edition, Gerhard Sauter, ed. [Zürich: Theologischer Verlag, 1982], 390f.). Cf. also Bonhoeffer's rendering of Barth's view that "God is free inasmuch as God is bound to nothing, not even the 'existing,' 'historical' Word. The Word as truly God's is free" (*AB*, 82).

"haveable," graspable in the Word within the church. Here the formal understanding of God's freedom is countered by a substantial one. (*AB*, 90-91)[36]

There is no doubt: this is a Lutheran protesting against the Calvinian *"non capax."* Yet, Bonhoeffer's purpose is similar to Barth's, namely, to disturb the theological system. But the disturbance is to arise from Christ, whom Bonhoeffer thinks of less over against the church but much more as "existing as community" (*AB*, 112). For "from such a position," that is, from that of ecclesiology, "the problem of the theological system, too, could be raised and solved in quite a different way" (*AB*, 91).

It is in the congregation where "God's freedom" manifests itself precisely in "that God binds God's self to human beings," and that "the revelation is somehow held fast here" (*AB*, 112). If this is true, the question of the "continuity of revelation," namely, a continuity which "impinges on existence," raises itself unavoidably. It is obviously not sufficient for Bonhoeffer to say with Barth that God's revelation impinges on the existence of the listening human being "in each instance." Rather, everything depends on revelation being "always present (in the sense of 'what is in the future')" (*AB*, 113). For "it is only in the community of faith itself that revelation can be understood in its real, existence-affecting being" (*AB*, 116). In this context Bonhoeffer even goes so far as to assert that in the congregation "every member of the church may . . . 'become a Christ' to the others."

Everything now hinges on understanding clearly that it is not at all Bonhoeffer's intention in his insistence on "the continuity of revelation" to nullify Barth's repudiation of the ideas of continuity found in liberal theology. The fact is that Barth's repudiation of any continuity whatever

36. Cf. the similar critique of Barth in Bonhoeffer's 1931/32 lectures on the history of systematic theology in the twentieth century. "The understanding of the *sola fide* calls for the radical concept of God's freedom. Barth's term 'in each instance.' . . . In contrast the Lutheran: (it is) God's freedom and honor to have bound Godself wholly to the Word. Not freedom from but freedom for. . . . The community lives of this in freely given continuity which is Christ himself present" (*DBW,* 11:211). According to *AB*, 82 n. 1, the most important reference in Luther is in the Weimar edition, 23:157: "It is the honor of our God, however, that, in giving the divine self for our sake in deepest condescension, entering into flesh and bread, into our mouth, heart and bowel and suffering for our sake, God be dishonorably handled, both on the altar and the cross."

between hither and yon was meant above all for Bonhoeffer's — and his own — teacher Adolf von Harnack and liberal theology as a whole. This is clearly stated in his correspondence with Harnack: "my rejoinder to your reproof of 'severing' . . . , is that you empty faith by asserting a continuity between the 'human' and faith just as you empty revelation by saying that there is a continuity between history and revelation. I do not sever; I do repudiate every continuity between hither and yon. . . . Parable, parable only can be all 'becoming' in view of the birth from death to life. . . ."[37] Bonhoeffer too is not concerned with the continuity between hither and yon, but with an endured, an imposed continuity in the opposite direction: from the there to the here, that is to say, from above to below. He could well endorse Barth's statement from the Tambach address, "always from above to below, and never the reverse, if we want to understand ourselves rightly" (WGWM, 324, T.a.).[38] But the Word really became flesh and, in Christ, "exists as community"; therefore, Bonhoeffer immediately ascribes a social and historical dimension to this vertical-from-above. He writes that "community with God by definition establishes social community as well" (SC, 63). "Thus revelation happens in the community of faith; it requires primarily a Christian sociology" (AB, 113). For that reason, "how existentiality and continuity come together in the concept of *pati*" must be examined in relation to "the concept of the church" (AB, 116). Consequently, Bonhoeffer could not possibly adopt for his purposes the programmatic statement of Barth's Tambach address: "*We* live more deeply in the No than in the Yes, more deeply in criticism and protest than in naïveté, more deeply in longing for the future than in participation in the present" (WGWM, 311-12).[39] In relation to the church, Bonhoeffer would stress the exact opposite. In the community of faith, the naïveté of the child is quite possible; "Home is the community . . . of Christ, always 'future,' present 'in faith' because we are chil-

---

37. H. Martin Rumscheidt, *Revelation and Theology: An Analysis of the Barth-Harnack Correspondence of 1923* (Cambridge: Cambridge University Press, 1972), 49.

38. In his lectures on "new publications in systematic theology," delivered in the winter term of 1932/33, Bonhoeffer comments approvingly: "Human speech" concerning God must correspond to God's way coming from above to what is below. In my thinking I "must take note of this from above to the below" (DBW, 12:154).

39. "The Christian's Place in Society," 311-12. But note the later "retraction" of this theological "negativism" in Barth's 1956 essay "The Humanity of God." (See below, 132-33.)

dren of the future . . ." (*AB*, 116). Here what is yet to come is already present and — albeit in a preliminary way — at our disposal "in faith" (*AB*, 112).

According to Bonhoeffer, Barth's "fateful mistake . . . to have substituted for the concept of creator and lord that of the subject" (*AB*, 125)[40] was symptomatic of his formalization of God's freedom. For that ultimately means that God is not understood "as person" (*AB*, 125). Bonhoeffer insists that "the Protestant idea of the church is conceived in personal terms — that is, God reveals the divine self in the church as person. . . . Hence, the gospel is somehow held fast here. God's freedom has woven itself into this personlike community of faith, and it is precisely this which manifests what God's freedom is: that God binds God's self to human beings" (*AB*, 112).

The acuity of the critique of Barth present in the habilitation dissertation should not deceive one into ranking Bonhoeffer with the colleagues at the Berlin faculty in their opposition to Barth. The converse is more likely: precisely because he feels close to him — the many approvingly cited quotations affirm this perception — Bonhoeffer endeavors to work out as clearly as possible the differences which nevertheless exist between them. In fact, he rather tries to keep in conversation with each other the controversial positions of Barth, on the one side, and those of the Berlin faculty, on the other. "But that does not make him an ordinary theologian of mediation, even though *Act and Being* is a masterpiece of mediating theology. Rather, he senses that the existing contrasts are no real and final contrasts. The remarkable theological freedom Bonhoeffer exercised during the Church Struggle, while rigorously maintaining his place in what was the real front, manifests itself here as the ability to rise above phantom-like confrontations in a theologically legitimate manner."[41]

Another example of Bonhoeffer's mediating position at the time of his habilitation is how he spoke about the controversy between his teacher

40. Cf. Barth's *Die christliche Dogmatik im Entwurf*, 127; new critical edition, 166: "It is quite simply the logical question about the subject, predicate and object of the little sentence: 'God speaks,' *Deus dixit*." Note Barth's comments on these "then in fact . . . unguardedly and ambiguously" used words in *CD* I/1, 296, *340*.

41. Hanfried Müller, *Von der Kirche zur Welt. Ein Beitrag zu der Beziehung des Wortes Gottes auf die societas in Dietrich Bonhoeffers theologischer Entwicklung* (Leipzig: Koehler & Amelang, 1961), 152.

Adolf von Harnack and Karl Barth[42] in the memorial address for Harnack on 15 June 1930: "And if he [scil., Harnack] ever spoke anxiously, or uttered warnings in respect of the most recent developments in our field of scholarship, this was motivated exclusively by his fear that the view of the others might perhaps be in danger of confusing something alien with the pure quest for truth" (*NRS,* 26). It is the scientific theologian Harnack, of all people, whom Bonhoeffer then depicts as a secret church dogmatician in Barth's (and Bonhoeffer's own) sense. ". . . Adolf von Harnack . . . was a theologian, a conscious theologian, and we believed that this was the only standpoint from which it was possible to understand him. . . . Theology means speaking of God. . . . In Harnack, the theologian, . . . truth and freedom found their true connection without becoming arbitrariness. It was like him to say too little, indeed many words too few, rather than to say one word too many on these matters" (*NRS,* 26). In the eyes of Bonhoeffer, in other words, Harnack practiced an "arcane discipline" in relation to the bond of theology to the church, which bond made the freedom of theology possible in the first place as a scholarly discipline. Harnack's theological liberalism was theologically legitimate only on the basis of this "arcane" bond.

The controversy between the Berlin faculty and Barth is similarly softened in Bonhoeffer's inaugural lecture, "The Question of the Human in Contemporary Philosophy and Theology," at that faculty on 31 July 1930. On one hand, Bonhoeffer salutes the "return" of contemporary theology to Luther; on the other, he also cites approvingly the lively opposition on the part of dialectical theology against Karl Holl, the initiator of this "Luther renaissance," and his reduction of Luther's faith to a religion of conscience (cf. *NRS,* 57f.). Bonhoeffer still repudiates every "fixed *finitum incapax*" because "there can be no mention of a possibility for revelation independent of the reality of this revelation itself" (*NRS,* 60). What is decisive now is that humans understand "that their nature is not to be *capax* or *incapax infiniti,* . . . but that their nature is determined by 'Thou art under sin' or 'Thou art under grace'" (*NRS,* 62).[43] The controversy between Lutherans and Calvinists is obviously relativized, as is that between the Berlin faculty and dialectical theology, by the "reality of the church of Christ" (*NRS,* 65). In this me-

---

42. Cf. Rumscheidt, 29-53.
43. Cf. the similar wording in *CD* I/1, 407, *466.*

diating effort it may well have been Bonhoeffer's purpose to make Barth's theology worthy of discussion in the context of the Berlin faculty, where it was viewed as scandalous.

4. As a "Barthian" in the United States of America

Bonhoeffer made a similar effort at mediation while studying at Union Theological Seminary in New York in 1930/31. He presented himself as so decidedly an advocate of the new theology that he was seen by U.S. American theologians as "the most convinced disciple of Karl Barth," as John Baillie put it (*DBE*, 117). This "Barthianism" becomes apparent above all in Bonhoeffer's address "The Theology of Crisis and Its Attitude toward Philosophy and Science" (see *DBW*, 10:434-49). Bonhoeffer declares "that I do not see any other possible way for you to get into real contact with his [scil., Barth's] thinking than by forgetting at least for this hour everything you have learned before concerning this problem." What is actually new in Barth's theology is that we stand again "in the tradition of Paul, Luther, Kierkegaard, in the tradition of genuine Christian thinking" (*DBW*, 10:435),[44] which philosophy of religion had abandoned long ago. Barth tries to let "the world of biblical thinking" come alive again.[45] "The logic of the Bible," however, is "God's coming which destroys all human attempts to come" (*DBW*, 10:438). Into the place of "general thinking and especially religious thinking," there enters "the category of the Word of God, of the revelation straight from above, from *outside* of man [*sic*], according to the justification of the sinner by grace." Theology as a scholarly discipline of the Word of God faces the difficulty, however, that it has to describe precisely this category which resists every form of general thinking, in terms of "general, formal presuppositions of think-

44. On the ancestry of Barth's theology given here, cf. also Bonhoeffer's article of 1931/32, "Concerning the Christian Idea of God." According to it, it is "the foolishness of the Christian idea of God" in the Christian paradox "which has been witnessed to by all genuine Christian thinking from Paul, Augustine, Luther, to Kierkegaard and Barth" (*DBW*, 10:432).

45. Cf., for example, Barth's essay "The Strange New World within the Bible," in *WGWM*, 28ff. Cf. also *Die christliche Dogmatik im Entwurf*, sec. 24: *"biblische Haltung"* and *"Denkform"* ("biblical attitude" and "thought-form"), new critical edition, 556 and 558.

ing." Here lies "the deepest contradiction in the task of theology" (*DBW,* 10:440).[46] And the task Bonhoeffer takes upon himself now is to present the relation of theology to philosophy and the natural sciences from the perspective of "theology of crisis" (as he calls it), even though Barth himself "has never published any comprehensive treatment of our problem" (*DBW,* 10:435). Bonhoeffer knows very well that however much he depends on Barth, he is very much on his own in seeking a solution to this problem which the theological situation in the United States seems to have posed for him. It appears that he feels himself especially qualified to undertake this task precisely because of his background in the theological liberalism of Berlin.

This constellation is most likely behind the view — such as that of Eberhard Bethge — that "it can be shown in the essays [Bonhoeffer] wrote for the Seminary that his proselyting zeal caused him, no doubt without realizing it, to mingle propositions of his own with Barth's and actually attributing them to him" (*DBE,* 117). It is not so much that Bonhoeffer "completely suppressed" his critical questions to Barth, as Bethge surmises; rather, he tries to carry Barth's thinking forward by integrating his own reservations, to "mingle" them with Barth's conception so as to relativize them on the basis of Barth's point of departure. It appears erroneous, therefore, to distance Bonhoeffer from Barth, as Hans Pfeifer does. Pfeifer suggests that the absolute contrasting of idea and reality which he discerns in Bonhoeffer's statement that "the revelation of God" is not executed "in the realm of ideas, but in the realm of reality" (*DBW,* 10:436), is "precisely not in line with Barth's intentions."[47] Indeed, Bonhoeffer does differ from Barth here in terminology while very much corresponding to his intention, which was to place the reality of revela-

---

46. Cf. again "Concerning the Christian Idea of God," where Bonhoeffer says: "Theological thinking is not a construction a priori, but a posteriori, as Karl Barth maintained. Therefore, it has to be conscious of its limitations. . . . That means that there is not one theological sentence which could presume to speak 'truth' unless it refers to the reality of God and the impossibility of embracing this reality in theological sentences. Every theoretical sentence generalizes. But God does not permit of generalization. Because he is reality, he is absolutely free of all theoretical generalization. Even a sentence like 'God is love' is, in the last analysis, not the truth about God, because it is not a matter of course that by such a sentence I could calculate that God is love. On the contrary, God is wrath as well as love and this we also should know" (*DBW,* 10:426).

47. Pfeifer, 79. Cf. *DBE,* 117 n. 30.

tion into priority over its possibility.[48] Even in the essay which Pfeifer cites as being opposed to Bonhoeffer, Barth seeks to understand "God as *reality*," and as "real in the *eminent* sense." The thought of God, "to be taken seriously . . . must be an expression of reality, indeed of the great reality which includes and surpasses all other reality in itself. It must represent the one reality present in all other realities, hidden but not entirely hidden there."[49] Bonhoeffer would have had such statements in mind in the United States when he referred to Barth in claiming that revelation occurred "in the realm of reality." In the essay Pfeifer cites, Barth is not prepared to exclude "the concept of idea" from theological thinking, not — as Pfeifer seems to believe — in order to subtract something from the reality of revelation, but to secure[50] the concept of reality against being misunderstood as flat "reality" in the sense of the merely factual, and to keep it open for changes.[51] Barth would therefore agree with Bonhoeffer that God's revelation "is not executed in the realm of ideas but in the realm of reality"; but it "is executed" (*DBW*, 10:436), that is, it enters into "all other reality" in that it distinguishes itself as the reality of revelation from that other reality in order to change it materially. In his habilitation dissertation Bonhoeffer had put it as follows: "There is no God who 'is there'" [Einen Gott, den "es gibt," gibt es nicht] (*AB*, 115); he would surely have felt himself misunderstood were this sentence read as implying a contesting or diminishing of God's "reality."

48. Cf. Barth's 1927 *Dogmatics*, sec. 14 ("The Objective Possibility of Revelation"), 227 (new edition, 306f.): "We did not construct and shall wisely avoid constructing . . . the Word, God's Son, Jesus Christ himself, the reality of revelation, without which we would be in no position to give an account to ourselves about its possibilities."

49. Barth, "Fate and Idea," 37. There is a similar passage in the Barth-Harnack correspondence: "The Scriptures . . . witness to revelation. . . . *genuine* revelation that is, and not to a more or less concealed religious possibility of [the human being] but rather to the possibility of God, namely that [God] has acted under the form of a human possibility — and this as *reality*. According to this testimony, the Word became flesh, God himself became a human-historical *reality* and this took place in the *person of Jesus Christ*" (Rumscheidt, 44).

50. Cf. Barth, "Fate and Idea," 36: "The exact foreign word corresponding to the [concept] *Wirklichkeit* here would not be 'reality' but 'actuality.'"

51. Cf. Barth's discussion of "the fact . . . that materially changes all things and everything in all things . . . that God is" (*CD* II/1, 258). On this point, see Friedrich-Wilhelm Marquardt, *Theologie und Sozialismus. Das Beispiel Karl Barths,* 3rd ed. (Munich: Chr. Kaiser Verlag, 1985), 240f.

Erroneous too is the assumption of Gerhard Krause that in this particular lecture Bonhoeffer meant to highlight the task of a "general philosophical thinking" in the field of theology.[52] Indeed, Bonhoeffer wants to address the problem of the "relation between theology and philosophy with regard to the use of forms of general philosophical thinking in theology" (*DBW*, 10:440), but with the result that — as he approvingly cites Barth — "there is no Christian philosophy or philosophical terminology at all." Thus Barth could say that "it does not make very much difference what philosophy a theologian has, but everything depends upon how strongly he [*sic*] keeps his eyes on the category of the word of God, on the fact of revelation, of justification by faith" (*DBW*, 10:447). The use that theology makes of philosophy is therefore eclectic, as may be seen in how "Barth and his friends . . . try to point out what seems to them the most important trend in Kant's thought" instead of worrying about "a complete presentation of the manifold sides of Kant's philosophy" (*DBW*, 10:444). Such words tend at least to relativize the critique Bonhoeffer had made in *Act and Being* of Barth's Kantian transcendentalism, whereas conversely, the Berlin faculty is judged for disregarding the concreteness of revelation. "Ritschl, on whose theology I was brought up in Berlin, could not succeed in his attempt to free theology from the wrong metaphysical premise because he had not thought through the Christian category of revelation, as becomes obvious in his Christology, doctrine of sin and of justification" (*DBW*, 10:442).

5. The Meeting in Bonn and Its Consequences

The first face-to-face meeting of the "Barthian" Bonhoeffer with Karl Barth took place in July 1931 in Bonn, just after Bonhoeffer's return from the United States (cf. *DBE*, 131f.). Bonhoeffer wrote about it in a letter to his friend Erwin Sutz on 24 July 1931. "I don't think that I have ever regretted anything that I have failed to do in my theological past as much as the fact

---

52. G. Krause, "Dietrich Bonhoeffer," in *Theologische Realenzyklopädie,* vol. 7 (Berlin and New York: Walter de Gruyter, 1981), 58. Cf. my "Dietrich Bonhoeffer — wissenschaftlich verharmlost. Anmerkungen zu Gerhard Krauses Bonhoeffer-Artikel in der Theologischen Realenzyklopädie," in *Bonhoeffer-Rundbrief. Mitteilungen des Internationalen Bonhoeffer-Komitees, Sektion Bundesrepublik Deutschland,* no. 17 (Düsseldorf, 1984), 2ff.

that I did not come here earlier" (*NRS*, 115). In Bonn, Bonhoeffer had the opportunity to hear something of the new formulation of dogmatics which then began to be published in 1932 as *Church Dogmatics*. He wrote to Sutz: "It is important and surprising in the best way to see how Barth stands over and beyond his books. . . . I have been impressed even more by discussions with him than by his writings and his lectures" (*NRS*, 115-16).

Next to dogmatics, Bonhoeffer apparently was very interested while in Bonn in the question of ethics; the fact that he obtained a copy of lecture notes taken during Barth's "Ethics II" course presented in Münster during the winter semester of 1928/29 would support this observation (*NRS*, 115).[53] Quite to his surprise, he recognized in his conversations with Barth about ethics that in spite of much agreement, there were differences which could not entirely be removed. "He would not make concessions to me where I expected that he would have to. Beside the one great light in the night, he said, there were also many little lights, so-called 'relative ethical criteria'; he could not, however, make their significance and application and nature comprehensible to me — we didn't get beyond a simple reference to the Bible" (*NRS*, 116, T.a.).[54] Bonhoeffer himself did not want to turn grace into a principle (something he apparently judges Barth to be doing), but he cannot understand "why everything else should *not* be killed" (*NRS*, 116).

In spite of such differences, Bonhoeffer left Bonn believing that Barth was "really someone that one can get things out of!" whereas there was no one anymore "in poor old Berlin" with whom he could talk seriously (*NRS*, 116).

That is why Bonhoeffer repeatedly sought contact with Barth by letter and in person during his time as an instructor at the University of Berlin from 1931 to 1933. "On their first meeting, and in the years that

53. This is probably a copy prepared by R. Pestalozzi and circulated in 1929 by the World Student Christian Federation.

54. On this early version of Barth's "doctrine of lights," see "Church and Culture," delivered in Amsterdam in 1926; *Theology and Church: Shorter Writings, 1920-1928*, trans. Louise Pettibone Smith (London: SCM, 1962), 343: "The work of culture *can* be parabolic, *can* be a reference to what the human being, as God's creature and in God's image, is to become, can be a reflection of the light of the eternal Logos who became flesh, and yet was, is and is to be also king in the whole domain of nature. [The work of culture] *can* be witness to the promise which was given human beings at the beginning. 'It can,' I say. In Christ, it *is*. Reconciliation in Christ is the restoration of the lost promise" (T.a.).

immediately followed, the whole complex of Bonhoeffer's early critical questions to Barth dating from 1927 and 1929 seemed to have been buried and forgotten. . . . They do not occur at all in the documents relating to the personal meetings between the two in the years from 1931 to 1933" (*DBE*, 134-35). Bethge finds it necessary to qualify that the early questions "recur in the university lectures beginning in 1931," but even there they are held within the now "overriding purpose of presenting Barth's theological revolution to the Berlin forum in as positive a light as possible" (*DBE*, 135).

This may be seen in Bonhoeffer's first course in the winter semester of 1931/32, "The History of Systematic Theology in the Twentieth Century." In the context of a detailed presentation of the "revolution" wrought by Barth, he describes Barth's position by saying that "the object of theology [is] solely the *logos theou*," the Word of God. Human beings can "no longer" go "behind this beginning" (*DBW*, 11:99). However, it is plain that Barth's theology is also "affected by the war-experience," and "one hopes that this is so in every theologian." Still, Barth's "critical theology [is] . . . not to be explained in terms of the collapse of the war . . . but in terms of a new reading of Scripture, of the Word which God has spoken in God's self-revelation." The "revolution" is described precisely in saying that Barth no longer wants to confuse "religion with God. . . . This is not war-psychosis but listening to God's Word. Barth does not come from the trenches but from a Swiss village pulpit" (*DBW*, 11:194f.). Also, in Barth's "dialectical manner of speaking," Bonhoeffer now sees that some of his own concerns about the constraints of theological systems are being taken up. The point of that speaking is "to safeguard the freedom of God; it is about the mystery of predestination. . . . Genuine dialectics" places "speech and counter-speech" one against the other, while the "truth" itself remains "beyond the imperceivable middle." "God remains free also over the dialectics." Barth is intent precisely on "not affixing God to his theology. He intends so much more to set God free from it" (*DBW*, 11:202). Similarly, Bonhoeffer now salutes Barth's *habitus practicus* (the practical turn) by means of which "theology is placed wholly into the service of the church" (*DBW*, 11:203).[55] The following may

---

55. The whole section from which those citations are taken bears a title that recalls the title of Barth's first collection of essays: "The Word of God and Theology" (*DBW*, 11:199). [In its English translation, that volume is entitled *The Word of God and the Word of Man*. Trans.]

serve as a summary of his theological agreement with Barth. "This is a theology which once again wants to understand wholly the *sola fide,* and for that reason speaks on the grounds of predestination and, hence, dialectically. . . . There is nothing in all of recent literature that seriously poses a challenge to Barth" (*DBW,* 11:211). But Bonhoeffer does want to "pose a challenge" to Barth, which is why he cannot silence critical questions. The earlier reservations retreat quite noticeably; only at the conclusion of those lectures on "systematic theology" does he recollect the denominationally determined polemics from *Act and Being.* "The interpretation in terms of pure act does not do justice to the thinking of the New Testament and of Luther." Here "the denominational problem [emerges] anew." Barth had "seen and discovered the boundary line Calvinism had drawn against Catholicism." But now the polemical edge is directed primarily against "contemporary Lutherans": it is a "shameful situation" that Lutheran theology "no longer sees its boundary line against Catholicism." Bonhoeffer now wants to put a Lutheran profile on Barth's "radical concept of the freedom of God." He does so by understanding "God's freedom and glory" not as a "freedom from" but as a "freedom for" which becomes event not only "in each distinct instance" but "in a freely granted continuity" present in the community of faith as "the present Christ" (*DBW,* 11:211).[56]

There are reverberations of Bonhoeffer's early critique of Barth that had been motivated by an ecclesiological interest in the lectures delivered in the summer of 1932 on the nature of the church. Barth is reproached, for example, for individualism. With Barth, as with Troeltsch, the "starting point" is "the *individual's* knowledge of God." Against that, one must maintain with Luther that "the knowledge of God has primarily the *community* for its subject" (*DBW,* 11:259). Even in his seminar on problems of a "theological psychology," conducted in the winter semester of 1932/

56. There is still a reminiscence of this early critique in the introduction to Bonhoeffer's course on the church in 1932 where, in reference to Barth's actualism, Bonhoeffer says: "We must speak of the being and the act of the church together" (*DBW,* 11:243). On the problem of continuity, cf. the extensive discussion of Barth in Bonhoeffer's seminar on "theological psychology," winter term 1932/33. "The continuity of the historically existing person is not to be found in discernible religiousness but in the person-like church. . . . Human existence has continuity only through the other person. It is not possible to conceive of ourselves as human beings other than as being bound to the neighbor. . . . (In the sense of continuous existence) we *are* as a person only in the church" (*DBW,* 12:187 [text plus n. 51]).

33, in a like manner and against Barth, Bonhoeffer insists on a "continuity" of revelation in the church (*DBW,* 12:187).

In a manner of speaking, Barth's book *Anselm: Fides Quaerens Intellectum: Faith in Search of Understanding,* published in 1931, complied with Bonhoeffer's insistence on a "freely given continuity" of revelation in the community of faith. This did not escape Bonhoeffer's notice: in his lectures on recent theology, delivered in the winter of 1932/33, he comments in relation to that book, where the shift from "Christian" to "church" dogmatics was made, that "theology is a thinking that is bound to the church as the place of revelation. . . . Its object is the creed, spoken and affirmed beforehand. That is why theology is possible only within the domain of the church. Its presupposition implies that it can be begun only with prayer. If it does not begin that way, then it is neither appropriate to its object nor scholarly" (*DBW,* 12:160-61).[57]

In 1932 Bonhoeffer reviewed Karl Heim's *Glauben und Denken,* published the year before.[58] Eberhard Bethge believes that in the review one may hear echoes of Bonhoeffer's early "epistemological criticism of Barth," although he adds that his critique now entirely "lacks the sharpness of 1929." Bethge surmises that "the 1944 observation about 'positivism of revelation'" intimates itself here (*DBE,* 136, T.a.), so that one may speak of a subterranean continuity of Bonhoeffer's early questions into his late criticisms. However, Bonhoeffer's review of Heim is actually a clear defense of Barth against Heim's attack, even though "Heim's whole push toward concreteness" seems to correspond to Bonhoeffer's own quest for ethical concreteness, particularly in view of "the question: what must I do?" (*DBW,* 12:228). But Bonhoeffer unmasks Heim's procedure of beginning with the "ultimate questions" as an attempt to do theology without presuppositions, that is to say, from without the church in the final analysis (*DBW,* 12:161). Heim's charge that Barth lacks concreteness therefore turns "directly back on himself" (*DBW,*

57. See also the letter to Erwin Sutz of 25 December 1931: "Barth's book about Anselm is a great delight to me; you must read it when you have time. He shows the countless academic cripples, once and for all, that he really does know how better to interpret and still remain sovereign." Bonhoeffer continues: "Nothing of course has in fact become any less questionable," which quite likely is in reference to Bonhoeffer's ethical questions to which, as before, the answers were still outstanding (*NRS,* 136).

58. Cf. Bonhoeffer's critique in the lectures "Recent Publications in Systematic Theology," in contrast to Barth's book on Anselm (*DBW,* 12:161).

12:228). For, if Barth is in danger of "making God an object of thought," as Heim remarks, then it is the crux of every theology. "The idiosyncratic feature" of Barth's theology, what distinguishes it from every other theology, is Barth's belief "that he cannot secure himself against this danger while consistently doing his thinking with an eye on this danger" (*DBW*, 12:228).[59] Therefore, Barth was quite correct in his written communication to Bonhoeffer when he thought that the latter had shown agreement with his theology in the article on Heim (*NRS*, 201).

6. The Question of Ethical Concreteness

The extensive agreement between Barth and Bonhoeffer, particularly in the hitherto disputed question of epistemology, must not blind us to the fact that the controversy about ethics which broke out surprisingly during the first meeting in Bonn remained unresolved between the Bonn theologian and his Berlin ally on the eve of the rise of fascism. Eberhard Bethge remarks quite accurately that Bonhoeffer did not receive, "in the form that he desire[d]," "Barth's support in his concern for the concrete ethical commandments" in the "phase of eagerly sought meetings between 1931 and 1933" (*DBE*, 134). Again it is not surprising that precisely the ethical question appeared to Bonhoeffer in those years as the most urgent of all questions. His letter of 8 October 1931 to Erwin Sutz indicates that he, in face of "the unprecedented state of our public life in Germany" resulting from the economic crisis, was under "the very definite impression that they are standing at a tremendous turning point in world history. Whether it will lead to Bolshevism or to a liberal compromise, who knows? And after all, who knows which is the better? But the coming winter will leave no one in Germany untouched. Seven million unemployed, that is, fifteen or twenty million people hungry; I don't know how Germany or the individual will survive it" (*NRS*, 118). Ten days later, in a letter to Helmut Rössler, he writes: "One thinks that something very big

---

59. Cf. also *DBW*, 12:203: "Because Barth knows that the *whole* of reason is for nought, he can speak 'according to reason' more courageously and with less constraint than someone who seeks to hold on to a final claim of reason." On this basis there arise for Bonhoeffer also "other possibilities of interpreting Luther."

is about to happen any moment now, but all one can do is wait. Will this Winter bring the great change? I do hope so but fear that it won't." In the midst of the confusing situation and looking at the church, Bonhoeffer feels that "Christianity's great dying" is upon us; "it is becoming more and more incomprehensible that 'the city will be spared' for the sake of *one* righteous person. . . . Who believes that anymore? This invisibility does us in. . . . This maddening, persistent condition of being thrown back upon the invisible God — no human being can stand that any longer." It must become visible "in our personal life that Christ was here" (*DBW,* 11:33f.).

In striving for a visible actualization of the eschatological expectation in the reality of society, Bonhoeffer seems at first glance to move in the direction of what Otto Dibelius's book *Das Jahrhundert der Kirche,* published in 1928, had propagated as "the flight into visibility." Karl Barth diagnosed the book's substance in those words.[60] Even Bonhoeffer's phrasing of the question is reminiscent of Dibelius's thematic.[61] However, at the political level Bonhoeffer is at the opposite pole in that he seeks ethical concreteness, contrary to the clericalism of Dibelius, in terms of pacifism and socialism. At that time and with the help of Franz Hildebrandt, he makes contact with Friedrich Siegmund-Schultze and his "social work alliance" (Soziale Arbeitsgemeinschaft), in Fruchtstrasse, located in Berlin's eastern section (*DB,* 233f.). His interest is consumed now by the question of socialism and pacifism as the forms of an ethically concrete propagation of the gospel.

Bonhoeffer's ethical question to Barth had appeared initially in his "History of Systematic Theology in the Twentieth Century" lectures. These lectures concluded with this question: "Barth's conception" of ethics as "demonstration" not only excludes "an ethics of principles," but also "every concrete" ethics. How then is it possible to develop "a Christian ethics as a scholarly discipline"? "How am I to preach the Law?" (*DBW,* 11:212-13). The concern with preaching the Law was also quite likely the reason why Bonhoeffer was one of the very few German theologians who had taken notice not only of the completely revised second edition of

60. See Karl Barth, "Die Not der evangelischen Kirche," *Zwischen den Zeiten,* no. 2 (1931): 89ff.
61. Cf. Otto Dibelius, *Friede auf Erden? Frage, Erwägungen, Antwort* (Berlin, 1930).

Barth's *Epistle to the Romans,* but also of the more religious-social first edition. At the center of the first edition was "God's visible approach to the world," while the second edition emphasized the God who comes ever anew to the world in each distinct instance (*DBW,* 11:209).[62] Bonhoeffer, too, was concerned with God's visible coming and with a corresponding preaching of the Law as a concretization of Barth's actualism. And that is why his ethical questions to Barth may be understood also as recollections of the unresolved issues of the first edition of *Romans* which the revised second edition had not settled.

In this search for the "principle of concreteness of the general demands of obedience," Bonhoeffer was not at all interested in creating a denominational difference between himself and Barth. He makes this plain when he speaks of the general "dire need of the church,"[63] which is that it does not know how to preach the concrete commandment. "Luther could write his *de servo arbitrio* and his pamphlet on usury at one and the same time. Why can't we do so any more? *Who will show us Luther?*" (*DBW,* 11:213).

In his seminar conducted in the summer of 1932, "Is There a Christian Ethics?" Bonhoeffer seeks further clarification of the ethical question. In the introduction, speaking about Barth's contribution to the solution of the problem, he says Barth understood God's will in essence as "gift-making, giving; he sees it as something indicative and independent of the doings of humans (predestination)." That is obviously not enough for Bonhoeffer; he is interested in the "connection" between the "self-acting and working" will of God and the "action of human beings" (*DBW,* 11:305). Bonhoeffer draws on two essays on this subject that Barth had

---

62. The compiler of the first edition of the lectures, Otto Dudzus, assumed on the basis of Joachim Kanitz's lecture notes that Bonhoeffer's distinction between a first and a second edition referred most likely to Barth's *Romans.* (See *GS,* 5:225.) The editors of the new edition of these lectures in the *DBW* now assume, instead, that the distinction is between Barth's *Christliche Dogmatik im Entwurf* and the first volume of *Church Dogmatics.* This creates a difficulty in that they have to acknowledge a Bonhoefferian misunderstanding of Barth's intention. If one follows Dudzus, this difficulty disappears. The phrasing "first and second edition" in relation to Barth's different dogmatics proposals is nowhere to be found in Bonhoeffer, and would be quite unusual, whereas it had become customary in connection with the two *Romans* editions since 1922.

63. See Barth's address "Die Not der evangelischen Kirche," delivered at the University of Berlin on 31 January 1931. It met with the vehement protest of Otto Dibelius, whereas Bonhoeffer expressly shows his agreement here.

published in the space of seven years.[64] According to the text reconstructed by Otto Dudzus, Bonhoeffer states that in the later of the two essays, Barth had gone "in no small manner" beyond his earlier position "in relation to the concreteness of our actions" (*GS*, 5:283). In the first essay, entitled "The Problem of Ethics Today," written in 1922, the ethical question is raised wholly under the impact of the revision of *Romans,* that is, "only from a position of permanent and depressing not-knowing," which requires great care so as not "to turn the ethical crisis all too quickly into a fixed position by means of dialectics" (*GS*, 5:280).[65] According to Bonhoeffer, while "the continuity of ethical endeavor" is secured in the essay solely through the "uncertain connection between the light of forgiveness and the shadowy area of ethics" (*GS*, 5:282),[66] the second essay, entitled "The Holy Spirit and the Christian Life," written in 1930, can speak quite positively in its eschatological perspective of a continuity of Christian existence in ethics. "The Christian life is new life in hope born from the Holy Spirit. The Holy Spirit is a spirit of promise and, for that reason, the new life is present only eschatologically. 'Eschatological' means the repudiation of every continuity presumed by human beings to exist between them and God. But when understood eschatologically, a positive, genuine continuity to our existence comes into being" (*GS*, 5:283). On the other hand, "the chiliastic basis of our ethical action," found in the earlier essay, has "disappeared. Gone is its future-image of history" (*GS*, 5:284). However much this change must have suited Bonhoeffer the Lutheran, he was nevertheless very concerned about the loss of political unambiguity in ethics. In the earlier essay Barth had raised the ethical question still "in terms of the image of the thousand year reign" and came to the conclusion that "without an ounce of chiliasm . . . [there could be] no ethics"; this had also put the question of "the socialist hope for the future" on the agenda (*GS*, 5:281; cf. *DBW,* 12:307 n. 14).[67] Was that hope no longer pertinent at the beginning of the thirties?

Contrary to Karl Barth, Dietrich Bonhoeffer was not a socialist. Nonetheless, the question of social justice and international peace took

64. K. Barth, "The Problem of Ethics Today," in *WGWM,* 136ff., and *The Holy Ghost and the Christian Life* (London: Muller, 1938).

65. Cf. Barth, "Problem of Ethics Today," 145f. and 151f.

66. Cf. Barth, "Problem of Ethics Today," 172f.

67. Cf. Barth, "Problem of Ethics Today," 157f.

on extreme urgency for him in the moment of danger, on the eve of Germany's turn to fascism.[68] But how does "the commandment 'Have faith now!' become the concrete 'Do not go to war!'"?[69] If it is not possible to provide a basis for a binding proclamation of the commandment "from within the cut-off sphere of humankind," then one must obviously search for an "ethics of revelation" in which the "gap is once again bridged," and that "as God's own action" (*DBW*, 12:308 n. 20). It is precisely in this search for an "ethics of revelation" as the theological foundation for socialism and pacifism that Bonhoeffer feels himself abandoned by Barth in 1932. After a meeting with him in Berlin, where on 11 April 1932 Barth had delivered a lecture entitled "Theology and Mission in the Present," Bonhoeffer wrote to Erwin Sutz (17 May 1932) that "in this matter" — the question of the theological basis of a socialist and pacifist ethics as God's concrete commandment — "Barth himself" did not side with him. However, Barth had admitted that "this point just was still uncannily troublesome for him" (*DBW*, 11:89).

Bonhoeffer searches for a solution in "the concept of sacrament" which he wants to "draw into" the discussion of ethics (*DBW*, 11:89).[70] "The gospel becomes concrete through the sacrament, the commandment through reality. The Word proclaimed without sacrament is in need of concreteness (the commandment!)" (*DBW*, 11:311 n. 42). Unlike conservative Lutheranism, which speaks of "orders of creation," an ethics of revelation, according to Bonhoeffer, can speak only of *"orders of preservation"* that are oriented "toward Christ"; "orders that are not closed in

68. Cf. Wolf-Dieter Zimmermann's reminiscences, "Years in Berlin," in the work edited by him and Ronald Gregor Smith, *I Knew Dietrich Bonhoeffer: Reminiscences by His Friends* (New York: Harper, 1966), 67: "With considerable astonishment I learned that he was a convinced Socialist and a pacifist. This attitude was so incomprehensible that for a time I mistrusted his ethics."

69. It must be kept in mind that Bonhoeffer's thought moves here from the already discovered content of ethics (pacifism) toward the theological foundation of it and not vice versa. Therefore, the question to Barth is one of dogmatics on the basis of the agreement that existed between them in ethics. On the question of peace in ethics, cf. his address of 26 July 1932 in Černohorské Kupele, "Zur theologischen Begründung der Weltbundarbeit," *DBW*, 11:327ff.; ET, "A Theological Basis for the World Alliance?" *NRS*, 153ff.

70. In this context, Bonhoeffer makes reference to his despairing sermon on 2 Chron. 20:12: "We do not know what we are to do but our eyes look for you" (*DBW*, 11:417). Cf. my *Dietrich Bonhoeffers Forderung einer Arkandisziplin*, 188ff.

themselves but point beyond themselves to Christ" (*DBW,* 11:312). Bonhoeffer's address "A Theological Basis for the World Alliance," delivered on 26 July 1932, shows that, just like socialism, "international peace" is for him such "an order of preservation of the world oriented toward Christ" which, in view of the emergence of fascism and the concomitant threat of war, had taken on "today" an "absolute urgency" (*NRS,* 163f.).

Two things become plain here. On the one hand, Bonhoeffer makes his own Karl Barth's rejection of the "teaching of Lutheranism" according to which "there is a hierarchy of sacred offices which are to be appropriated from an allegedly sacred order of creation." This teaching is for Bonhoeffer, too, "nothing but an evasion of the question of what we are to do" (*GS,* 5:282; cf. *DBW,* 12:312).[71] On the other hand, his discussion of the "orders of preservation" is meant to fill in a gap in Barth's understanding precisely where the theological foundation ought to be for a binding proclamation of peace and social justice as concrete commandments. While Barth depicted socialism during the revolutionary period after World War I as "the opposition to the old order,"[72] as an analogy that "demands continuity,"[73] Bonhoeffer was confronted by the same problem but in reverse order. It confronted him at a moment when the order of society was in grave danger;[74] he spoke of "the order of preservation" which presupposes a continuity of revelation in the ecumenical church. In the Tambach address of 1919, Barth could not help but, "at the crucial point, *give in* to the protest which . . . *socialism,* with concen-

71. Cf. Barth, "Problem of Ethics Today," 170-71; in his lectures on ethics at the University of Münster in 1928/29, Barth reverted to speaking of "orders of creation," but he refused to publish the lectures on account of this concession to the Lutherans.

72. Barth, "Christian's Place in Society," 319: the place of Christians in society should be "as hope-sharing and guilt-sharing comrades within social democracy, within which the problem of the opposition against what exists now has been raised and the parable of God's kingdom been given for our time" (T.a.).

73. Barth, "Christian's Place in Society," 317: "We *cannot* rest content with seeing in things transitory *only* a likeness of Something Else. There is an element in analogy that demands continuity."

74. In July 1932 Vice Chancellor Franz von Papen declared in the name of his government that all further participation of Germany in the Geneva negotiations on disarmament was halted. At the end of July the elections for the German Parliament took place; with 230 seats, the National Socialist German Workers Party (the Nazis) became the strongest party.

trated weight [makes] against the whole structure of society, intellectual and material" (*WGWM,* 315), whereas Bonhoeffer was most intent in 1932 to preserve this structure. His conservative justification of socialism is not meant to relativize the ethical problem socialism raises; on the contrary, the "absolute urgency" of it is to be made plain "by daring to put the commandment, definitely, exclusively and radically. In that case the church will dare to say, 'Do not engage in this war,' 'Now be Socialists,' uttering this commandment as the commandment *of God . . .*" (*NRS,* 159). A "certain partiality for those who are oppressed," for socialism as an ethical possibility that has "a greater parabolic capacity" (*Romans,* 2nd ed., 462f., T.a.), is not good enough for Bonhoeffer.[75] His words about socialism and international peace as "orders of preservation" contain certain relativizations, especially in relation to the conservative Lutheran ethics of orders;[76] yet, in stressing their orientation "toward Christ," Bonhoeffer seeks to prevent their utter seriousness as "concrete commandments" from being softened.[77] Thus, he repeats his question to Barth at the beginning of his lectures on "new publications in systematic theology" in the winter of 1932/33. "The question now is only this: 'where and how is ethics to be founded?'" (*GS,* 5:305; cf. *DBW,* 12:156f.). And for that reason the decisive question to the church is: Can

75. In *Romans* Barth says socialism is a protest movement that seeks not to preserve but to "transform" the existing order. Since Christianity also does "not set its mind on *high things*" (cf. Rom. 12:16) but finds "truth more in the 'No' than in the 'Yes,'" it "displays a certain partiality for those who are oppressed, deprived of their due, immature, sullen and . . . ready to rise up. There is, *for that reason,* much in the cause of social democracy that evokes the approval of Christianity" (462f., T.a.).

76. Cf. *DBW,* 11:312: since orders of preservation "point beyond themselves to Christ," they are "fragile orders and no longer very good ones, valuable in themselves." Bonhoeffer's use of "orders of preservation" is given its foundation in the creation theology lectures of the winter term of 1932/33 known as *Creation and Fall.* In connection with Gen. 3:21 — "And Yahweh God made cloaks of skin for Adam and for his wife and clothed them with these" — Bonhoeffer says: "The Creator is now the preserver; the created world is now the fallen but *preserved world.* . . . All orders of our fallen world are God's orders of preservation that uphold and preserve us for Christ. They are not orders of creation but orders of preservation. They have no value in themselves; instead they find their end and meaning only through Christ" (*CF,* 139-40).

77. According to Otto Dudzus (*GS,* 5:292), the concept of orders of preservation "was a polemic concept in intention right from the start in the debates of that time and probably goes back to Bonhoeffer." Bonhoeffer dropped it again when it was exploited by conservatives for political reasons.

the church proclaim God's commandment? Can it proclaim it as "the word now to this concrete situation" of humanity, of people now? . . . All questions thus flow into two questions of ethics, that is, the question of "human beings in their natural bonds" and the "question of the church" which is to proclaim the Word of God as the word of this hour (*DBW,* 12:157f.).[78]

Barth later came to recognize how right Bonhoeffer had been in pushing so hard for ethical concreteness. It was an "energetically upheld supplement" — as Barth put it — to his own concerns, particularly in the political arena.[79] It had been precisely the question of politics which, in face of the emerging fascism, had divided the "dialectical theologians." Barth wrote Bonhoeffer that "Over the past months I have begun to feel more and more strongly that a great many of the theological alliances claimed to have been seen in Germany in recent years have been deceptive" (*NRS,* 201). When the "turn" to National Socialism came in 1933, it seemed to Barth as if he had been "thrown back into the same solitude" from which he "rode into this peculiar arena twelve years ago" (*NRS,* 201, T.a.). Bonhoeffer himself had long been aware of the crisis within the "theology of crisis" which led to Barth's renewed isolation and to his "farewell to *Between the Times.*"[80] Bonhoeffer wrote Erwin Sutz on 8 October 1931, telling him how surprised he was again about "how great the difference is between . . . Barth" and Gogarten; "I would not feel particularly drawn to Breslau [where Gogarten was teaching. Trans.], whereas I would go to Bonn again any day" (*NRS,* 11, T.a.). On Christmas Eve 1932, having visited Barth in September on the "Bergli" [a cottage in Switzerland where in those days Barth spent many of his holidays. Trans.], Bonhoeffer expressed that "I have a peculiarly sure feeling that the way you see things

78. See also the letter to H. Rössler of 25 December 1932: "There is agreement about one thing, namely that our church today cannot declare the concrete commandment. It may be asked whether this is part of its nature, that is, in its limitation by the *eschata* [what pertains to the last things], or whether it is due to apostasy and loss of substance. . . . The decision ought not to be withheld for fear of gambling away authority or for fear of chaos. (Compare Luther and Erasmus on the demoralizing consequences of the doctrine of predestination!)" (*DBW,* 12:39).

79. Cf. Barth's letter to Eberhard Bethge in Karl Barth, *Fragments Grave and Gay,* ed. H. Martin Rumscheidt, trans. Eric Mosbacher (London: Collins, 1971), 121.

80. Cf. K. Barth's "Abschied von *Zwischen den Zeiten,*" *Zwischen den Zeiten* 11, no. 6 (1933): 536ff.

is somehow right . . . that somehow the point of it all is being touched on" (*NRS,* 200, T.a.). After he had aligned himself with Barth in the "Günther Dehn case" of 1931, in solidarity with the defamed theologian [Dehn had been attacked by Nazi students at the University of Halle for "unpatriotic" attitudes. Trans.], Bonhoeffer openly sided with Barth in the winter of 1932/33 and campaigned — in vain — that he be called to the University of Berlin (cf. *NRS,* 201-2).

On the eve of political power being handed over to the Nazis, the fronts are already clearly demarcated; in spite of Bonhoeffer's ethical criticism of Barth, Bonhoeffer stands unambiguously on Barth's side. How very much Bonhoeffer wished for a final theological unity may be seen in his "Christology" lectures of the summer of 1933. In the context of the old controversy between Lutherans and Calvinists over the *capax* or *incapax,* he makes a proposal to settle the issue. While seemingly asserting the Lutherans' formulation, in substance his proposal fully embraces the Calvinists' concern: *"Finitum* capax *infiniti, non per se sed per infinitum!"* [The finite can hold the infinite, not by itself, but it can by the aid of the infinite!] (*CC,* 93).[81] In order to avoid "unbiblical" abstractions on either side of the controversy, Bonhoeffer searches for "a criterion for . . . decision . . . in the Scripture" (*CC,* 93). He does so after he had come across "conflicts with biblical statements" also in Lutheran Christology that extend all the way to the "danger of bringing back monophysitism" (*CC,* 91, T.a.).

7. The "Aryan Clause" as *Casus Confessionis*

After the Nazi rise to power, when the Church of Prussia voluntarily aligned itself with the new legislation, Bonhoeffer's question about the concreteness of the commandment in the church's proclamation intensified. At this time it received a dogmatic, or more precisely, an ecclesiological, foundation. In the question of the church's "conformity to the race," the existing agreements and differences between Bonhoeffer

81. In the letter of 26 February 1932 to Erwin Sutz, Bonhoeffer writes about his habilitation dissertation, *Act and Being,* in which he had built his most important arguments against Barth precisely on the basis of this difference between Lutheran and Reformed theology, that "in the meanwhile I've taken quite a dislike to it" (*NRS,* 146).

and Barth came to the fore with new urgency. Characteristic for this controversy once again is the fact that, in his ecclesiological concerns, Bonhoeffer believed himself to be following entirely the directions Barth had signaled in his polemical pamphlet *Theological existence today!*, published on 25 June 1933. Bonhoeffer wanted to address how the church-political implications of that alignment were to be made concrete. And thus, on 9 September 1933, three days after the "brown" synod of Prussia had voted to adopt the "Aryan Clause," he wrote Barth. "In your booklet you said that where a Christian church adopted the Aryan Clause it would cease to be a Christian church. . . . Now the expected has happened . . ." (*NRS*, 226, T.a.). Barth had not expressed the matter quite as unambiguously as Bonhoeffer interpreted it; nevertheless, the prompt reply from the "Bergli" shows that Barth did not feel misinterpreted. "Naturally the decision of the General Synod has at least partly realised the possibility which I considered. They do not, or apparently do not yet, want to go as far as excluding non-Aryans from church membership. But even the decree about officials and pastors is intolerable." And when Bonhoeffer declares that "there can be no doubt at all that the *status confessionis* has arrived," Barth concurs: "I too am of the opinion that there is a *status confessionis*" (*NRS*, 227). The question that concerns Bonhoeffer above all else is what this ecclesiological perception will mean concretely in terms of church politics. "What we are by no means clear about," he writes, "is how the *confessio* is most appropriately expressed today" (*NRS*, 227). Bonhoeffer indicates what his own thoughts are when he says that "Several of us are now very drawn to the idea of the Free Church" (*NRS*, 226). Together with his friend Franz Hildebrandt, who was himself victimized by the "Aryan" legislation, Bonhoeffer was advocating a "widespread resignation from office. They believed that, with the Aryan clause, their opponents had brought schism to the realm to which they all belonged. Nothing therefore remained but to accord that fact material recognition" (*DBE*, 238). However, this plan of action failed to gain majority support among the pastors in Berlin who were of the "Young Reformers Movement" and who resisted the legislation of the Nazis. Accordingly, Bonhoeffer wrote Barth: "I know that many people now wait on your judgment; I also know that most of them are of the opinion that you will counsel us to wait until we are thrown out" (*NRS*, 227f.). But against this majority Bonhoeffer and Hildebrandt obviously stayed firm, insisting tenaciously "that to effect an immediate exodus

would not only be more logical theologically but would also be more suc-
cessful in the field of church-politics than would a delay" (*DBE*, 238).
First, however, they wanted Barth to answer the question when there is
"any possibility of leaving the church" (*NRS*, 227). To their disappointment, his answer was as "most" had expected. "Otherwise I am for waiting. When the schism comes, it must come from the other side. . . . It
could then well be that the collision might take place at a still more central point. . . . Perhaps in that case it may not be absolutely necessary to be
willing to wait until one is expelled or dismissed. Perhaps one will then really have to 'walk out.' But that should only be a last resort for us. . . . We
will in no way need to regret at a later date an extremely active, polemical
waiting . . ." (*NRS*, 228-29, T.a.).[82]

Eberhard Bethge describes the reaction of Bonhoeffer and
Hildebrandt to Barth's answer: "What point, though, could be more
'central' than the Aryan clause? This time, Bonhoeffer, and more especially Hildebrandt, were somewhat disappointed with Barth. . . . The
actual question respecting Hildebrandt himself had not been given a direct but a rather reserved response" (*DBE*, 239). It is true that, without
Barth's support, a move toward a Free Church, which Bonhoeffer and
Hildebrandt continued to consider to be imperative,[83] was unthinkable,
or at least open only to individuals. Initially Bonhoeffer solved the
problem for himself. He accepted a call to a congregation in London
without, as he had first planned, making that move contingent on
Barth's counsel. (Cf. *NRS*, 230: "I simply believed that you would tell
me the right thing.") He seeks to "justify" his action to Barth only after
the fact, obviously because he feels "as if I had become personally un-
faithful to you by my going away" (*NRS*, 232, T.a.). On 24 October
1933 he writes Barth from London that, after the adoption of the
"Aryan Clause" in the Prussian Church, he knew "that I could not accept the pastorate I longed for in this particular neighbourhood without giving up my attitude of unconditional opposition to the church
. . . without betraying my solidarity with the Jewish Christian pastors"

82. When Barth was himself finally removed from his position in Bonn (1935), his
membership in the Social Democratic Party of Germany played a significant role in having him removed. Was this a theologically "more central place"? On this whole development, see Hans Prolingheuer, *Der Fall Karl Barth 1934-1935. Chronographie einer
Vertreibung* (Neukirchen-Vluyn: Neukirchener Verlag, 1984).
83. Cf. Franz Hildebrandt, "Zehn Thesen für die Freikirche," in *GS*, 2:167f.

(*NRS*, 231). The same day, Hildebrandt communicates to Martin Niemöller his disappointment with the halfheartedness of the Pastors' Emergency League. "For some time now, I have been unable to go along with anything of the 'Young Church' [Young Reformers Movement. Trans.] and the Pastors' League, just as little or even less so than Barth claims for himself. . . . But I do not wish, either as a 'young man' or as someone otherwise burdened, to repeat and make public the verse that I have recited in our circle again and again since the end of June and harm your cause. What does 'public' mean among us anyway? My part now is to be silent . . ." (*GS*, 6:278). Just like Bonhoeffer's "justification" to Barth, this letter shows that despite their differences with Barth in church politics, the two "Young Ones" from Berlin were, as before, aligned with him in matters of theological fundamentals and, like Barth, on the side of "unconditional opposition," a side the emerging Confessing Church embraced ever so reluctantly.

Bonhoeffer had quite correctly assumed that Barth would not endorse his "marching off to London." On 20 November 1933 Barth wrote: "[Y]ou were quite right not to ask for my wise counsel first. I would have advised against it absolutely, and probably by bringing up my heaviest guns. . . . No, to all the reasons or excuses which you might perhaps still be able to put in front of me, I can and I will give only one answer: And the German church? And the German church? — until you are back again in Berlin to attend faithfully and bravely to the machine-gun which you have left behind there. Don't you see yet that an age of completely undialectical theology has dawned?" (*NRS*, 233-34). Bonhoeffer did, indeed, not return "by the next ship" or "the ship after next," as Barth had urged him to (*NRS*, 235), but only in April 1935, shortly before Barth was himself finally driven out of Nazi Germany.[84] For that reason, Bonhoeffer's return may not be seen as an undivided agreement with Barth's advice, especially because it did not lead him into the pastorate. It became his first step into illegality; for, in taking on the direction of a preachers' seminary of the Confessing Church, Bonhoeffer entered into a space ungoverned by the law, halfway between the institutionalized, territorial church (*Volkskirche*) and the Vol-

---

84. Barth returned to Switzerland in June 1935 after he was felt to be an unbearable "burden" even within the Confessing Church. Cf. Prolingheuer, *Der Fall Karl Barth 1934-1935*.

untary Free Church *(Freiwilligkeitskirche)*. Subsequently, Barth expressed his full agreement with Bonhoeffer's position in this matter. On the occasion of the publication of Bethge's biography of Bonhoeffer, he wrote to Bethge that "for a long time now I have considered myself guilty of not having raised [the question of the Jews] with equal emphasis during the church struggle."[85]

8. An "Ongoing, Silent Discussion"

Bonhoeffer's return to Germany in April 1935 must not blind us to the fact that, in essence, his theological position was as different as ever from the understanding of the other protagonists in the Confessing Church.[86] In describing the relationship to Barth, Bethge rightly notes that the "church struggle to some extent served again to strengthen the alliance between Barth and Bonhoeffer against secessionists and renegades, but in [this] phase of their relations it was not only the spatial distance between them that grew greater. . . . Bonhoeffer showed his gratitude and loyalty, not by repeating what had already been said, but in courageous and critical new thinking or at least new foundations. The Sermon on the Mount now moved into the foreground of his thought, and here he did not yet find anything helpful in Barth" (*DBE*, 141).

His turn to the Sermon on the Mount took place while he was in London. Yet, in his lectures at Berlin University, when he dealt with the concreteness of the commandments, there were already signs of this turn.[87] Writing to Erwin Sutz on 28 April 1934 — before the meeting of the Synod of Barmen — he says: "although I am investing all my energies

85. Karl Barth, "Letter to Eberhard Bethge," in *Fragments Grave and Gay*, 119. Barth is thinking particularly also of "the two Barmen Declarations I composed in 1934." In his view, a different text would not have been accepted then, "but this does not excuse the fact that I (my interests lay elsewhere) did not offer at least formal resistance in this matter at that time."

86. Cf. my "Bonhoeffer und das Barmer Bekenntnis," *Neue Stimme*, no. 12 (1984): 13ff.

87. Cf. the seminar on "Christian ethics," summer term 1932: "The Sermon on the Mount shows us what the one commandment of faith might look like. It is the residue of the concrete hearing of the one commandment. The 'why' is always the same but there is each time a different 'how'" (*DBW*, 11:312 n. 49).

working in the church opposition, it is quite clear to me that this opposition is no more than a provisional stage in transition to an entirely different kind of opposition. . . . You know, I believe — perhaps you are surprised by this — that the whole matter will be resolved through the Sermon on the Mount" (*TF,* 434-35). Bonhoeffer wants to know how Sutz preaches on the Sermon on the Mount. "I am currently trying to preach on it, very simply, without pretension. And I speak always for *keeping* the commandment and against evading it. *To follow Christ* — I would like to know what that is — is not wholly explained in our concept of faith. I am at work at something that I would call 'exercises,' a sort of preliminary step" (*DBW,* 13:128f.). This mention of "exercises" is Bonhoeffer's first reference to what he then was to present to the seminarians at Finkenwalde (and, until February 1936, also at the faculty in Berlin) under the title *Nachfolge* (ET: *The Cost of Discipleship*), which was then published in 1937 under the same name.[88]

This discovery of the Sermon on the Mount constitutes the point of departure for Bonhoeffer's church struggle; it is from here — after the Confessing Church had been called into being at Barmen — that he decides to return to Germany. Once again it is in a letter to Sutz, dated 11 September 1934, where Bonhoeffer puts the matter clearly. "The entire training of the budding theologians belongs today in church, monastery-like schools in which pure doctrine, the Sermon on the Mount, and worship can be taken seriously. . . . We must also finally do away with the theologically grounded restrictions in regard to action by the state — after all, it is only fear" (*TF,* 435). Thus: the cloister as a breeding place of resistance, as the organized center of an antifascist church of opposition. At the time when the Confessing Church declined more and more, Bonhoeffer tried to bring together in the communal house of Finkenwalde people who would be prepared to try out "the uncompromising at-

---

88. Cf. the letter of 13 July 1934 to Reinhold Niebuhr, written after Barmen. "The dividing line lies . . . with the Sermon on the Mount. And now the time has come when the Sermon on the Mount has to be brought to mind again on the basis of a partially restored Reformation theology — although, to be sure, with a different understanding than the Reformation's. And precisely at this point the present opposition will divide again. Before we reach that juncture, everything is only preparation. The new church which must come about in Germany will look very different from the present opposition church." Cited in Larry Rasmussen, *Dietrich Bonhoeffer: Reality and Resistance* (Nashville: Abingdon, 1972), 220.

titude of a life lived according to the Sermon on the Mount in the following of Christ" (*TF,* 447).[89]

Here it seemed insufficient to build a "common life" focused in following after Christ upon the theology of Karl Barth. Writing to Sutz, Bonhoeffer remarks that Barth's theology "both delayed once again . . . but also made for" the realization "how everything comes to a head through the Sermon on the Mount" (*DBW,* 13:128). In commenting on this, Bethge writes that the "answers to his questions that Bonhoeffer obtained at this stage from Barth did not take him far enough. When he himself provided an answer in *The Cost of Discipleship,* it was only after his death that Barth expressed the agreement and approval that he so badly wanted" (*DBE,* 142).

And so it was that, while working on his *Nachfolge,* Bonhoeffer was on the lookout for other theological teachers; Søren Kierkegaard in particular clearly seemed to be of help to him. In an undated letter from 1934 concerning the development of the church struggle, he expresses — as he does in other letters from that year to Sutz and Niebuhr — his belief that, after the "skirmishes" to date, there will be a second, real battle which "cannot and will not be waged in hale and hearty militancy" but, instead, will "be won only by the one who fully endures it." This battle will lead "to the utter division and destruction of the so-called opposing fronts, of those who want to be Christians," and will lead "into their isolation. It will be utterly impossible to confuse church and church-political association," so that "everything will once again depend on the individual, as it did at the beginning." "The individual will be discovered anew and with the individual — and in no other way — will it be known again what it means to follow Jesus. Only then will it be clear also what confessing means" (*DBW,* 13:177).

This massive reference to the "individual," on the basis of whom alone the idea of a confessing church that is worthy of that name can be erected, signals Bonhoeffer's intensive preoccupation with Kierkegaard; it

89. See the letter of 14 January 1935 to his brother Karl-Friedrich: "I believe I know that inwardly I shall be really clear and honest only when I have begun to take seriously the Sermon on the Mount. Here is set the only source of power capable of exploding the whole enchantment [Hitler and his rule] so that only a few burnt-out fragments are left remaining from the fireworks. The restoration of the church will surely come from a sort of new monasticism which has in common with the old only the uncompromising attitude of a life lived in accordance with the Sermon on the Mount in the following of Christ. I believe it is now time to call people to this" (*TF,* 447).

is highly likely that it was the selection from Kierkegaard's late journals, published in 1934 by W. Kütemeyer under the title *Der Einzelne und die Kirche. Über Luther und den Protestantismus* [The individual and the church. On Luther and Protestantism], to which Bonhoeffer alludes here. He had read this work, and its substance flowed into the conception of *The Cost of Discipleship*.

Bonhoeffer's discovery in 1934 of the Kierkegaardian "individual" is psychologically quite understandable — his "marching off to London" was symptomatic of the isolation he clearly felt himself to be in — but it is also in many ways theologically astonishing. He had long been familiar with Kierkegaard,[90] yet his 1927 dissertation on the community of saints shows his critical assessment of Kierkegaard's "individualism" and the use Barth had made of it in his revised edition of *The Epistle to the Romans* of 1922.[91] Bonhoeffer discovered Kierkegaard's "individual" for himself[92] at the time Barth was turning his back on the "Kierkegaard Renaissance" of the twenties[93] — not least because that "individual" had in the meantime become problematic to Barth.[94] Bon-

90. In November 1925 Bonhoeffer's fellow student and friend R. Widmann had called his attention to Kierkegaard's "attack" (cf. *DBE*, 58). Bonhoeffer in turn acquaints his fellow student Helmut Goes with Kierkegaard (cf. *DBE*, 45).

91. *SC*, 212 n. 12: Kierkegaard "lays the foundations for an extreme sort of individualism in which the significance of the other for the individual is no longer absolute but only relative" (*SC*, 57). See also *SC*, 162 n. 20: Kierkegaard moved from the loneliness of the individual in the sphere of "the paradox" to the rejection of "the idea of the church." The same charge of individualism is made against Barth on 169 n. 28; Kierkegaard is also referred to in that note.

92. Correspondingly, Bonhoeffer makes extensive use in his Christology lectures of 1933 of Kierkegaard's terms "paradox" and "incognito," which had such great significance for Barth in the second edition of *Romans* when it came to describe the *"extra Calvinisticum,"* even though this terminology completely disappears entirely no later than the Anselm book.

93. Karl Barth, "A Thank-You and a Bow," in *Fragments Grave and Gay*, 98: "The second edition of my *Epistle to the Romans* is the very telling document of my participation in what has been called 'the Kierkegaard Renaissance.' . . . It is true, however, — and this several people have pointed out — that in my later books, writings, and sermons, express references to Kierkegaard have become fewer and fewer."

94. "[W]hat about the individual in whose existence nearly everything seems to be centred in Kierkegaard? . . . We may perhaps raise the historically pointed question whether his teaching was not itself the highest, most consistent, and most thoroughly reflective completion of pietism. . . ." Barth, "A Thank-You," 99-100.

hoeffer devotes a whole chapter of his *Nachfolge* to "the individual," and in the section on the discipleship faith of Abraham he makes use of the interpretation of Kierkegaard that he had criticized in *Sanctorum Communio* (*CoD*, 84ff.).[95] It appears as if Bonhoeffer wanted to reactivate in *The Cost of Discipleship* the critical movement against the "church become bourgeois" that Barth had already initiated in his *Romans* as he faced the shock that World War I had caused, but he wanted to do so now at the moment when that church was totally collapsing. Kierkegaard's "attack" upon Christendom, launched in the middle of the nineteenth century, became significant for Bonhoeffer in 1933, just as it had for Barth earlier. With Barth, he was suspicious of the ecclesial opposition that had come together and organized itself at Barmen, but whereas Barth had become suspicious of Kierkegaard, it was Kierkegaard who fueled Bonhoeffer's mistrust of the opposition even *after* Barmen. For Bonhoeffer it was the "uncompromising dimension" of the "individuals" who oriented themselves by the Sermon on the Mount, that is, the core group of the "fraternal community" *(Bruderhaus)*, which represented the actualization of the "monastic idea."[96]

It is hardly surprising, therefore, that Bonhoeffer's description of the motivations of early monasticism and of Luther's way through the cloister in *Nachfolge* is shaped by Kierkegaard's journal entries, right into the very words he uses. For Bonhoeffer "the fatal error of monasticism lay . . . in that it allowed its aim to become an individual and special achievement of a select few and claiming for it a special merit of its own" (*CoD*, 39, T.a.). Kierkegaard had said about "the monastery" that "Christianity sustained its first fracture when the emperor became Christian, the second and far more dangerous one when the idea arose that there had to be extraordi-

95. Cf. Søren Kierkegaard, *Fear and Trembling,* cited in *SC,* 162 n. 20, and (without indication) in *CoD,* 88-89. Cf. *Romans,* 2nd ed., 118f. The only explicit reference to Kierkegaard in *CoD* is on p. 43, in connection with the observation that "acquired knowledge cannot be divorced from the existence in which it is acquired."

96. The "idea of the cloister" appears in an undated letter fragment of 1934 on "the development of the Church Struggle" (*DBW,* 13:178), and also in his letter to Erwin Sutz of 11 September 1934 (*TF,* 435-36). Earlier, in his letter to Sutz dated 28 April 1934 (*DBW,* 13:129) and in his letter to Niebuhr of 13 July 1934 (Rasmussen, 220), Bonhoeffer, when speaking of "following after Christ," makes reference consistently to "India," that is, the ashram of Gandhi that he intended to visit. Cf. as well the letter to J. Winterhager dated 25 May 1934: "here or the university or something *totally* different — India, the monastery" (*DBW,* 13:148).

nary Christians whom one would recognize as such without any problem. The mistake was not in entering a monastery but in the title: 'extraordinary Christians' who are venerated through the admiration paid them by their contemporaries."[97] Bonhoeffer calls "Luther's return from the cloister to the world" a "frontal attack" (CoD, 40); Kierkegaard had written this about "Luther's swing away from the monastery": "Out, cries Luther, out with all these imaginary pious acts, with fasting and the like! Everyone, remain in your vocations, for that is true worship. But, dear Luther, hold on a minute . . . : in contrast to the error of monasticism, your swing away looks so simple. On close examination, however, what enormous collisions here, precisely because it is characteristic of Christianity not to fit into the world."[98] Finally, Bonhoeffer's distinction between costly "grace as answer to the sum" and "grace as the data for our calculations" (CoD, 42) clearly goes back to Kierkegaard,[99] which Bonhoeffer notes there explicitly.

Several years of silence ensued; it was not until 19 September 1936 that Bonhoeffer again wrote Barth. The work for the book Nachfolge was nearly completed. "The whole period was basically a constant, silent discussion with you, and so I had to keep silent for a while. The chief questions are those of the exposition of the Sermon on the Mount and the Pauline doctrine of justification and sanctification. I am engaged in a work on the subject and would have asked and learnt a very, very great deal from you." Even if he is clearly aware that in relation to Barth and Reformation theology he is moving on new paths with his interpretation of the Sermon on the Mount, Bonhoeffer wants to make explicit that his independent thinking not be misunderstood as a separation from Barth. Even though he is "not counted as one of the theologians associated with you,"[100] he himself knows well "that it is not true." And usually, "most of us who feel that they had to keep away from you for a while . . . seem to

97. Søren Kierkegaard, *Der Einzelne und die Kirche. Über Luther und den Protestantismus*, ed. W. Kütemeyer (Berlin, 1934), 161.

98. Kierkegaard, *Der Einzelne und die Kirche*, 171ff.

99. Kierkegaard, *Der Einzelne und die Kirche*, 182f.: "What if I were a tapster in a saloon, unable to read or write, and therefore knew that I didn't have the necessary preconditions like the learned man, the very preconditions that justified his saying 'it is not science that matters,' what if I did not dare to accept this as a result and say that sentence myself?"

100. Much to his disappointment, Bonhoeffer had not been invited to contribute to the Festschrift for Barth's fiftieth birthday in 1936.

find that afterwards, in a personal conversation with you, they learn that once again they have seen the whole question in far too crude terms" (*WF*, 116). Concerning the "life together" in the fraternal community, Bonhoeffer mentions explicitly that he perceives it to be "only the consequence of what you have made very clear in 'Anselm.' The charge of legalism does not seem to me to fit at all" (*WF*, 117).

The reference to Barth's book on Anselm as what gave the inducement to Bonhoeffer's experiment in Finkenwalde could not reduce Barth's suspicions about the "theoretical-practical system" he saw taking shape there. Barth does tell Bonhoeffer, however, that he has "much sympathy with that" and does not think it to be an "impossible" undertaking on principle. But what troubles him about an "Introduction to Daily Meditation" in Finkenwalde, composed by Eberhard Bethge (cf. *WF*, 57ff.), is the "odour of monastic eros and pathos" for which "at the moment I still have neither a positive feeling nor a use." In addition, he preferred not to "go with the distinction in principle between theological work and devotional edification" (*WF*, 121). And he "looked forward openly, but not without concern," to the attempt in the new book to raise in a new way "the inexhaustible theme of justification and sanctification." He considered it a mistake to resign "in the face of the original Christological-eschatological beginning in favour of some kind of realisation (in fact becoming more and more abstract) in a specifically human sphere." Nevertheless, Barth did not wish his questions to be understood "as a criticism of your efforts, simply because the basis of my knowledge and understanding of them is still far too scanty" (*WF*, 120-22).

We may leave open the question as to what extent Bonhoeffer's *Cost of Discipleship* contained features of resignation "in the face of the original Christological-eschatological beginning."[101] And yet, Bonhoeffer complains that his real concern is being misunderstood when Barth once again detects in it "the *whole line from Ragaz to Buchman* [of the movement that came to be known in 1938 as "Moral Rearmament"] or, rather, an extension of it" (*DBW*, 14:256). In this letter of 24 October 1936 to

---

101. Bonhoeffer's own later concerns about *The Cost of Discipleship* certainly seem subsequently to confirm Barth's "keen nose" of 1936. "I thought I could learn to have faith by trying myself to live a holy life, or something like it. I suppose I wrote *The Cost of Discipleship* as the end of that path. Today I clearly see the dangers of that book, though I still stand by what I wrote" (*LPP*, 369).

Erwin Sutz, Bonhoeffer shows that his Finkenwalde experiment ought not be aligned with the "groups movement" [such as Buchman's Oxford Group, as it was still known in 1936] and its sanctimonious retreat to the backwoods of religion. That movement was indeed taking on "an extremely serious appearance" in Germany so that suspicion was quite appropriate. "All the people of the church's mainstream, including church committees, are full of interest and immediately rushing to look at this unpolitical, living phenomenon, and to flirt with it. . . . We of the Confessing Church could give ourselves over to this and everything would be ours. The price we pay is only that we are no longer church, that is, that we are no longer city *(polis)*, that we can no longer preach the gospel to the city *(polis)*. We would have become, in all the publicity we would enjoy then, a fringe church without influence" (*TF,* 436-37, T.a.).

What Bonhoeffer wants to accomplish in Finkenwalde is not at all a softening of the confrontation by means of withdrawal into the pious group but, on the contrary, a strengthening of the Confessing Church's intransigent position on the basis of the decisions reached at the Synods of Barmen and Dahlem. He made that abundantly clear in his essay on the coexistence of the churches, entitled in English "The Question of the Boundaries of the Church and Church Union" (*WF,* 75ff.). It was written in April 1936, after the founding on 18 March 1936 of the compromise-prone "Lutheran Council." Reporting to Karl Barth, he writes: "Unfortunately I am at the moment involved in a big battle over my article on the churches' coexistence. People are getting frightfully excited about it. And I thought that I was writing something obvious. I would be very glad to have a word from you on the matter" (*WF,* 118, T.a.). Helmut Gollwitzer's "Hinweise und Bedenken" [Comments and concerns] may to some extent be taken as Barth's "word" on the matter. He called attention at the time to Bonhoeffer's hotly disputed sentence, "Those who knowingly cut themselves off from the Confessing Church in Germany cut themselves off from salvation" (*WF,* 93-94, T.a.), and asserted that this sentence could indeed not be interpreted as something "legalistical," but that it was actually an actualization of what the church had declared from the beginning: *extra ecclesiam nulla salus* [Outside the church, no salvation] (*WF,* 97-98). On the other hand, there are formulations in Bonhoeffer about which doubts may be raised (*WF,* 99). This goes especially for the assertion that "we can no longer go back behind Barmen and Dahlem . . . because we can no longer go back behind the Word of God"

58

(*WF,* 87). Gollwitzer counters that "the confession of the church is not the Word of God but the church's testimony of the Word of God. It is not God, but the church which has spoken at Barmen and at Dahlem, however great the part played by God may be thought to have been" (*WF,* 101).[102] In opposition to the Lutherans' accusation that the Barmen Declaration belongs to the tradition of "the Enthusiasts," Gollwitzer — understanding himself throughout as Barth's "spokesperson" — retorts that "Karl Barth of all people has described the better knowledge of the provisional character of the church's confession and of its difference from the Word of God as an advantage of Reformed thought over the Lutheran . . . the same Karl Barth who is now said to have become an enthusiast all of a sudden!" (*WF,* 102, T.a.). Thus, if anyone has misunderstood the Barmen Declaration in an "enthusiastic" manner, it was the Lutheran Bonhoeffer in his "Barthian" zeal.[103]

No matter, Bonhoeffer believes himself to be wholly with Barth, the author of that Declaration, when he writes that the Synod of Barmen could "not be justified by the letter of the Lutheran Confession," while insisting nonetheless that "since Barmen, Lutherans and Reformed have been speaking with one voice in Synodal declarations. Schismatic differences of confession no longer make it impossible to form a Confessing Synod" (*WF,* 89).[104] And that is why Bonhoeffer can turn to Barth (in the letter already referred to) and ask precisely of him to bring out into the open and to discuss "some of the questions of substance which divide Lutherans and Reformed." Of course, Bonhoeffer aligns himself with Barth against the Lutheran Sasse (*WF,* 118).[105]

---

102. One may ask, however, whether the statement of Bonhoeffer's under judgment here really has to be interpreted in such a way that the Barmen Declaration itself is "God's Word." What Bonhoeffer wants to stress is simply that, in the decision of Barmen, God's Word has become effective. Gollwitzer does not dispute that. (The author thanks M. Loerbroks for this insight.)

103. One might see in Bonhoeffer's "zeal" a late expression of his earlier identification of the "Sanctorum Communio" with "Christ existing as community"; what must be noted is that he uses this "Lutheran" understanding of the church now to depict what Barth meant.

104. Bonhoeffer recognized the possibility that differences that separate churches may turn into differences that separate schools and vice versa; cf. *WF,* 84. Cf. *LPP,* 382: "the Lutheran versus Reformed [controversies], and to some extent the Roman Catholic versus Protestant, are now unreal."

105. In subsequent years, Gollwitzer wholly abandoned the "concerns" about Bonhoeffer that he expressed at this time. (He indicated this in conversations with the author.)

There is something that has escaped those who, without much ado, made Bonhoeffer's later charge of "positivism of revelation" against Barth part of the confessional controversy between the Lutheran and the Calvinist. In 1936, at the latest, while preparing a speech entitled "The Inner Life of the German Evangelical Church since the Reformation," to be delivered in connection with the Olympic Games,[106] Bonhoeffer learned to dread "the consequences of the *finitum capax infiniti.*" Working on hymns by Zinzendorf, he wrote Eberhard Bethge and exclaimed: "What rottenness there is beneath all this piety! . . . Yes, such is the human being! The pious human being! . . . By all means, avert the eyes from the human being! It is disgusting!" (*WF,* 72, T.a.).[107] Thus, at a certain time Bonhoeffer began to dread the consequences of his own Lutheran origins. One may, therefore, wonder whether it is really true that during the church struggle Bonhoeffer distanced himself theologically from Barth. In any case, Bonhoeffer later expressed his "Barthian" diffidence about *The Cost of Discipleship* (cf. *LPP,* 369), and Barth, on his part, later spoke about that book with unconcealed admiration,[108] so that one may indeed speak of a reversal of positions.

9. Bonhoeffer's Swiss Visits and the *Ethics*

It was not until the war years that Bonhoeffer again met with Karl Barth face-to-face. Bonhoeffer traveled to Switzerland three times; under the cover of the military's intelligence section, he carried secret communica-

106. As part of a series of events sponsored by the Confessing Church, the address was delivered on 5 August 1936. Contrary to a competing series of addresses arranged for by the governing body of the Reich-Church and presenting theology professors from the Berlin faculty, the address was attended by vast congregations that listened with deepest devotion. (Cf. *WF,* 73.)

107. To Eberhard Bethge, written on 31 July 1936; the only interpreter of Bonhoeffer that I know of who took notice at all of Bonhoeffer's dread of the consequences of the Lutheran *"capax"* is Eberhard Bethge, to whom this letter is addressed. He refers to it in his address "The Challenge of Dietrich Bonhoeffer's Life and Theology," in *WCA,* 63. Still, it is in precisely this address where Bethge states that Bonhoeffer had fought "all his life" against the *extra Calvinisticum* (36).

108. Cf. Karl Barth, *CD* IV/2, 533-34, where Barth feels "tempted" to insert the first chapters of Bonhoeffer's book as "an extended quotation" into the chapter entitled "The Sanctification of the Human Being."

tions of the conspiratorial group around Beck. In the course of those visits, Barth and Bonhoeffer again had extensive theological discussions; very little of them was recorded, seeing that the two had to confine themselves to oral exchanges. But in the letters Bonhoeffer thanks Barth repeatedly for the "conversations" that the Swiss visits had made possible.[109] The topics they addressed in those conversations can be named with relative clarity.

During the first of those visits, between 24 February and 24 March 1941, Bonhoeffer was able to obtain the latest volume of Barth's *Church Dogmatics,* published in 1940. Before having the volume sent to Berlin, he removed the binding and title page as a matter of precaution. This was volume II/1 on the doctrine of God. In a letter dated 30 May 1941, written after his return to Germany, Bonhoeffer tells Barth what great joy it was for him to take possession of that volume. "I am well into it by now and am pleased every day to be reading real theology again" (*MBBC,* 2). At that time Bonhoeffer himself was working on his *Ethics* every free day available to him (cf. *DBE,* 635). He regarded that work as "his actual life work" (*E,* 7; cf. *LPP,* 163). It remained a fragment and thereby points clearly to the "ethical situation" of its genesis.

Upon his return from Switzerland, Bonhoeffer was served with an official prohibition to publish. He writes Barth about it: "Like others, I too have been prohibited from publishing." Then he announces a further visit to Switzerland, for the late summer of 1941, hoping to be able to work and write during that visit. "Lately I have made good progress in my work, stimulated particularly by my trip. But it is often difficult for me to concentrate, and I would like very much to discuss certain concerns of my work with you at length" (*MBBC,* 2). In March, and again in the second Swiss visit from 29 August to 26 September 1941, it is above all questions of the *Ethics* that Bonhoeffer raised in the "conversations" with Barth in Switzerland. The new, critical edition of *Ethics* presupposes that in 1941 Bonhoeffer was occupied primarily with the chapter "Guilt, Justification and Renewal" (*E,* 110ff.), that is to say, with the chapter that also contains a concrete confession of guilt on the part of the church. Moreover, at the same time, Barth was also working primarily with questions of ethics; in the summer of 1941 he was composing the ethical sec-

109. *MBBC,* 2,6.

tion of his doctrine of God. (Cf. Karl Barth, *CD* II/2, chap. 8, "The Command of God.")

On this second visit, Bonhoeffer apparently discussed with Barth the idea of an anthology, to which the latter was to contribute; the plan did not come to fruition (*MBBC,* 3-4). On the basis of a communication by Charlotte von Kirschbaum, Eberhard Bethge concludes what Bonhoeffer's interests were in relation to that project. "Bonhoeffer was now concerned less with the hermeneutical problems of interpretation raised by Bultmann, and much more with the way Christians are drawn into contemporary history. In addition, it was questions of an ethics of responsibility and, thirdly, how the church handles the guilt it had incurred through its complicity that interested him, as did the question of how he himself and his associates in the conspiracy had to bear guilt."[110] The questions of "Christian responsibility" that Bonhoeffer was himself addressing at that time would have been the very ones that Barth was to deal with in the proposed anthology.

Finally, in May 1942, the third of Bonhoeffer's Swiss visits took place (from 11 to 26 May). He immediately procured the page proofs of the as yet unpublished, newest part-volume of Barth's dogmatics, *The Doctrine of Election* (*CD* II/2). Still in Switzerland, and even before the visit to Barth, Bonhoeffer initially studied the second part of that volume, the one dealing with ethics (cf. *MBBC,* 5). The interest in ethics remains constant; Eberhard Bethge comments: "Since Bonhoeffer was working on his own 'Ethics' and was grappling with new approaches, and because earlier he had critically questioned Barth precisely in relation to ethics, he particularly wanted to know how the master approached this complex of issues."[111] The last chapters Bonhoeffer wrote for his *Ethics,* before his work was halted by his arrest, were clearly influenced by his reading of this volume of Barth's *Church Dogmatics.* At issue is "the 'ethical' and the 'Christian' as a theme" as well as "the concrete commandment and the divine mandate" (*E,* 263ff. and 286ff.). Bonhoeffer later managed to have Barth's "doctrine of predestination

---

110. Eberhard Bethge, "Bemerkungen," in Dietrich Bonhoeffer, *Schweizer Korrespondenz 1941/42,* Theologische Existenz heute, n.s., no. 214 (Munich: Chr. Kaiser Verlag, 1982), 26. As far as Bultmann is concerned, Bonhoeffer makes reference at least in a letter to Barth of 13 May 1942 to the pamphlet *New Testament and Mythology* of 1941, calling it "the last theological happening" (*MBBC,* 5).

111. Bethge, "Bemerkungen," 28.

(unbound)" smuggled across the border and even into prison (cf. *LPP,* 171, T.a.).

While on his second visit to Switzerland, Bonhoeffer apparently also had a very open exchange with Barth about his secret activity that subsequently led him to believe that everything was "now clear" between him and Barth in relation to this matter. He refers to this when, at the beginning of the third visit, he learns of the rumor that this newest visit to Switzerland was "uncanny" for Barth "because of my commission." In the interest of "the admittedly difficult effort to continue our solidarity," he tells Barth "that, at least in the eastern part of Germany, there are few who have declared their loyalty to you as often as I have tried in recent years" (*MBBC,* 6-7). Bethge comments: "Bonhoeffer takes for granted that what existed now between them in questions of church and politics was the same agreement that he, Bonhoeffer, had accorded the author of the open letter to Professor Josef Hromádka during the Czech crisis of 1938. This was contrary to most of the brethren in the Confessing Church at home."[112]

In his 1937/38 Gifford Lectures on the Scottish Confession (Karl Barth, *The Knowledge of God and the Service of God: According to the Teaching of the Reformation*), and subsequently in the biblically based argument in the publication *Rechtfertigung und Recht* (1938; ET, "Church and State," 1939), and finally in the letter to Josef Lukl Hromádka already mentioned, Barth repeatedly called for resistance against Hitler. That call and, in particular, his call for "tyrannicide" also earned him disavowal in the ranks of the Confessing Church. Again, Bonhoeffer took no part in the widespread abandonment of Barth at this time; rather, by his entry into the activities of the political underground, he gave practical expression to Barth's call for political resistance. According to Bethge, Bonhoeffer "no doubt knew about" the pamphlet *Rechtfertigung und Recht* and, in terms of substance, "comes close to it later in his *Ethics.*" But there is not "a single line" in Bonhoeffer's writings explicitly "commenting" on that publication (*DBE,* 525). Only Reinhold Niebuhr recalled some years later that, during a conversation in London in 1939, Bonhoeffer explicitly asserted "that Barth was right in becoming more political." However, he held that "a little pamphlet" was, in this respect, too little in comparison to the size of Barth's dogmatics (*DBE,* 526). It seems

112. Bethge, "Bemerkungen," 30; cf. also *DBE,* 510-11.

that Bethge has distanced Bonhoeffer further from Barth than is neces-sary. A letter by Bonhoeffer dated 7 March 1940, which Erwin Sutz sent from Switzerland to Bonhoeffer's brother-in-law, the jurist Gerhard Leibholz, who had emigrated from Germany and was living in Oxford, contains an affirming comment that appears to refer to Barth's pamphlet; here Bonhoeffer breaks his silence on this explosive topic.

> Karl has now made the attempt, based on the rigorously Reformed the-sis, nevertheless to avoid relativizing the historical. That is very tempt-ing. (In good biblical fashion) he relates every order of the created world strictly to Christ and says that they can be properly understood only in relation to him and that they need to find their orientation from him. One simply must read this. Once these problems have been dealt with, the question of the relationship of law, justice and love (in the sense of the Sermon on the Mount) has to be raised, in my judg-ment. Do they exclude one another? Or do they belong together after all (albeit in the form of antitheses)? I would think yes. Law that is ori-ented toward justice and becomes a historical reality through the use of force (rather than remaining an abstract idea!) is "a tutor to conduct us to Christ," as Gal 3:24 puts it. (NEB) (*DBW,* 15:298f.)[113]

That excerpt from the letter is significant: however affirming of Barth's "rigorously Reformed" attempt, Bonhoeffer pushes forward indepen-dently, his specific concern being the integration of the Sermon on the Mount into the Reformation's approach and the ethics corresponding to it. If he now judges the isolation of "love (in the sense of the Sermon on the Mount)" from law to be something characteristic of enthusiasts (*DBW,* 15:299), then we have an indication that, in comparison to the approach of *The Cost of Discipleship,* a shift of emphasis has taken place that might have something to do with the new political experiences of the conspiracy. As a result, we may assume that the chapter entitled

---

113. Cf. Karl Barth, "Church and State," in *Community, State, and Church: Three Essays* (Gloucester, Mass.: Peter Smith, 1968). "Is there a connection between justification of the sinner through faith alone, completed once and for all by God through Jesus Christ, and the problem of justice, the problem of human law?" (101). "Clearly we should know not only that the two are not in conflict, but first and foremost that and to what extent they are connected" (102). It was a "gap" in the teaching of the Reformers that they did not provide "a gospel foundation, that is to say, in the strictest sense, a Christological foundation," for human law and political power (104).

"The Last Things and the Things before the Last" in Bonhoeffer's *Ethics,* on which he was working during the winter of 1940/41 in Ettal (cf. *E,* 12), was influenced by Barth's pamphlet on *Rechtfertigung* ("justification," as the *last* thing) and *Recht* ("law," as the *penultimate* thing). This would be especially true in relation to the coordination of the *last* and the *penultimate* depicted in the section of that chapter entitled "The Preparing of the Way."[114] Bonhoeffer's distinction between *"the last"* and *"the penultimate"* may well go back terminologically to the early Barth who, in his Tambach address, firmly maintained that "the last thing, the *eschaton,* the synthesis, is *not* the continuation, the result, the consequence, the next step after the next to the last, so to speak, *but,* on the contrary, is forever a radical break with everything next to the last; and this is just the secret of its connotation of Origin and its moving power" (*WGWM,* 324).[115] Bonhoeffer himself speaks of "the complete breaking off of everything that . . . is before the last" by the last (*E,* 123), but his chief concern now is the "relation" of "the things before the last . . . to the ultimate" (*E,* 125), the "preparing of the way" for the ultimate in the penultimate. All told, one may interpret Bonhoeffer's

---

114. Compare Bonhoeffer, *Ethics,* 120ff., "The Last Things and the Things before the Last," with Karl Barth, "Church and State," 119, according to which the task of the state, in christological perspective, is to "administer justice and protect law [and] . . . in so doing, voluntarily or involuntarily, very indirectly yet none the less certainly, [grant] the gospel of justification a free and assured course." Bonhoeffer refers to this as "making the way ready" for the last in the penultimate (*E,* 134).

115. Cf. *Romans,* 1st ed. (Bern: Bäschlin, 1919), new, critical edition (Zürich: TVZ, 1985), 509; here Barth declares that Christians, as a matter of course, belong to the "most radical left," for which reason "the possibility of arbitrarily anticipating, and thereby relegating to the very back, the revolution coming in the Christ" is so dangerously present to them. But "the substance of what is God's renewing must not be intermixed with the substance of human progressing. . . . Whatever your position is in the things before the last, you must keep yourselves free for the last thing. Under no circumstances must you seek the decision, the victory of God's reign in what you undertake against today's state." This is presented as an exegesis of Rom. 13! Cf. Barth's explanation of why he joined the Social Democratic Workers' Party in his letter to Eduard Thurneysen dated 5 February 1915. "Precisely because I endeavor Sunday after Sunday to speak of the last things, I felt no longer permitted to hover personally in the clouds above today's wicked world; now is the time to show that faith in the greatest does not exclude work and pain in the imperfect but, rather, includes them." In *Karl Barth–Eduard Thurneysen Briefwechsel. Vol. 1, 1913-1921* (Zürich: TVZ, 1973), 30.

Ethics drafts as attempts to concretize Barth precisely in relation to the "political worship of God"[116] with the necessary completeness.

On the matter of Barth's alleged mistrust in connection with Bonhoeffer's travels, Charlotte von Kirschbaum informs Bonhoeffer that there was indeed, in Barth's circle of friends, "some surprise about the ease with which you can move," but that this was now "completely dropped" after "Karl's conversation with you. . . . But when all is said and done, there actually is something 'uncanny' for Karl Barth," not in relation to Bonhoeffer's person but in relation to "all the attempts to save Germany from the evident misery into which it has now been plunged by still more 'national' undertakings. This includes those that the generals might venture. He has told you so himself and is ready to talk to you about it" (*MBBC*, 7-8). Here one may indeed detect a difference in relation to the concrete forms that the "political worship," jointly called for and practiced by Barth and Bonhoeffer, would need to take in the resistance against the fascism of Hitler.[117] In a letter to Jørgen Glenthøj dated 7 September 1956, Barth recalls that the "main topic" of his "conversation with Bonhoeffer at the time" had been the "question whether the planned new German government would be conservative and authoritarian, or have a democratic form."[118] It has to be noted at this point that immediately following his third Swiss visit, Bonhoeffer traveled to Sweden for a conspiratorial meeting with Bishop George Bell of Chichester. On that occasion he told Bell that, in divergence from the German generals' interest in "self-assertion," he was praying and working for the military defeat of

---

116. Cf. Barth, "Church and State," 101: "Is there something like a political service of God?" (T.a.). See how Barth speaks of this already in his *Knowledge of God and the Service of God: According to the Teaching of the Reformation,* trans. J. L. M. Haire and Ian Henderson (London: Hodder & Stoughton, 1938), 217ff. and esp. 229-32: "active resistance!" [The particular chapter referred to is entitled in English "The State's Service of God," while in German it is "Der politische Gottesdienst" (The political worship of God). Trans.]

117. In his otherwise quite readable article "Das patristische Erbe in der Theologie Dietrich Bonhoeffers," *Berliner Theologische Zeitschrift,* no. 2 (1988): 190, R. Staats claims that Barth "refused to receive Bonhoeffer in Basel in May 1942." There is not a trace of such an action on Barth's part in the correspondence. The construction built on that allegation, namely, that Barth had left Bonhoeffer "in the lurch during the difficult years after 1942" (190), expresses no more than an anti-Barthian prejudice.

118. Eberhard Busch, *Karl Barth: His Life from Letters and Autobiographical Texts* (London: SCM, 1976), 315.

Germany.[119] Might this be regarded as a political consequence of the conversations with Barth about the "commission"?

Barth's mistrust toward the *coup d'état* planned by the German military has its parallel in his later critique of the "doctrine of the mandates" that Bonhoeffer used since 1940 in his sketches for *Ethics* in order to make more precise what he had spoken about earlier in his "orders of preservation."[120] In the context of his "ethics of creation," Barth wondered in 1951, in face of this concededly constructive attempt, whether an enumeration of precisely those four mandates with an appeal to Scripture "does not still contain some arbitrary elements" and whether those mandates had to be about relations of authority rather than relations of freedom. "In Bonhoeffer's doctrine of the mandates, one cannot entirely shake that little taste of North German patriarchalism. . . . Would it not be advisable . . . [not to be] rushing on to the rigid assertion of human relationships arranged in a definite order, and the hasty assertion of their imperative character?" (*CD* III/4, 22).[121] In a certain way, Bonhoeffer took up Barth's concern in the course of working on the *Ethics;* in his draft "The 'Ethical' and the 'Christian' as a Theme" of early 1943, he wanted to understand "the commandment of God" as *"permission,"* namely, the "permission to live as a human being before God." Following closely Barth's ethical argumentation in *Church Dogmatics* II/2, he writes

119. Cf. my "Dietrich Bonhoeffers theologische Begründung der Beteiligung am Widerstand," *Evangelische Theologie,* no. 6 (1995): 507-10.

120. Bonhoeffer's first experimental use of the concept of "mandate" appears to be the one in the manuscript "Church and State," probably written in April 1941. Here "marriage and labor" are designated as the "two institutions" that the "Bible discloses . . . to us already in Paradise," for which reason they find themselves right "from the beginning subject to a definite divine mandate" (*E,* 344). The notion of "the four mandates of God" appears first in an insertion, made in 1941, into the first outline of *Ethics,* entitled "Christ, Reality and Good ('Christ, the Church and the World')," of 1940. Bonhoeffer discerns the "relativeness of the world to Christ" becoming concrete in "labor, marriage, government and the Church" (*E,* 207). Cf. furthermore the manuscript on "'Personal' and 'Real' Ethos?" (*E,* 329f.), dating probably from the summer of 1942, and the final draft section for the *Ethics,* "The Concrete Commandment and the Divine Mandates," from January to April 1943 (*E,* 286ff.).

121. On the other hand, Jürgen Moltmann refers of all things to the doctrine of the mandates as "the best and today still most helpful concept" for the meeting of church and world in their common resistance. "Die Wirklichkeit der Welt und Gottes konkretes Gebot nach Dietrich Bonhoeffer," in *Die Mündige Welt III* (Munich: Chr. Kaiser Verlag, 1960), 59.

the following about the commandment of God: "This is how it differs from all human law in that it *commands freedom*" (cf. *CD* II/2, 585).

Attention must be drawn in this context to the fact that during the war, as the so-called Operation Seven was being prepared — an attempt in 1942 to rescue a group of endangered Jews from the "Final Solution" that was in full course then and to bring them across the Swiss border — Barth and Bonhoeffer were cooperating in a very practical manner. After Bonhoeffer's first Swiss visit and as a result of his mediation, Willi Rott interceded with Barth on behalf of Charlotte Friedenthal, a coworker in the Confessing Church, who was in grave danger on account of her Jewish origin. In early November that year, Barth successfully obtained valid immigration papers for Mme. Friedenthal. In the meantime, Himmler had ordered a total prohibition of Jewish emigration, so that for her a legal departure from Germany was out of the question. Bonhoeffer thereupon asked his brother-in-law, Hans von Dohnanyi, to place Mme. Friedenthal under the protection of the "intelligence" in order to prevent her from being deported. In the course of Operation Seven, she was brought safely across the Swiss border on 5 September 1942, in the "disguise" of a spy of the "intelligence."[122]

In his letters and papers from prison, Bonhoeffer relativizes his "doctrine of the mandates" in a way that to a great extent anticipates Barth's later critique. In his letter of 23 January 1944, addressed to Renate and Eberhard Bethge, Bonhoeffer writes: "Our 'Protestant' (not Lutheran) Prussian world has been so dominated by the four mandates that the sphere of freedom has receded into the background." On the basis of this "sphere of freedom," which for Bonhoeffer includes friendship, culture, education, he wants to relativize the "sphere of obedience" (*LPP,* 193). It would appear, therefore, that not only was the earlier, intense dispute between Barth and Bonhoeffer about the concrete commandment settled in the war years, but that they also finally came to agree (but without being able to have the other confirm this!) particularly in their critique of an inflexible "doctrine of the mandates" on the basis of the freedom of the gospel.

122. Winfried Meyer, *Unternehmen Sieben. Eine Rettungsaktion für vom Holocaust Bedrohte aus dem Amt Ausland/Abwehr im Oberkommando der Wehrmacht* (Operation Seven. A rescue action for persons threatened by the Holocaust undertaken by the department "foreign countries/intelligence" of the supreme command of the armed forces) (Frankfurt am Main: Anton Hain, 1993), 70-82 and 290-306.

In a letter from prison to Eberhard Bethge dated 8 June 1944, in which Bonhoeffer is critical of Barth, he writes: "It was not in ethics, as is often said, that he subsequently failed" — as Bonhoeffer himself had often maintained in his earlier years; "his ethical observations, as far as they exist" — he would have had *Church Dogmatics* II/2 in mind, among other things — "are just as important as his dogmatic ones" (*LPP,* 328). On his part, Barth could later regard Bonhoeffer's insistence on ethical clarification as an "overdue completion[,] . . . for which [Bonhoeffer] stood up so strongly," of what Barth himself had had in mind. "Germany, burdened with the problem of her Lutheran tradition, was very much in need of a 'refresher course' in just the outlook which I presupposed without so many words and emphasized merely in passing, namely ethics, brother/ sisterliness, a servant church, discipleship, Socialism, movements for peace — and throughout all these in politics. Obviously, Bonhoeffer sensed this void and the need to fill it with increasing urgency right from the start and gave expression to it on a very broad front."[123]

10. An Interim Summation

It has become clear that we may speak at best only in a very convoluted way of a continuity between Bonhoeffer's early questions about Barth and his later charge of positivism of revelation. From the period when Bonhoeffer lectured at the University of Berlin onward, the early epistemological critique of dialectical theology is hardly to be found anymore. Similarly, at the latest during the church struggle and the "union" of the Synod of Barmen in 1934, the insistence on the Lutheran *"capax,"* concomitant with that critique, completely recedes. In fact, it recedes so completely that Bonhoeffer actually comes to "dread" the pietistic consequences of the *capax.* The question of "ethical concreteness" that had moved Bonhoeffer in the early thirties was obviously reshaped by the events of 1933 into an attempt, influenced by Kierkegaard, to appropriate grace "existentially" in "discipleship." When Bonhoeffer became a participant in the political resistance, he recognized that this attempt was fraught with the danger of "enthusiasm." It appears on the whole that Barth's political direction since 1937 and the first "ethical" section of his

123. Barth, in *Fragments Grave and Gay,* 120-21 (T.a.).

dogmatics corresponded to a large degree to Bonhoeffer's own political-ethical interests. Earlier, Barth's turn from a "Christian" to a "church" dogmatics had corresponded to Bonhoeffer's ecclesiological interests. All in all, in the way Eberhard Bethge presents it in his superb Bonhoeffer biography, the theological closeness between Bonhoeffer and Barth is minimized more than it is overstated.

CHAPTER III

Once Again: What Is "Positivism of Revelation"?

1. "Positivism of Revelation" in Luther

The use of the term "positivism of revelation" was proof enough for Gerhard Krause to allege that Bonhoeffer was permanently stamped by the theological faculty of Berlin. Bonhoeffer is not to be counted among the proponents of dialectical theology; rather, he criticized their ethics as well as "the questionable understanding of the world resulting from their rejection of 'natural theology'" with arguments "derived from the faculty in Berlin."[1] According to Krause, the term "positivism of revelation" had been coined by the church historian Erich Seeberg, who used it fequently in his 1929 book on Luther's theology.[2]

What needs to be said concerning Bonhoeffer's ethics questions to Barth has already been indicated; continued repetition does not make the assertion more correct that between Bonhoeffer and Barth a difference remained until the end.[3] As for the "rejection of 'natural theology'" by dia-

1. Gerhard Krause, "Dietrich Bonhoeffer," in *Theologische Realenzyklopädie,* vol. 7 (Berlin and New York: Walter de Gruyter, 1981), 58.

2. Krause, "Dietrich Bonhoeffer," 54 n. 1; cf. Erich Seeberg, *Luthers Theologie. Motive und Ideen,* vol. 1, *Die Gottesanschauung* (Göttingen: Vandenhoeck & Ruprecht, 1929).

3. Bonhoeffer's final word on this matter is this: Barth's "ethical observations, as far as they exist, are just as important as his dogmatic ones" (*LPP,* 328).

lectical theology, it was never a unanimous matter. One need think only of the controversy between Barth and Brunner on this subject.[4] One may, indeed, read in Bonhoeffer's charge of "positivism of revelation" a critique of Barth's "understanding of the world" insofar as here "the world is in some degree made to depend on itself and left to its own devices, and that's the mistake" (*LPP,* 286). But this critique is not made at all on the presupposition of a "natural theology." Krause wishes to conclude from the relative rehabilitation of the "natural" in Bonhoeffer's *Ethics* ("Natural Life," 149ff.) that "this — anonymous but actual — distancing from the total rejection of 'natural theology' Barth had made at that time . . . was the theological foundation of *Ethics.*"[5] However, the rehabilitation of the *"natural"* in Bonhoeffer's thinking means something utterly different from the rehabilitation of "natural *theology*" as Krause alleges. He has to admit that the openness to the world of Bonhoeffer's *Ethics* is throughout legitimated christologically, so that "no created thing can be conceived . . . without reference to Christ, the Mediator of creation" (*E,* 296). This christologically based rejection of natural theology is not an inconsistency within Bonhoeffer's new openness to the world,[6] but precisely its very core. This is indicated in the sketch "On the Possibility of the Word of the Church to the World," probably composed in the autumn of 1942. "For the Church too, therefore, there is no relation to the world other than through Jesus Christ. In other words, the proper relation of the Church to the world cannot be deduced from natural law or rational law or from universal human rights, but *only* from the gospel of Jesus Christ" (*E,* 357).

Krause's reference to the faculty in Berlin is quite likely accurate in relation to the term "positivism of revelation." The work on Luther by Erich Seeberg that Krause refers to uses that term only twice,[7] not relatively frequently, and does not define it in detail. This may support the

---

4. Cf. Emil Brunner, "Nature and Grace," and Karl Barth, "No! Answer to Emil Brunner," in Emil Brunner and Karl Barth, *Natural Theology,* trans. Peter Fraenkel (London: Centenary Press, 1946). Not even Krause alleges that Bonhoeffer drew on Brunner in arguing against Barth.

5. Krause, "Dietrich Bonhoeffer," 62.

6. This is contrary to Krause, who maintains ("Dietrich Bonhoeffer," 62) that the decisive "weakness" of Bonhoeffer's view lies in his "christological" assessment of the natural. But we cannot have Bonhoeffer without his "christomonism."

7. Erich Seeberg, 185 and 218.

assumption that the term was indeed part of the Berlin faculty's parlance and that its meaning needed no specific defining for the "adept."[8] E. Seeberg seems to have meant something like this: in "positivism of revelation" the word of God revealed in Jesus Christ is accepted as something positively given, that is to say, as a truth of faith natural reason cannot analyze or question. The context in which E. Seeberg discusses Luther's "positivism of revelation" suggests this meaning in juxtaposition to "natural" knowledge of God.

The central theme of E. Seeberg's study of Luther is Luther's term *deus absconditus,* the hidden God. In that language, Luther both related himself to and differentiated himself from the "unknown God of nominalism that had come under the influence of mysticism."[9] For Luther, God is "the hidden God because he acts in oppositeness, that is in suffering and death, creating life." God is the hidden One because God is a "God concealed from reason and known only to faith," and not so much because God "is to be described through negations only," as Neoplatonic tradition and its *via negativa* had maintained.[10] Hence, to believe means for Luther "to believe in the hidden God or to acknowledge the hidden God as God, i.e. to affirm the God who everywhere in nature and history as well as, and particularly in, salvation-history acts in opposition to and against the whole of reason." Thus, "faith in the hidden God essentially coincides with faith in Christ" (98). However, E. Seeberg admits that in relation to the decisive question of the origin of the "idea of the *deus absconditus,*" there is a "dilemma" in Luther: "Neo-Platonism *or* the contemplation of the Cross of Christ" (143). It is true, on the one hand, that "the concrete God Christ . . . [is] the hidden God" (144), but then, on the other, one also finds in Luther "the 'hidden God' in the ordinary sense of that term," namely, "the unsearchable God of predestination" (154). This becomes apparent in the "question of how this non-objective God be-

8. For a comparison, cf. how Erich Seeberg's father, Reinhold Seeberg, speaks of the "ecclesial positivism" of the nominalists in his *Dogmengeschichte,* vol. 3, 5th ed. (Darmstadt: Wissenschaftliche Buchgesellschaft, 1959), 724.

9. Erich Seeberg, 20. Page references in the following two paragraphs of text are to Erich Seeberg's *Luthers Theologie.*

10. "Quite likely, the difference lies most deeply in the relation to the idea of revelation: the hidden God is the God of revelation while the unknown God is the God who is enthroned beyond all revelation in the dark inaccessibility of his non-materiality." Erich Seeberg, 60f.

comes concrete," which, according to Seeberg, Luther discusses especially in his writings on the Eucharist (182).[11] In this connection, Seeberg also refers to Luther's "positivism of revelation": Luther's doctrine of the Eucharist relies on the connection between "God's omnipotence," wherein God is able to see more than we, and "the positivism of revelation," by means of which we believe God's words against all reason (185).

Here, E. Seeberg notes a "connection with Franciscan positivism," in that Luther understands faith as "the power of the invisible" that "discerns true but hidden reality. . . . What reason does not see, faith sees; what reason judges to be good, faith judges to be bad" because faith bases itself solely on the word, i.e., on the "authority of Christ" (208f.). "Therefore, to believe means to accomplish with a mighty affect of the will and the spirit what reason cannot, namely, to know the seemingly alien and cruel God in spite of this veiling as the merciful and good God who is near" (210).[12] In connection with "Luther's idea of the Spirit," E. Seeberg refers once again to "Ockhamist positivism" and its impact on Luther. The Spirit is thought of by Luther as "concrete-historical": "the Spirit is not *'an sich,'* as such, but always in a concrete presence, in the word, the sacrament, and the saints of God, i.e. in the church. . . . In Christ, the Spirit really became history. He is the *deus incarnatus et absconditus*" (216). And so, in the idea of the Spirit, Luther's "transcendentalism" is

---

11. See also Erich Seeberg, 183: "The basis of the understanding of God in the eucharistic writings . . . is the . . . idea of the God who in a manner that is simply contrary to reason acts contrariwise in 'hiddenness' and 'concealment.'" Or 184f.: "an understanding of God arises beyond this faith in the antirational omnipotence of God for which the perception of the dynamically conceived aseity of God is characteristic." According to this understanding, God is "by nature action," "a life force" that is thought of "dynamically as a power that creates movement and is deeply inward and one's own as well as most remote." Behind this "dynamic-voluntaristic metaphysics" hides the "scholastic concept of *actus purus.*" In Luther's "transcendentalism," the "otherworldly God" reveals himself "not utterly . . . in his this-worldly activity"; rather, there remains "beyond all revelation a domain that is not wholly accessible to us."

12. See also Erich Seeberg, 193: "According to its will, the all-embracing and all-creating divinity becomes concrete and graspable in the word; the word, however, leads us to the human being Christ. . . . Here, the ungraspable eternal becomes temporal reality, here God has become personal-historical, so we are capable of having him in faith." Or 194: "In the proper sense, the word is revelation that unlocks what would as such remain locked." It does so by bringing God's work, which would remain barred without the word, close to human beings and interprets it to them. See Bonhoeffer's *AB*, 91, on the terminology of "haveable" and "graspable."

connected with "positivism of revelation," wherein "God becomes real for us in the historical revelation that God desired to be thus, i.e. in the anti-rational formation of life unveiled and lived by Christ and in which God establishes the reign of God" (218).

Accordingly, "positivism of revelation" means the "irrational" assertion of divine revelation as the "positively" given reality against all reason, in opposition to the possibility of natural knowledge of God. Such "positivism of revelation" has for its presupposition in theological history the separation of, and finally the conflict between, natural reason and revelation, knowing and believing. The ancient church had already expressed it, and Tertullian gave it its classic formulation;[13] late scholasticism, above all Ockham, knew it as "Franciscan positivism," which Gabriel Biel and Johann Staupitz transmitted to Luther.[14]

What is remarkable in E. Seeberg's attempt to describe Luther's theory of revelation as "positivistic" is the fact that it is utterly beyond him to chide Luther for this aspect of his teaching. On the contrary, given the irrationalistic trend of that time, Luther's "revelation-positivistic" demand that the intellect be sacrificed was, according to E. Seeberg, the true greatness and depth of his theology. Bonhoeffer made similar use of the Berlin terminology in his habilitation dissertation when he described the basic concern of Ockham's theology: "Revelation . . . is a contingent event that is to be affirmed or denied only in its positivity [!; AP] — that is to say, received as reality; it cannot be extracted from speculations about human existence as such" (*AB*, 82). And now Bonhoeffer draws a "revelation-positivistic" line from late nominalist scholasticism via Luther to Barth's "actualism." But the difference between Barth and Ockham seems to lie for him in that "the concept of the freedom of God of late scholasticism" conceded the validity of "the positivity of the church's order," whereas "in Barth, God's freedom is asserted within the positive order as the explosive disruption of all historical forms" (*AB*, 85 n. 7). According to Bonhoeffer, Luther here clearly stands on the side of the "ecclesial positivism" of late

13. Cf. Tertullian's statement: "credo quia ineptum est," in *De carne Christi* 5.
14. On the whole subject, cf. Reinhold Seeberg, *Die religiösen Grundgedanken des jungen Luther und ihr Verhältnis zum Ockamismus und der deutschen Mystik* (Berlin, 1931); R. Seeberg does not speak of "positivism of revelation" in Luther but of "ecclesial," "Ockhamist," or "biblical" positivism. In contrast, Karl Holl emphasized the differences in the relation of Luther to Ockham; see "Was verstand Luther unter Religion?" in *Luther,* 4th ed. (Tübingen, 1927).

scholasticism and against Barth in that the revelation of God's word, in correspondence with the Lutheran *"capax,"* is somehow "haveable" in the church. This is exactly what Barth's "critical proviso" prevents. "What binds God to the church is God's freedom. Dialectically to leave open a freedom of God beyond the occurrence of salvation is to formalize, to *rationalize,* the contingent positivity of that occurrence. . . . We 'know' of the revelation given to the church from preaching" (*AB*, 124).

No doubt: in his habilitation dissertation, Bonhoeffer himself is one who represents positivism of revelation, for whom the positivity of revelation concretizes itself in that of the church. On the basis of this Lutheran understanding of the positivity of revelation in the church, he chides Barth for *insufficient "positivism"* inasmuch as the positivity of revelation evaporates dialectically in him. In the face of this, Barth's turn to ecclesial "positivity" in the Anselm book and in the *Church Dogmatics* has to look like a long overdue move onto the "ecclesio-positivistic" line of Luther.

However, everything is different in the prison letters. "Positivism of revelation" suddenly is a reproach, something that could not have been anticipated at all on the basis of the parlance associated with the Seebergs. And now it is Karl Barth, of all people, whom Bonhoeffer chided for insufficient "positivism" when he was an assistant and instructor at the faculty in Berlin, who is supposed to have planted this "positivism of revelation" in the Confessing Church.

2. "Positivism of Revelation" in the Confessing Church

In the face of Bonhoeffer's "Barthianism," the charge of "positivism of revelation" laid against Barth in the prison letters is surprising. Where does the charge come from? It is to be noted that this charge is regularly preceded by an acknowledgment of Barth's "great merit" in having initiated the critique of religion.[15] In the first "theological" letter, dated 30 April 1944, we read that Barth was "the only one to have started along the line of thought" of "religionless Christianity" (*LPP,* 280), and a week later, on 5 May 1944, "Barth was the first theologian to begin the criti-

15. This has been ignored by all of Barth's despisers who, in calling on Bonhoeffer, charge him with "positivism of revelation" without being prepared to accept Bonhoeffer's critique of religion and its approach.

cism of religion, and that remains his really great merit" (*LPP*, 286). And again, on 8 June 1944, Bonhoeffer writes that Barth was the first to recognize the error of all apologetic attempts by Heim, Althaus, and Tillich, in that they were "leaving clear a space for religion in the world against the world" (*LPP*, 328). Only then does Bonhoeffer make the charge that Barth's doctrine of revelation itself also became positivistic.

A second qualification is needed here: Bonhoeffer's charge is in fact directed less against Barth himself than it is against a certain conservative "Barthianism" in the Confessing Church as represented, among others, by the Lutheran Hans Asmussen. Thus, in the letter of 8 June 1944 Bonhoeffer gives the charge this pointed formulation: "The Confessing Church has now largely forgotten all about the Barthian approach, and has lapsed from positivism into conservative restoration" (*LPP*, 328). Bonhoeffer's concern in response to that development is to overcome liberal theology, which, albeit negatively, still determines even Barth, by genuinely taking up and answering its question (*LPP*, 329), something that the positivism of revelation of the Confessing Church had not done (*LPP*, 329). This is stated in a similar summary in the "Outline for a Book" that was appended to the letter of 3 August 1944. "Barth and the Confessing Church bring about that one entrenches oneself persistently behind the 'faith of the church' and never asks and declares what one really believes. That is why there blows no fresh breeze in the Confessing Church either" (*LPP*, 382, T.a.).[16]

It was Asmussen who, as early as the Synod of Barmen, interpreted the *Theological Declaration* Barth had composed in the sense of a neo-orthodox position against theological liberalism and neo-Protestantism, thereby making the declaration acceptable for the "positive" Lutherans.[17]

16. Krause, "Dietrich Bonhoeffer," 64 n. 6, sought to trace back Bonhoeffer's reference to "fresh air" to Richard Rothe. He probably had in mind Ernst Troeltsch's anniversary address, *Richard Rothe. Gedächtnisrede gehalten zur Feier des hundertsten Geburtstages* (Freiburg, Leipzig, and Tübingen, 1899), 23, which contains a statement allegedly by Rothe: "*An freier Luft fromm zu sein, das ist's, worauf es ankommt* — to be religious in the open (fresh) air, that is on which all depends."

17. Cf. Hans Asmussen, "Vortrag über die Theologische Erklärung zur gegenwärtigen Lage der Deutschen Evangelischen Kirche," in *Die Barmer Theologische Erklärung*, ed. H. Burgsmüller and R. Weth (Neukirchen-Vluyn: Neukirchener Verlag, 1983), 48. When the synod protested the claim "that the events of 1933 are to be acknowledged as binding upon proclamation and scriptural interpretation, . . . we do not protest as members of the people against the most recent history of our people, not as citizens against the new state, nor as subjects against the government. We raise our protest

Eight years later, it was Asmussen once again who took a stand against Rudolf Bultmann's address of 1 June 1941, "New Testament and Mythology,"[18] delivered at Alpirsbach; it was almost as if the devil had to be driven away.

In his capacity as chair of the Berlin Council of Brethren *(Bruderrat)*, Asmussen sent a strong letter of protest to Ernst Wolf, who was responsible for the publication of Bultmann's address.

> I have been authorized to inform you that the General Convention is alarmed about the arguments of the address as well as about the fact that the few opportunities still open to the Confessing Church to publish are made available to a publication of this kind. . . . Christianity cannot meet arguments of such nature any differently than the errors of the German Christians. Being presented intelligently and with reason does not make them any more acceptable to Christianity. . . . We Christians in Berlin live by God's miracles which he [*sic*] performs among us in the manner of the miracles performed at the time of God's incarnation. We implore God that he protect us against the rule of demons like those Christ drove out and whose terrible reality we do indeed experience. We pray to God that still today he send forth his angels to our service. We, too, have already become well aware that this world in which we live is in a state of contrast to the age of radio, telephone and aircraft. We envy no one for whom the experience of that age has become overwhelming. Nor do we want to dispute with them. But they cannot and never shall be discussion-partners within our walls.[19]

Hans Asmussen's and the Berlin Council of Brethren's excommunication of Rudolf Bultmann from theological discussion is a classic exam-

---

against the very phenomenon that for more than 200 years has slowly been preparing the devastation of the church." It is against this background that one may interpret Bonhoeffer's charge against Barth in the sense that he is guilty of "positivism of revelation" insofar as he did not make it clear enough how his intention differed from Asmussen's "conservative-restorationist" interpretation.

18. Cf. Bultmann, "New Testament and Mythology," in *Kerygma and Myth,* ed. Hans-Werner Bartsch (New York: Harper & Row, 1961), 1-44.

19. Hans Asmussen's letter to Ernst Wolf, dated 21 March 1942, cited in Enno Konukiewitz, *Hans Asmussen. Ein lutherischer Theologe im Kirchenkampf* (Gütersloh: Gütersloher Verlagshaus, 1984), 236.

ple of the lack of "fresh breeze" in the Confessing Church that Bonhoeffer laments in his "Outline" from prison. In this sense, here would be a clear case of "positivism of revelation." In replying to Asmussen, Ernst Wolf objected to the identification of Bultmann's program of demythologization with the heresy of the German Christians. An "ecclesiastical censure" that excludes Bultmann from theological discussion would turn the Confessing Church "into a sect with a sectarian 'orthodoxy' which, I am afraid, would not be distinguishable in essence from 'modern-positive' party-lines." Moreover, Bultmann's questions and judgments "can only be useful to the theology of the Confessing Church . . . in that they call back the knowledge that, as theologians of the Confessing Church, we, too, do not 'possess' anything but are ourselves struggling human beings in this age, laboring for knowledge and struggling with our own 'intellectual conscience.'"[20] Asmussen, however, persisted in his "modern-positive" doctrine of revelation, which he did not hold to be a party line but, rather, an *articulus stantis et cadentis ecclesiae,* something on which the church stands or falls.[21] Invitations to discuss the matter further were turned down by Asmussen (*DBE,* 615).

If one considers the moment of time at which this controversy occurred, the pointedness with which Asmussen defended the positive-theological position and substance against Bultmann's alleged demonism takes on a phantomlike character. The mass destruction of European Jewry was in full course — the Wannsee Conference had been held on 20 January 1942 — and for Asmussen the most dangerous enemy seemed to lurk in Bultmann's neoliberal course of questions, which themselves were far away, indeed, from perceiving the decisive dangers for "modern humanity."

Bonhoeffer referred to the controversy around Bultmann in a letter to Barth dated 13 May 1942. "The most recent theological happening that took place among us is the pamphlet by Bultmann which has sparked

20. Wolf to Asmussen, cited in Konukiewitz, 236.

21. Cf. Asmussen's letter to Wolf, in Konukiewitz, 237: "Comments of that kind represent in our view just as strong a danger to Christian proclamation as the comments of German Christians. . . . We ministers of the Confessing Church in Berlin stand and fall with the truth and reality of the New Testament accounts. Professor Bultmann's statements controvert the ground we stand on, indeed, the Christian church as such." Asmussen's polemic is "revelation-positivist" also in the sense of the antirational understanding of revelation that, according to Erich Seeberg, has to be called "Lutheran."

a huge fight between Asmussen and Wolf and beyond. In spite of everything, I enjoyed the essays in the pamphlet very much. Asmussen is beside himself. But more on that by word of mouth."[22] We would like to know more of this, but unfortunately there are no records about the conversation between Bonhoeffer and Barth about Bultmann in May 1942.[23] Bonhoeffer did welcome Bultmann's article on demythologization and, together with Bultmann's commentary on the Gospel of John, recommended it as "the most important event among the latest theological publications" (DBE, 615). In a letter to Ernst Wolf dated 24 July 1942,[24] Bonhoeffer defends Wolf and Bultmann against the "presumption" of certain "pompous individuals," obviously quite unaware of the fact that in Berlin the judgment on Bultmann and its anchorage in "positivism of revelation" had become "official" some time ago.

> I am delighted with Bultmann's new booklet. I am continually impressed by the intellectual honesty of this work. It would appear that, at a recent gathering of the Berlin Convention, D. delivered himself on Bultmann and you in a rather idiotic fashion. I was told that a proposal to send a protest to you against Bultmann's theology was turned down by the slimmest of margins! And that from the Berliners of all people! I should like to know whether any one of those people has worked through the commentary on John. The presumptuousness that flourishes there — I believe that it is due to the influence of a few pompous folk — is a real scandal for the Confessing Church. (DBE, 616, T.a.)

In a letter to Winfried Krause, written a day later, Bonhoeffer welcomed the fact that "Bultmann has let the cat out of the bag. . . . He has ventured to say what many people inwardly repress (I include myself) without having overcome it. In that way he has rendered a service in intellectual integrity and honesty. The credal pharisaism that many brethren are now calling up against it I regard as fatal. Now is the time for giving an account. I should like to talk to Bultmann about it, and I would willingly expose myself to the breath of air that he brings. But then the window

---

22. MBBC, 5 (T.a.).

23. Barth's views on Bultmann may be consulted in "Rudolf Bultmann — an Attempt to Understand Him," in Kerygma and Myth: A Theological Debate, ed. Hans-Werner Bartsch (London: SPCK, 1962), 83-132, and CD III/3, xii.

24. Cf. John A. Phillips, Christ for Us in the Theology of Dietrich Bonhoeffer (New York: Harper & Row, 1967), 249.

must be shut again, or the susceptible people will catch cold too easily" (*DBE*, 616, T.a.).

On the basis of this passage, Bonhoeffer is viewed as being with Bultmann on the same "liberal" track against Barth's alleged "positivism."[25] And indeed, there is no doubt that the infelicitous term "credal pharisaism," with which Bonhoeffer describes the "many brethren" around Asmussen, is a prelude to the charge of "positivism of revelation" that sets up "in the last analysis, a law of faith" (*LPP*, 286), which Bonhoeffer lays against Barth and the Confessing Church in his prison letters. On the other hand, one needs to pay heed to the fact that in the letter to Winfried Krause already mentioned, Bonhoeffer does welcome the "breath of air" of free discussion while, no matter how much sympathy he has for Bultmann's "intellectual integrity," he wants in no way to be understood as being in agreement with him on what he says. Rather, he deplores the "double approach" in Bultmann's booklet: "the argument on the basis of Jn 1:14 and the radio should not be mixed together. I recognize the second as a genuine argument, only the separation needs to be made more clearly."[26] For his part, Bonhoeffer in the prison letters lets the theological cat out of the integrity bag when he writes that "Bultmann's approach is fundamentally still a liberal one (i.e. abridging the gospel), whereas I'm trying to think theologically" (*LPP*, 285). In the letter of 8 June 1944 from Tegel Prison to Eberhard Bethge, there may be an echo of the conversation with Barth about Bultmann. "Bultmann seems to have somehow felt Barth's limits, but he misconstrues them in the sense of liberal theology, and so gets caught in the typical liberal process of reduction — the 'mythological' elements of Christianity are removed, and Christianity is reduced to its 'essence.' — My view is that the full content, including the 'mythological' concepts, must be kept . . . this mythology (resurrection etc.) is the thing itself — but the concepts must be interpreted in such a way as not to make religion a precondition of faith" (*LPP*, 328-29, T.a.).

This passage shows that it is not possible either to settle Bonhoeffer in the "golden middle" between Barth and Bultmann. According to Bon-

---

25. Cf. Gerhard Krause, "Dietrich Bonhoeffer und Rudolf Bultmann," in *Zeit und Geschichte. Dankesgabe an Rudolf Bultmann zum 80. Geburtstag* (Tübingen: J. C. B. Mohr, 1964), 439ff.

26. Phillips, 249-50, T.a.

hoeffer's own perspective, Bultmann, in his justified attempts to think beyond Barth, fell back once again behind Barth's critical approach to religion. Bonhoeffer, too, wants to think beyond Barth — the charge of
"positivism of revelation" is an aspect of this! — and to do so as "a 'modern' theologian," i.e., as a dialectician formed by Barth, "who still carries
within himself the heritage of liberal theology" (*LPP,* 378, T.a.).
Bonhoeffer is committed genuinely to take up and answer the liberal
question in this way, but with the intent of overcoming liberal theology
that determines, though negatively, even Karl Barth (*LPP,* 329). This
means that Barth's critical approach to religion remains the presupposition for this entry "into the open air of intellectual discussion with the
world" (*LPP,* 378). Whoever falls back behind Barth will soon catch cold
from that "breeze of air," and whoever with Asmussen keeps the windows
closed for fear of infection will suffocate from clerical malodor.

Hans Asmussen's evident "positivism of revelation" confirms once
again that this charge leveled against Barth in Bonhoeffer's prison letters
was primarily a critique of conservative Lutheranism and its theology in
the Confessing Church. One may speak of an inheritance of the Berlin
faculty, insofar as Bonhoeffer was concerned, on the basis of the theological change wrought by Barth to find a connection nonetheless with theological liberalism.[27]

3. Once More: "Positivism of Revelation" in Karl Barth?

An inescapable question arises now. How is it that Karl Barth was subject
in Bonhoeffer's perspective to the verdict of "positivism of revelation"
even though he had engaged in vehement battle with German
Lutheranism, particularly during the church struggle? Later, Barth was to
admit that he had "indeed on occasion behaved and expressed myself
'positivistically'" (*WCA,* 90). There are, indeed, such expressions in accordance with Erich Seeberg's parlance, particularly in Barth's "dialectical" phase.

One thinks, for example, of the way the critical approach to religion
in the first edition of *The Epistle to the Romans* is systematized in the sec-

27. It is no coincidence that Bonhoeffer lauds above all Bultmann's "intellectual integrity," something that had already impressed him about his teacher Harnack.

ond edition. In Barth's own words, that edition's "system" consists in being as mindful as possible of what Kierkegaard called "the infinite qualitative difference" between time and eternity (*Romans,* 10). To such a systematization of the *"finitum non capax infiniti"* corresponds Barth's frequent use of Kierkegaard's concept of "paradox" in connection with faith.[28]

Another example of "positivism of revelation" in this sense might be a statement in Barth's Tambach address, "The Christian's Place in Society." "The Divine is something whole, complete in itself, a kind of new and different something in contrast to the world. It does not permit of being applied, stuck on, and accommodated. It does not permit of being divided and distributed, for the very reason that it is more than religion. It does not permit itself to be used: it seeks to overthrow and to build up. It is complete or it is nothing" (*WGWM,* 277, T.a.).[29] Indeed, there are sentences that may be taken to express "positivism of revelation" if one reads them in light of the last sentence just cited and its all-or-nothing stance. It could well be that Bonhoeffer had just such sentences in mind when he chided Barth for his "positivistic doctrine of revelation" in his letter to Eberhard Bethge, written in prison on 5 May 1944. In that doctrine, "each is an equally significant and necessary part of the whole, which must simply be swallowed as a whole or not at all" (*LPP,* 286).

Nonetheless, we must ask whether there is not a fundamental misunderstanding of the Tambach address on Bonhoeffer's part if the charge of "positivism of revelation" was coined with that address in mind. Contrary to Asmussen's defensive position toward Bultmann's liberal questioning — a position that could be described as a "safe stronghold of transcendence" without provision for sorties[30] — Barth is very much concerned in his address with a sortie on existing society, namely, the assault of God's Word on the world. The issue for him is not the unrelatedness of "the divine" to the world or how alienated the church is from the world. His concern precisely in the "negativism" is, rather, a rela-

28. Cf., e.g., Barth, *Romans,* 112: "The paradox of faith can *never* be circumvented nor can it *ever* be removed."

29. Cf. also *WGWM,* 82: "Jesus will be understood wholly or not at all."

30. That is how Ernst Bloch phrases his charge against Barth (*Atheism in Christianity: The Religion of the Exodus and the Kingdom,* trans. J. T. Swann [New York: Herder & Herder, 1972], 42ff.). It seems that Bloch's charge rests on the same misunderstanding as that of Bonhoeffer's charge of "positivism of revelation."

tion to the world that is indeed polemical: the newness of God's Word that overturns everything, the revolution of God. Only when one completely overlooks this can one interpret such statements as "positivism of revelation." But then the charge would be restricted to Barth's claim to absoluteness, to his apodictic "authoritarian" style of arguing,[31] which itself is no more than an expression of the theologically indeed nonnegotiable "claim to absoluteness" of God's Word. In terms of its substance, the idea would not have been foreign to Bonhoeffer that the relation of God's Word to society takes the form that, particularly in dark times, is above all negative: an assault on the world. In his book *Discipleship,* he had explicitly spoken of the Christians' "true alienation from the world" ("otherworldliness" — *CoD,* 239), and in his "baptismal letter" from prison, he sensed "in the words . . . handed on to us . . . something quite new and revolutionary" (*LPP,* 300, T.a.).

Finally, it remains to be asked whether, beyond occasional statements, the all-or-nothing position may really be understood as a "pervasive feature" of Barth's doctrine of revelation so that the comprehensive charge of "positivism of revelation" would be justified. Here it becomes apparent that for Barth himself the "authoritarian" style of arguing and the manner in which the questions of natural reason were simply beaten down with a claim to absolute truth on the part of revelation were by no means without problems. It is significant that this became apparent to him in the work of no less than Martin Luther. "We have all come upon those places in Luther — in his teaching about the Trinity, for instance — where we are simply left standing with instructions to give up thinking, lift our hat, and say Yes. We feel in spite of ourselves that it will not do thus to slay the harlot reason, and we remember with dismay how often we who are not Luther have done so, in public and even more in private. Why will it not do? Because by this kind of answer the human being's question for God is simply quashed" (*WGWM,* 202, T.a.). And while Barth could still clearly call for a *sacrificium intellectus* in the second edition of *The Epistle to the Romans,* where he refers with approval to the *credo quia absurdum* [I believe because it is absurd] (*Romans,* 112), it is

31. Eberhard Bethge's question in his letter of 3 June 1944 to Bonhoeffer seems to point in this direction: "What has attracted people to Barth and to the Confessing Church? The feeling that they can find a certain shelter of truth here, the 'Old Testament-prophetic' . . . ?" (*LPP,* 317, T.a.).

equally clear that no later than his book on Anselm he decidedly inquires about the *ratio* in the church's creed. "By its very nature, the *quaerere intellectum* is really immanent in *fides*."[32] Herein is also achieved the ecclesial concretization of the "positivism of revelation" Bonhoeffer had called for in his habilitation dissertation. "Faith . . . is related to the *Credo* of the Church into which we are baptized. Thus the knowledge that is sought cannot be anything but an extension and explication of that acceptance of the *Credo* of the Church, which is already implicitly accomplished in faith itself. Those who ask for Christian knowledge ask, '*to what extent* is it thus?', on the basis of the presupposition that is never for a moment questioned, namely, *that* it is as they, being Christians, believe."[33]

Yet, it is this ecclesial positivity of theological knowledge which in his "Outline" from prison seems problematic to Bonhoeffer in Barth and the Confessing Church. Bonhoeffer writes: "Barth and the Confessing Church bring about that one entrenches oneself persistently behind the 'faith of the church' and never asks and declares what one really believes" (*LPP,* 382, T.a.). This means that in Barth, in good biblical fashion, "in the place of religion there now stands the church . . . but the world is in some degree made to depend on itself and left to its own devices" (*LPP,* 286). "For the religionless worker or human being in general, nothing decisive is gained here." In a religionless world, the decisive question is: "How do we speak of God — without religion . . . ? In what way are we 'religionless-secular' Christians . . . ?" (*LPP,* 280, T.a.).

The question is whether a difference between Barth and Bonhoeffer that has to do with the respective social position or function that both attribute to theology as an "ecclesial science" crystallizes itself in the term "positivism of revelation." While during Barth's Safenwil period it still could seem that the workers' movement also provided the primary social context for his theological thinking,[34] theology is understood exclusively in orientation toward the church and as one of its functions when Barth

32. Karl Barth, *Anselm — Fides Quaerens Intellectum* (Cleveland: World Publishing Co., 1962), 16 (T.a.). Cf. *CD* I/1, 135, *153:* "The Word of God — and at this point we should not evade a term so much tabooed today — is a rational and not an irrational event."

33. Barth, *Anselm,* 26-27, T.a.

34. Cf. Friedrich-Wilhelm Marquardt, "Der Aktuar. Aus Barths Pfarramt," in *Einwürfe III* (Munich: Chr. Kaiser Verlag, 1986), 93ff.

began to publish the *Church Dogmatics,* if not even earlier than that. Thus, social reality is chiefly reflected only indirectly, i.e., mediated by the church in its social function.

As we have already noted, this ecclesial concentration of theology corresponds to an early concern of Bonhoeffer's. During the Finkenwalde period and its "life together" in the *Bruderhaus,* he himself is governed by this concern almost to an extreme degree. However, after having had to learn "the view from below" (*LPP,* 17), up to and including imprisonment, in his prison letters he suddenly turns himself into the spokesperson of the "religionless worker and human being in general" (*LPP,* 280) or of "the masses" (*LPP,* 381), that is to say, of the social reality outside the church. Similar to the early Barth, the "religionless world" itself — without mediation by the church — now seems to form the primary frame of reference for theological thought. In a manner of speaking, Bonhoeffer wants to do theology "vicariously" for the dependent masses, for "the excluded, the suspect, the maltreated, the powerless, the oppressed, the reviled — in short, . . . those who suffer" (*LPP,* 17, T.a.), who are far removed from the church.[35] And he discovers that if one were to pounce upon these "religionless workers and human beings in general" with the *Church Dogmatics* left uninterpreted, all they could grasp is "positivism of revelation."

To be sure, the last thing Barth would have wanted was that his *Church Dogmatics* should be misused in such a "positivism of revelation" manner. The very title expresses this: in concentrating on the ecclesial function of theology, Barth practices an "arcane discipline." Bonhoeffer, in his personal correspondence, for his part, calls on the churches to engage in just such a discipline. What is left unanswered is the question

---

35. The project is problematic enough exactly in the light of Bonhoeffer's own earlier approach, not to speak of the contradictions a "deputy" *(Stellvertreter)* politics seems almost determined to land in; the conspiracy against Hitler provides a clear example of this. But Bonhoeffer's theological project appears in a different light immediately when the jail situation is understood beyond the biographical dimension — a Protestant pastor who gets Soviet fellow prisoner Kokorin to teach him Russian (*DB,* 1033) and who is prepared to conduct a meditative worship with the other prisoners only with his explicit consent (*DB,* 1037) — as an illustration of the situation of people — the exploited, starved, imprisoned, and murdered masses — in the "world come of age." When seen under the signature of Nazi-fascism as a manifestation of the historical leaning of late capitalism, church, theology, and society enter into a new relationship one with another.

about the directly "liberating and redeeming" effect of the Word of God (*LPP,* 300) among the "religionless workers and human beings in general" outside the church. It is the question Bonhoeffer addressed in terms of "non-religious interpretation"; it is one that he no longer wants to leave outside of theological reflection. But this is where Barth's doctrine of revelation appears unsuitable to him, although it has its very proper place within the "hiddenness" of the community gathered to listen to God's Word.

4. Critique of Religion and "Nonreligious" Christianity

It was in reference not only to the charge of "positivism of revelation" but even more particularly to how Bonhoeffer's "program of non-religious language" was to be carried forward that Karl Barth expressed perplexity. "Can he really have meant anything other than a warning against Christian babble *(Papperlapapp),* all unthought-out recitation of biblical and traditional images, phrases, and combinations of ideas, meaningless to the 'world' because the 'religious' speakers or writers basically have either no idea at all or nothing substantive in mind about what they are presenting?" (*WCA,* 91, T.a.). Barth obviously did not notice that in the concept of being Christian in a "religionless-worldly" manner, Bonhoeffer connects with Barth's own critique of religion as stated in the interpretation of *The Epistle to the Romans* and other earlier essays.

Bonhoeffer explicitly refers to Barth, who "brought in against religion the God of Jesus Christ, *pneuma* against *sarx.* That remains his greatest service (his *The Epistle to the Romans,* second edition, in spite of all the neo-Kantian egg-shells)."[36] And "through his later dogmatics, he enabled

36. Cf. Barth's *Romans* on this point, "The Spirit," 271ff., in particular "The Decision" (on Rom. 8:1-10): "Spirit means the eternal decision taken by God for humans and by humans for God . . . Spirit means struggle, superior power, victory and dictator-like rule in one and never, never, calm, equilibrium, synthesis, toleration at the same time. Spirit means either-or, but an already determined either in face of an already done with or. . . . What the Spirit knows as an alternate possibility is only the one already excluded, done with, non-existent. This no longer existing possibility is the existence of humans in the flesh" (283, T.a.). Barth had expressed the same alternative in the first edition of *Romans,* but in a less neo-Kantian manner and, above all, much less in the terminology of Kierkegaard's dialectics of existence. In that edition it had much more a cosmological-

the church to effect this distinction, in principle, all along the line" (*LPP,* 328). It would appear almost as if it was only in prison that Bonhoeffer became fully aware of the full range of Barth's critique of religion and its approach, namely, its scope as a *critique of the church*. It is precisely this critique of the church that Bonhoeffer seeks to hold up in and through the concept of "religionless Christianity." He does this in response to a Barth who now seemingly has taken a "positive" position vis-à-vis church. This is how Bonhoeffer seeks to move forward critically with Barth's approach to religion. Bonhoeffer obviously did not notice that in his endeavor to move forward with Barth's approach in both agreement and critique, he was working to a large extent along the lines of the first edition of Barth's *Romans*.[37]

Bonhoeffer's statement, "The Pauline question whether *peritomé* [circumcision] is a condition of justification seems to me in present-day terms to be whether religion is a condition of salvation. Freedom from *peritomé* is also freedom from religion" (*LPP,* 281), is not only an allusion to that edition of *Romans,* but an almost verbatim citation from it, albeit an unconscious one. Speaking of "circumcision, religion and church," Barth said something very similar in that interpretation of Paul's Epistle to the Romans. "For Abraham, [circumcision] was not the *condition for salvation* but merely an expression of the community between him and God that had already been given at the time when circumcision was a purely *worldly* thing."[38] Bonhoeffer's concern with "religionless Chris-

---

speculative aura; cf. 218ff. ("The Spirit") and in particular 244f. ("What Is Past"): "In the midst of the world of flesh, an enclave of God's world has come into being whose area is increasing continuously. . . . Among us is new power, the power of the coming world of God, to walk no longer according to the flesh but according to the ways of the spirit. . . . What must finally be understood is that entry into the new level of freedom is not a matter of religiosity, of spirituality or morals, but a matter of power, of the suppositions, conditions and powers we are subject to; it is a matter of the old or the new world to which we belong."

37. Cf. Hanfried Müller, "Das 'Evangelium vom Gott der Gottlosen' und die 'Religion an sich,'" *Weissenseer Blätter,* no. 4 (1986): 34f.

38. Barth, *Romans,* 1st ed., 88 ("Faith and Religion," on Rom. 4:9-12, emphasis added). In the second edition and under the heading "Faith Is Beginning," Barth, commenting on the same passage, asks: "Does religion, in its historical reality, claim to be the presupposition and condition of the positive relationship between God and humans?" His dialectical answer is that "in its historical reality, religion is *not* presupposition and condition of the positive relationship between God and humans and this assertion is in com-

tianity" has its clear prelude here, not only in the repudiation of religion as condition for salvation, demonstrated in terms of circumcision, but also in the emphasis on community with God in Hebrew Bible "worldliness." There is yet no thought here at all that beyond religion "in its reality" one might speak even of a "truth of all religion." This notion emerges in the second edition of *Romans* as the dialectical suspension of the critique of religion,[39] and is extensively discussed in *Church Dogmatics* in terms of the church as "the true religion."[40]

But it seems that in that language of the church as the "true religion," Bonhoeffer fears a shutdown of the critical movement in the bad dialectics of the endless "not only — but also," of justification of sin instead of sinners; he fears a reversal to the "religious *a priori*." " 'Christianity' has always been a form — perhaps the true form — of 'religion.' But if one day it becomes clear that this *a priori* does not exist at all, but was a historically conditioned and transient form of human self-expression . . . what does that mean for 'Christianity'?" (*LPP,* 280).[41] Eberhard Bethge

plete accord with the meaning of religion itself" (*Romans,* 126 and 128-29, T.a.). The critical move against religion "in its historical reality" suddenly appears now as "the meaning of religion itself" so that the reversal of the dialectic comes dangerously close to a justification of religion (in its "truth," of course). This reversal occurs also in the interpretation of Rom. 3:21 and above all in chap. 7, where the dubious equation between "law" and "religion" has to bear the argument. (See next note on this.)

39. Cf. *Romans,* 126, on Rom. 3:21: "We have come to know faith and its righteousness as something particular, new and different contrasted with religion in its whole reality. We have found faith to be the *truth* of all religion, its purely other-worldly *beginning*" (T.a.). Cf. 240ff., "The Meaning of Religion," commenting on Rom. 7:7-13, esp. 242: "For the veritable *krisis* under which religion stands consists in that humans can not only not rid themselves of it 'as long as they live,' but that they also *ought* not to rid themselves of it" (T.a.). And again 254: "Moving within the sphere of humanity, religion is without doubt *holy*, that which points away from the human to the divine." Here, a "religionless Christianity" must indeed look like an illusion and insolence, if it makes any sense at all.

40. Cf. *CD* I/2 (sec. 17), 326: "There is a true religion: just as there are justified sinners." And again 344: "That there is a true religion is an event in the act of grace of God in Jesus Christ. To be more precise, it is an event in the outpouring of the Holy Spirit. To be even more precise, it is an event in the existence of the Church and the children of God."

41. We may leave open the question whether in this implicit critique of Barth's discussion of "true religion" Bonhoeffer has correctly understood Barth's intention. Cf. Hans-Joachim Kraus, *Theologische Religionskritik* (Neukirchen-Vluyn: Neukirchener Verlag, 1982), 29f. Kraus believes there is a misunderstanding.

thought that in Bonhoeffer's treatment of the term "religion" the difference from Barth lay precisely in the fact that "for Bonhoeffer, the phenomenon of religion seems no longer to be an eternally present, basic
condition of human beings but an historical, transient and hence no
more recurring 'Western phenomenon'" (DB, 978).

Ernst Feil took up this differentiation and intensified it, suggesting
that "the dissimilarities between Barth and Bonhoeffer were greater than
were their affinities."[42] For Bonhoeffer's "concept of religion was no longer a systematic concept in the sense of Barth's dialectic but a concept of
Geistesgeschichte, a concept belonging to a specific period of history."[43]

Such an interpretation has to be opposed. No doubt there are differences in Bonhoeffer's and Barth's treatment of the concept of religion in its
systematic and historical aspects, but those are differences in accentuation
and not in approach. The actual difference lies in the issue rather than in
the concept. Already in Barth's first edition of Romans, religion appears as
one of the "basic conditions of human beings": "religion is the necessary reaction of the soul to the creative act of God, the church an unavoidable historical frame, containing, steering and channeling the spring of God gush-
ing forth" (Romans, 1st ed., 86).[44] His prison correspondence indicates that
Bonhoeffer actually reckons that a religionless world is emerging. But this
difference becomes relativized when one keeps in mind that Barth's concept
of religion was in no way void of a historical component,[45] and when one

---

42. Ernst Feil, The Theology of Dietrich Bonhoeffer, trans. H. Martin Rumscheidt
(Philadelphia: Fortress, 1985), 172.

43. Feil, Theology of Dietrich Bonhoeffer, 173.

44. Cf. Romans, 129: "Religion is the unavoidable reflection in the soul — in experience — of the miracle of faith which has occurred to the soul. The Church is the unavoidable framing, administration and canalization in history of that divine transaction in
humans which itself can never become a matter of history" (T.a.). And 269: "The religious
human being is 'as long as he or she lives' this human being in this world, the being of human possibilities whom we all know" (T.a.). But cf. also Bonhoeffer, arguing against
Barth: "It must be stated clearly that in the community of Christ faith takes form in religion and that, consequently, religion is called faith" (AB, 154).

45. Barth described the process of Christianity being individualized or interiorized,
which, according to Bonhoeffer, is a significant aspect of religion (see LPP, 344f.), in terms of
a historically concrete example, namely, eighteenth-century Pietism. "Here, in Pietism, was
the origin of the transformation of the concept of the church in Germany, . . . into that of a
free and voluntary religious assembly" (Protestant Theology in the Nineteenth Century [Lon-
don: SCM, 1972], 117). Cf. also the intellectual-historical excursus in CD I/2, 284ff.

acknowledges on the other hand that Bonhoeffer's interest in the trend of history toward religionlessness also is shaped in substance by systematic, or more accurately, by biblical, reflection. How Christ might "become Lord also of the religionless" is a christological question, within the context of Paul's critique of the law, before it is one of historical interest. The historical observation of the actual death of religion serves here only to illustrate the biblical-theological approach in the critique of religion.[46] It is precisely this approach that Bonhoeffer learned from Barth, "who is the only one to have started along this line of thought" (*LPP,* 280).

Apparently, it was only in prison that Bonhoeffer was prepared to accept Barth's "eschatological proviso" in its full, biblical legitimacy, also and particularly in relation to the church as religious institution. Not least among the reasons for this was his experience with the rather "unchurchy" character of a good number of the conspirators. Barth's early critique of the church is no longer suspect of being a critique from the outside, from the presuppositions of philosophical transcendentalism (cf. *AB,* 125). Rather, Bonhoeffer acknowledges it to be a critique from within, from the biblical presuppositions of the church. These presuppositions are not those of "religion," but those of a religionless "worldliness." When Bonhoeffer refers to Barth being the first to have begun thinking in this direction, he appears to have had statements from the essay "Biblical Questions, Insights and Vistas" of 1920 in mind, according to which "Biblical piety is not really pious; one must rather characterize it as well-considered, qualified worldliness. . . . The polemic of the Bible, unlike that of the religions to this day, is directed not against the godless world but against the *religious* world, whether it worships under the auspices of Baal or of Jehovah . . ." (*WGWM,* 66 and 70, T.a.).[47] This is "genuine worldliness"

---

46. Cf. Kraus, 78f.: "When Bonhoeffer describes the historical development . . . he must by no means be seen as providing an exclusively cultural-historical argument. His 'going beyond' Barth's critique of religion, which is undoubtedly said to be a matter of cultural history, gives no cause for the biblical motivation — decisive for Barth *and* Bonhoeffer — to be reduced or even eliminated. . . . Indeed, the biblical perspective serves in the cultural-historical analysis the function of grounding and unlocking cognition. . . . The collapse of the 'religious apriori' that Bonhoeffer can demonstrate in terms of the development of history still cannot be simply read off the pages of history. *A theological prejudgment is at work in (his) demonstration and interpretation.*"

47. Cf. *WGWM,* 285-86: "The new life revealed in Jesus is not a new form of piety. That is the reason why Paul and John are interested not in the personal life of the so-called historical Jesus but only in his resurrection" (T.a.). Cf. the already quoted citation from

as Bonhoeffer understood it (*E*, 297; cf. *TF*, 92, dating from 1932). It is worldliness "in the sense of the Old Testament and of John 1:14" (*LPP*, 286).[48]

It is this connection between Bonhoeffer's conception of a biblically qualified "worldliness" and Barth's critical approach to religion that Ernst Feil sought to dispute: while Barth in the early essays used "worldliness" synonymously with "otherworldliness" and "non-historicalness," Bonhoeffer understood "something wholly different" by "worldliness," namely — as one may deduce — this-worldliness, historicalness.[49] But the contradiction is only an apparent one; it dissolves when one examines Barth's "otherworldly," negativistic terminology from the beginnings of dialectical theology in relation to its societal context. What becomes obvious is that Barth is concerned here with safeguarding the unreplaceable dimension of the history of God that had become historically effectual in the event of the resurrection. And it is for that reason that Barth is concerned with the "otherworldliness" of the history of God over against the whole of known human history and its deadly laws. "There *must still* be a way from there to here. . . . This is not the act of the human being but the act of God in the human being. And for this reason God in *consciousness* is actually God in *history* — and no mere process of the mind. God causes something to happen, a miracle in our eyes" (*WGWM*, 287-88, T.a.).[50] Thus, in the second edition of *Romans* Barth could speak, in what on the surface looked like a contradiction in terms, of Abraham's "Genesis narra-

---

p. 88 in the first edition of Barth's *Epistle to the Romans* about "pure worldliness" in which the relationship between Abraham and God was said to have been founded.

48. It was Benkt-Erik Benktson who first drew attention to the connection between Bonhoeffer's understanding and Barth's early essays. See *DBE*, 55: "Perhaps it was these notes that were still ringing in Bonhoeffer's ears when he said that Barth had 'started' but 'had not finished.'"

49. Ernst Feil, *Die Theologie Dietrich Bonhoeffers. Hermeneutik — Christologie — Weltverständnis* (Munich and Mainz: Chr. Kaiser and Matthias Grünewald, 1971), 327 n. 1; cf. Feil, *Theology of Dietrich Bonhoeffer*, 233 n. 159.

50. Cf. Friedrich-Wilhelm Marquardt, *Theologie und Sozialismus. Das Beispiel Karl Barths* (Munich: Chr. Kaiser Verlag, 1985), 220: "It is in cognition, experienced as an event, that the boldness comes to view of taking one's *noetic* stand in the Easter-apriori and making Christ's victory the presupposition of one's *thinking*." On the Tambach address as a whole, see Marquardt, *"Der Christ in der Gesellschaft" 1919-1979. Geschichte, Analyse und aktuelle Bedeutung von Karl Barths Tambacher Vortrag*, Theologische Existenz heute, n.s., 206 (Munich: Chr. Kaiser Verlag, 1980).

tive" as a "non-historical history" (*Romans,* 146-47).[51] But in terms of substance, this corresponds exactly to the intention of Bonhoeffer when he — in a seeming paradox — says that "God is transcendent in the midst of our life" (*LPP,* 282, T.a.), so that "the Christian hope of resurrection . . . sends human beings back to their lives on earth in a wholly new way" (*LPP,* 336-37, T.a.). Bonhoeffer's "worldliness" too is the opposite of "shallow and banal this-worldliness" (*LPP,* 369).

Indeed, Bonhoeffer did not follow Barth in the latter's turn from a negative evaluation of the "reality of religion" to the positive assessment of its "truth"; he kept, rather, to the early version of Barth's critique of religion as expressed in the first edition of *Romans.* In addition, in the first version of his dogmatics, in the lecture "Instruction in the Christian Religion" — of which Bonhoeffer acquired stenographic notes in 1924/25 — Barth had still spoken with similarly undialectical abhorrence of "religion" as Bonhoeffer did later in prison.

> I have *no* interest in this concept, not even so much as to take part in the effort to derive new interpretations and contents from it. . . . I can't hear or speak the word "religion" any more without the repugnant recollection that it happens in actual fact to be the sign-post in recent intellectual history pointing to a place of refuge. This is where Protestant, and in part also Catholic, theology began more or less in flight to retreat to when it no longer had the courage to think from its object, that is, from the Word of God. Instead, it was ever so relieved to find a little

---

51. The section is entitled "Concerning the Value of History." Cf. the exceedingly sharp phrasing on the same topic in the first edition: "Mere 'interest' in what once was turns history *(Geschichte)* into a tangled chaos of meaningless relations and events and the writing of history *(Historie),* in spite of every bit of artful connecting, into a triumphant unfolding and description of that chaos, leaving what *truly* was surely hidden. Next to this 'interesting' kind of writing history another kind exists whose nature it is to let history talk to us and us to it about the one, the only topic of the coming reign of God. This is the Bible's kind of writing history. *Historia vitae magistra* says Calvin. The possibility to converse like that with the history in which the same light shall again and again shine in thousands of refractions, and the openness for the genius of the Old Testament, the key to the mystery of what was and shall be, will be ours to the extent to which we are participants ourselves in history. We *can* participate in Christ and, therefore, we also *can* understand history. For in Christ the meaning of time is revealed to us that is hidden in the diachronic section of past and future history" (102). And on 103: "God's word to us, which Abraham already heard without hearing it, is unmistakable: it is the resurrection of Jesus from the dead."

piece of real estate, an historical-psychological reality, precisely in the location where the little banner "religion" was waving, to which — renouncing everything else — it could address itself as a genuine "as-if" theology and in peace with the modern concept of science. . . . Even the most elegantly dialectical understanding about the all-told not half bad meaning of "religio" cannot dislodge in me today this intellectual-historical connection.[52]

This happens to correspond exactly to Bonhoeffer's allegedly "intellectual-historical" concept of "religion" as he depicts it, for example, in relation to "liberal theology." Its "weakness" was, in Bonhoeffer's words, that "it conceded to the world the right to determine Christ's place in the world; in the conflict between the church and the world it accepted the comparatively easy terms of peace that the world dictated" (*LPP,* 325). Barth did not come to a halt with this "intellectual-historical" rebuttal of the concept of religion. Already in his second edition of *Romans,* and then in his *Christian Dogmatics* and the subsequent *Church Dogmatics,* he took part in the endeavors to derive the "true" meaning of "religion" dialectically. It is precisely this endeavor that Bonhoeffer wants no part of in his period in prison; it appears to him, rather, that Barth "did not carry [the critical approach to religion] to completion" but, instead, wound up in a "restoration" to be described as positivism of revelation (*LPP,* 280).

5. "Prayer and Righteous Action"

According to the "baptismal letter" from prison, Bonhoeffer's "religionless" alternative to the transient and now overcome religious form of Christianity is to consist of the arcane discipline of a "silent and hidden" form of being Christian that manifests itself only in "prayer and righteous action among humans" (*LPP,* 300, T.a.). Looking to the future after the hoped-for destruction of fascism, Bonhoeffer also warns against the "attempt to help the church prematurely to a new expansion of its organizational power" and calls on Christians to "wait for God's own time" instead (*LPP,* 300, T.a.). But in so doing, Bonhoeffer connects this kind of arcane discipline materially with Barth's critique of the church in the situ-

52. Karl Barth, *Unterricht in der christlichen Religion,* vol. 1, *Prolegomena* (Zürich: TVZ, 1985), 224f.

ation following World War I. This is how Barth, in his 1919 Tambach address, emphatically warned against every attempt "to *clericalize* society": "for society shall be deceived about the help of God that we really have in mind, if we do not learn to wait upon God in a wholly new way but, instead, set to work building churches and chapels. . . . Let us withstand the new temptation of ecclesiasticism!" (*WGWM*, 281, T.a.). Half a year later, in the address "Biblical Questions, Insights and Vistas," Barth opposed rash "speculative dreams" and ecclesial "business": "For the sake of the suffering of the millions, for the sake of all the blood that has been shed . . . let us not be *so* sure! . . . If any utterance at all is in need of substantiation, attestation, and demonstration in corresponding moral, social, and political action, it is the Biblical utterance that death is swallowed up in victory." The problematic of every one of our actions ought to make it clear that "*we* should assuredly take the utterance upon our lips only with the greatest shame, confusion, and restraint." For, "truly to *name* the theme of the Bible, which is the Easter message, would mean to give it, to have it, to show it. The Easter message becomes truth, movement, reality, as it is expressed — or it is *not* the Easter message which is being expressed" (*WGWM*, 85-86, T.a.).

Correspondingly, Bonhoeffer too noted a quarter of a century later that "Our church, which has been fighting in these years only for its self-preservation," thereby placing great guilt upon itself (cf. *E*, 110f.), has become "incapable of taking the word of reconciliation and redemption to humankind. . . . Our earlier words are therefore bound to lose their force and cease. . . . All thinking, speaking and organizing in matters Christian must be born anew out of this prayer and action" among humans and in waiting for God's own time, that is, "the day . . . when people will once more be called so to utter the word of God that the world will be changed and renewed by it." These people will speak "a new language, perhaps quite non-religious, but liberating and redeeming — as was Jesus' language; it will shock people and yet overcome them by its power; it will be the language of a new righteousness and truth, proclaiming God's peace with human beings and the coming of God's reign" (*LPP*, 300, T.a.). In the posthumously published ethical fragment of the *Church Dogmatics* (IV/4), Barth once again came very close to this understanding of Christian life as prayer and righteous action among human beings instead of religious exercise of power on the part of the church. Barth writes there: "The action of those who pray for the coming of God's reign and, accord-

95

ingly, for the occurring of God's righteousness will be action that is *fitting to that reign* and, hence, righteous action on its lower plane and within its non-transcendable bounds."[53] Prayer for God's righteousness, according to Barth, will naturally be accompanied by "the struggle for human righteousness,"[54] so much so that, for Barth, "the life of Christians [appears] condensed and brought to its climax in an action of *praying to God.*"[55] Bonhoeffer's formulation seems in its emphasis to correspond to Barth's point, in that he declares the apex of prayer and righteous action of Christians to be "waiting for God's own time." But perhaps it is significant that, in contrast to Barth — who had above all stressed the unity of God's action and, consequently, the unity of the human reaction in the "praying to God" — Bonhoeffer is more inclined to speak of a twofold factor: prayer *and* action.[56] While for Barth this doing is naturally included in the praying, Bonhoeffer obviously fears that the doing could be neglected in the concern with praying unless it is explicitly called for.[57]

It is also clear to Bonhoeffer that this twofold factor is based finally in a unity, so that one side could never be stressed at the expense of the other but always already included it.[58]

<hr />

53. Karl Barth, *Das christliche Leben,* Die Kirchliche Dogmatik IV/4, Fragmente aus dem Nachlass. Vorlesungen 1959-1961, ed. H.-A. Drewes and E. Jüngel (Zürich: TVZ, 1976), 460.

54. Barth, *Das christliche Leben,* 347f.

55. Barth, *Das christliche Leben,* 76. Cf. on this whole topic Okko Herlyn, *Religion oder Gebet? Karl Barths Bedeutung für ein "religionsloses Christentum"* (Neukirchen-Vluyn: Neukirchener Verlag, 1979), esp. 125f. "There is no doubt that in his doctrine of prayer, Karl Barth took *the bull by the horns* as far as 'religionless Christianity' is concerned." Still, in his mistrust about Bonhoeffer's "enigmatic comments" from prison, Barth failed to point to the connection between his doctrine of prayer and Bonhoeffer's concern. However, Herlyn leaves righteous action, which is part of the call for prayer, quite underexposed. Cf. the critical response by Kraus, 48: "Prayer is no closed off domain in the communion with God; it is the open door to the action of faith." Cf. also 52ff.

56. Cf. *CoD,* 54: "Only they who believe are obedient, and only they who are obedient believe" (T.a.).

57. Bonhoeffer's apprehension here seems to correspond to that of the Epistle of James in relation to the Pauline conception of the righteousness of faith ("without works of the law"). Cf. James 2:14: "What good is it, my brothers and sisters, if you say you have faith but do not have works? Can faith save you?" (NRSV).

58. Cf. *E,* 58: "The more exclusively we acknowledge and confess Christ as our Lord, the more fully the wide range of His dominion will be disclosed to us."

6. A Difference in Method?

Given the extensive theological convergence between Bonhoeffer and Barth noted thus far, the sharpness of the charge of "positivism of revelation" in the prison letters must come as a surprise and, in the end, appear incomprehensible. And so, Heinrich Ott insisted "that in the controversy between Bonhoeffer and Karl Barth we are [not] dealing with a difference in *substance*."[59] After what we have said thus far, this assertion can only have our approval.

Ott sought to locate the difference "in *method*" instead (129).[60] But this is where doubts emerge. A difference in method in the midst of material agreement would mean, according to Ott, that positivism of revelation "*did assert* God's becoming human together with the incarnation," but that "none the less it did not *methodologically* treat that incarnation seriously" (126). Then it is the method of positivism of revelation to have "developed from this fundamental assertion, this axiom which it declared, a system of statements which, in so far as the basic presupposition, the axiomatic assertion, is right, must all be true the same way and with the same importance. The result is a monolithic block . . ." (126). "Now the method used by the *Church Dogmatics* is in fact that everything is deduced from a *Christological systematic principle*" (129). It is Barth's "doctrine of lights," of all things, that Ott uses to document that assertion. "[I]n its subject matter, in its *substantive* assertion, [it] points emphatically in the direction of a real Christian serious regard for the reality of the world" (130) and, for that reason, lies "within the stream of that theological trend that has come so powerfully into its own in the work of Dietrich Bonhoeffer, the trend towards a *radical theology of the Incarnation*" (134). But here Barth pretends to be methodologically deaf to all kinds of necessary questions, especially to the "monstrous problem of theological lan-

---

59. Heinrich Ott, *Reality and Faith: The Theological Legacy of Dietrich Bonhoeffer* (Philadelphia: Fortress, 1971), 129 (T.a.). Page references in the following paragraph of the text are to this work.

60. Cf. Ott, 129: "As regards the facts Bonhoeffer could be described as a 'Barthian,' at least in relation to the basic process *(Duktus)* of his thought which is Christocentric, not anthropocentric and 'religious.' He had joined the movement in theology which was given its decisive stamp by Barth. But as regards his style, his diction, the methodological purpose of his thought, he goes his own way from his early writings onward, a way which differs in characteristic fashion from that of Karl Barth."

guage, the problem which here in fact announces its presence in a way which cannot be avoided," in that he deduces everything from the unshakably established christological thesis. "But it was just this constructional method in the theological process of thought which Bonhoeffer, with an exaggerated polemical emphasis, but as a factual description not unfittingly, described as 'positivism of revelation'" (136). According to Ott, Bonhoeffer's own "method," the different "style" in his "presentation," means "that everything is not deduced from one principle, but that the revealed truth is discovered, piece by piece, in the study of the Bible and the study of the world." What finally remains hidden in such a piece-by-piece process, itself "never demanding legalistically, but demonstrating lovingly," ought to be worshiped in silence; "and this is what is meant by 'arcane discipline'" (126, T.a.).[61]

It is possible that, at times, Bonhoeffer perceived things in the same way; the phrasing about "the law of faith" in Barth (*LPP*, 286) and the treatment of religionlessness as a matter of "interpretation" seem to point in that direction. In fact, Bonhoeffer's earlier concern over "reactionary gestures" in Barth arose precisely at the time when Barth moved from biblical theology to dogmatics (*DBE*, 54).[62] To be sure, the method of interpretation in the two editions of Barth's *Romans* is no less assertive than in the dogmatics, where, in its mature form as *Church Dogmatics,* it has an explicitly "dialogical" character.[63] That character is evident already in the fullness of argumentation as well as in the small-

---

61. This presentation of the difference in method is governed by wistful thinking. Bonhoeffer's way of presentation can in fact be no less gripping and at least as stringently "deductive" as Barth's. One need only compare the sweeping opening section of *The Cost of Discipleship* or the lectures on *Creation and Fall* of 1932, where much of what would later appear in the prison correspondence is hinted at. That a "style" of presentation other than that of a "regular" dogmatics is present in the "irregular" form of theological letters, often hinting at rather than amplifying, should be obvious.

62. On the other hand, apparently only a few weeks later, when Bonhoeffer turned to working on his dissertation on the church, he defended Barth against the charge that he had become "reactionary" by staying in the church (*DBE*, 65). In the prison letters Bonhoeffer does not refer to Barth and the "Barthians" as "dangerous reactionaries," but to those (Oxford Group and the Berneucheners) who in the Confessing Church "miss the 'movement' and the 'life,' . . . [and] go right back behind the approach of the theology of revelation and seek for 'religious renewal'" (*LPP*, 328).

63. Ott, 37, makes reference to the "assertive" style of Barth's *Dogmatics,* over against which he wishes to set Bonhoeffer's "dialogical" style.

print excursus sections. Besides, Bonhoeffer's charge against Barth in the prison letters is in no way meant to address Barth's "dogmatic method" only; rather, he speaks no less approvingly of Barth's "later dogmatics" than of the beginnings of his critique of religion, only to arrive at the summary judgment that Barth's "doctrine of revelation" had become "positivistic" (*LPP*, 328).

Ott's reduction of the problem to a pure question of method is an inadequate reflection of the true state of things. His exemplification of the "problem of theological language" in terms of the style of preaching[64] constricts Bonhoeffer's concern so much to a pure "program of interpretation" that materially it completely misses the question that reverberates in that concern, namely, that of "religionless Christianity" in the Hebrew Bible's "worldliness."[65] Bonhoeffer himself was completely convinced that no method, not even nonreligious speech or dialogical-dialectical discourse, can guarantee that the real "matter" at issue is given theological expression. If Bonhoeffer's charge against Barth is to have any meaning, it has to be directed against more than Barth's "method"; it has at least to touch also the "matter" of his theology of revelation itself. It touches upon the "declaration" that Bonhoeffer finds in Barth: "*'Friss, Vogel, oder stirb'* — 'take it or leave it': virgin birth, Trinity, or anything else; each is an equally significant and necessary part of the whole, which must simply be swallowed as a whole or not at all" (*LPP*, 286, T.a.).

7. "Virgin Birth, Trinity, or Anything Else"

This appears to be an appropriate place to take a closer look at Barth's treatment of the doctrine of the Trinity and the virgin birth. Bonhoeffer focuses on these two components of doctrinal tradition as examples of the "mysteries of the Christian faith" that he seeks to protect against "profanation" by means of the "arcane discipline." And in the treatment of these two doctrines, he sees Barth fall victim to a "positivist doctrine of revelation" (*LPP*, 286).

It is true that in his dogmatics Barth did not wish to forgo a presen-

---

64. Ott confronts Eduard Thurneysen's preaching style, which he labels as one of "revelational positivism" (139), with Bonhoeffer's "dialogical" method.

65. Cf. *DB*, 986f.: "More than a program of interpretation."

tation of the doctrine of the Trinity and, in its proper place, also the doctrine of the virgin birth in a full manner. The dogmatics project of 1927 already elicited the charge that he "was going the way of scholasticism," since he clearly acknowledged that he regarded "the doctrine of the early Church as in some sense normative." In the preface to the first part-volume of the *Church Dogmatics,* Barth meets this charge with a whole series of counterquestions that climax in the very contextual question:

> Or shall I . . . bemoan the constantly increasing confusion, tedium and irrelevance of modern Protestantism, which, probably along with the Trinity and the Virgin Birth, has lost an entire third dimension — the dimension of what for once, though not confusing it with religious and moral earnestness, we may describe as mystery — with the result that it has been punished with all kinds of worthless substitutes, . . . and that many of its preachers and adherents have finally learned to discover deep religious significance in the intoxication of Nordic blood and their political *Führer?* (*CD* I/1, xiv, *xi*)

This much is certain: when it comes to Trinity and virgin birth, Barth too is concerned with the dimensions of "mystery." Obviously Barth does not consider prayerful silence sufficient in dealing with the mysteries of faith. Rather, he is concerned with discerning the mystery as a mystery, to interpret it with the help of human reason in order to deploy it as an antidote in the fight against the Nordic religion of National Socialism. Is such instrumentalizing of theology what appeared to Bonhoeffer as a "profanization" of the mystery? Bonhoeffer's course on "recent theology," delivered in the winter of 1932/33, may signal something in this direction. In response to the "Altona Confession," composed by Hans Asmussen, Bonhoeffer stressed the distinction between doctrine, proclamation, and confession in the church. While doctrine and proclamation are addressed to the public, confession is an event that is to occur only "in the congregation." A confession addressed to the world outside is a dangerous undertaking (*DBW,* 12:177f.). As praise of the mysteries of faith, confession here becomes an *arcanum* of the congregation that ought not become directly a matter of public teaching or, worse, of ideological engagement.[66]

---

66. As early as the lectures on the "church" which Bonhoeffer delivered in the summer of 1932, he said the following: "The confession of faith belongs . . . to the 'Discipline

But let us look in turn how, in his *Church Dogmatics,* Karl Barth engages these pieces of ancient church dogma.

In that work, contrary to the tradition of theological liberalism,[67] Barth gives the doctrine of the Trinity a prominent position, "at the head of all dogmatics," in that it is discussed already within the prolegomena as interpreting the central concept of "the revelation of God" (*CD* I/1, 300, *345*). In the doctrine of the Trinity, Barth's concern is the "biblical answer" to the question, "Who is God in God's revelation? . . . What is God doing? and What does God effect?" (*CD* I/1, 297, *341,* T.a.). By placing the doctrine at the front, Barth seeks to achieve the "practical recognition" that the "in every respect . . . very important term 'God' " is clarified as the "norm" of dogmatics. "The doctrine of the Trinity is what basically distinguishes the Christian doctrine of God as Christian, and therefore what already distinguishes the Christian concept of revelation as Christian, in contrast to all other possible doctrines of God or concepts of revelation" (*CD* I/1, 301, *346*).

We mentioned earlier that in *Act and Being,* Bonhoeffer had expressed regret about Barth's early version of the doctrine of the Trinity in the *Christian Dogmatics* of 1927. Here it was presented as the answer to the question concerning the subject, predicate, and object of the little sentence *deus dixit,* God says.[68] Bonhoeffer called that a "fateful mistake" because it formalizes the personality of God (*AB,* 125). Without referring explicitly to Bonhoeffer's critique, Barth admits in his *Church Dogmatics* that those words "were then in fact used unguardedly and ambiguously." But he does "repeat [them] today in due form" in explaining "how they

---

of the Secret' *(Arkanum)* in the Christian gathering of those who believe. . . . [Confession] is not . . . loudly shrieking out propaganda. [It] must be preserved as the most sacred possession of the community" (*TF,* 91). On confession as an *"arcanum,"* cf. my article "Aspekte der 'Arkandisziplin' bei Dietrich Bonhoeffer," *Theologische Literaturzeitung* 119 (1994): 755ff., esp. 758f.

67. Schleiermacher dealt with the doctrine of the Trinity only at the very end of his work *The Christian Faith* (New York: Harper & Row, 1963), since "this doctrine itself, as ecclesiastically framed, is not an immediate utterance concerning the Christian self-consciousness, but only a combination of several such utterances" (2:738). Liberal theology has followed Schleiermacher ever since in this marginalization and relativizing of the doctrine of the Trinity.

68. Karl Barth, *Die christliche Dogmatik im Entwurf,* vol. 1, *Die Lehre vom Worte Gottes. Prolegomena zur christlichen Dogmatik* (1927; new edition, Zürich: TVZ, 1982), 166.

were intended. . . . Naturally it was not my thought then, nor is it now, that the truth of the dogma of the Trinity can be derived from the general truth of such a dogma. Rather, it is from the truth of the dogma of the Trinity that the truth of such a formula can perhaps be derived in this specific application, namely to the dogma of the Trinity." Barth rejects the possible objection that there the "mystery of the faith" is turned into something rationalistic. In accordance with the meaning of *fides quaerens intellectum,* he declares instead that "All dogmatic formulations are rational, and every dogmatic procedure is rational to the degree that in it use is made of general concepts, i.e., of the human *ratio*" (*CD* I/1, 296, *340*).[69]

In his examination of the biblical-theological "root" of the doctrine of the Trinity and, even more so, in the subsequent presentation of "God's triunity," Barth speaks entirely in the sense of Bonhoeffer's personalist concerns of the triune God as "the Thou who meets the human being's I" (*CD* I/1, 348, *400*). Barth would prefer to avoid using the "concept of person" within the doctrine of the Trinity, given that concept's susceptibility to misunderstanding; but "as a *derivation* from the doctrine of the Trinity," the concept obtains its significance. "For it follows from the trinitarian understanding of the God revealed in Scripture that this one God is to be understood not just as impersonal lordship, i.e., as power, but as the Lord, not just as absolute Spirit, but as person" (*CD* I/1, 358, *412*). However, according to Barth, the meaning of this doctrine lies in its answer to "the question of the subject of revelation. . . . The subject of revelation attested in the Bible, no matter what may be that subject's being, speech and action, is the one Lord, not a demi-god, either descended or ascended. Communion with the One who reveals Himself there . . . means for human beings that this God meets them as a Thou meets an I and unites with them as a Thou unites with an I. Not otherwise!" (*CD* I/1, 380-81, *436-38*).

Does such an interpretation of the doctrine of the Trinity profane the mystery or render it banal? Could it not be understood as an appropriate approach to the mystery that does not exclude but very much presupposes praise? For purposes of comparison, we consult a sermon by Bonhoeffer on the "depth of divinity" (1 Cor. 2:7-10) preached in Lon-

---

69. Cf. also *CD* I/1: "Theology means rational wrestling with the mystery. But all rational wrestling with this mystery, the more serious it is, can lead only to its fresh and authentic interpretation and manifestation as a mystery" (368, *423*).

don on Trinity Sunday, 27 May 1934, a few days before the Confessing Synod of Barmen.

Characteristically, Bonhoeffer begins his sermon in a thoroughly anthropological manner in that he initially meditates on the concept of "mystery," on how "void modern life is of mystery" and what it would mean in face of this to live "with . . . respect for mystery" (*DBW*, 13:359f.). *"Mystery does not [mean] that one just does not know something."* Mystery "does not elude our grasp" because it is so incomprehensibly far away or so exalted; "on the contrary, the closer something comes to us and the better we know something, the more mysterious it becomes to us." Bonhoeffer then elucidates this first on the interhuman level. "The greatest mystery to us is not the one furthest away but the one closest to us. . . . It is the final depth of everything mysterious when two people come so close one to the other that they *love* each other. . . . The more they love each other and in that love know one of the other, the more profoundly they discern the mystery of their love. Thus, knowing does not dissolve mystery but deepens it. *That* the other is close to me, that is the greatest mystery" (*DBW*, 13:360f.).

It is only from there that Bonhoeffer moves on to speak of "God's triunity." God lives "in mystery," and none of the thoughts we have of God must serve to remove this mystery. Therefore, the task of the church's dogma may only be to "point to the mystery of God" (*DBW*, 13:361). Such pointing has a thoroughly critical significance for Bonhoeffer in that it opposes the human propensity to make God part of human calculation and to exploit God. "Those who in this world are on top live by calculating and exploiting; that is what makes them great in the world. But they do not discern the mystery; only children do." God's mystery, God's coming among us human beings, is closest to us "in the cross of Christ. . . . This is the undiscerned mystery of God in this world: Jesus Christ. That this Jesus of Nazareth, the carpenter, was the very Lord of glory, that was the mystery of God. It was mystery because here God became poor, lowly, insignificant and weak out of love for humanity" (*DBW*, 13:362).

The issue in the church's dogma is the praise of God's love, love being merely another word for God's mystery. Bonhoeffer elucidates this in a paraphrase of the doctrine of the Trinity that he left out of the actual delivery of the sermon. "There is no greater mystery in the whole world than this that God loves us and that we may love God. Incomparable to

103

every human love, just as the creator is incomparable to the creature. . . . The mystery means to be loved by God and to love God . . . but to be loved by God is named Christ and to love God is named Holy Spirit. Thus, God's mystery is named Christ and Holy Spirit; God's mystery is named Holy Triunity" (*DBW*, 13:362 n. 2).[70]

This much is clear: For Bonhoeffer "the meaning of the doctrine of the Trinity is everything but a rationalistic hardening or freezing of religion." Rather, it is "incredibly simple: the doctrine of the triunity is nothing but the feeble praise of human beings of the impetuousness of God's love, a love in which God glorifies Godself and in which God embraces the whole world; the doctrine is a call to adoration, to reverence and to a love that submerges itself in God" (*DBW*, 13:363). This could well be called a "doxological" structure of dogma.[71]

It was noted earlier that Bonhoeffer sees the mystery of "the love of God" to be revealed centrally in "the cross of Jesus Christ." This refers us to the other example of the "mysteries of the Christian faith" that Bonhoeffer seeks by means of the "arcane discipline" to guard against being swallowed up in positivism of revelation. This is the christological dogma which received its sharpest formulation in the ancient church's doctrine of the virgin birth.

It is not only in the prison correspondence that Bonhoeffer speaks of "mystery" in connection with Christology. Similar things may be found in the sentences that open his lectures on Christology at the University of Berlin in the summer of 1933. "Teaching about Christ begins in silence. . . . That has nothing to do with mystagogical silence which in its dumbness is the soul's secret chatter with itself. The silence of the Church is silence before the Word. In proclaiming the Word, the Church in truth falls down silently before the inexpressible." On the basis of such adoration alone is "scholarly study of this proclamation" possible: "In the humble silence of the sacramental congregation offering its worship we concern ourselves with christology. To pray is to be

70. The reason why this passage was deleted could be that the assertion concerning the incomparability of the inner-trinitarian relation with human love did not quite fit in with the anthropological beginning of the sermon. It spoke precisely of comparability under the encompassing term of "mystery."

71. Cf. Heinrich Vogel, *Das nicaenische Glaubensbekenntnis. Eine Doxologie* (Berlin and Stuttgart, 1963), 69: "According to its origin, essence and mission, *theology* is *doxology.*"

silent and at the same time to cry out, before God and in face of God's Word" (*CC*, 27, T.a.).

Like the trinitarian question, the christological one is formulated sharply by Bonhoeffer in terms of the question about the person. His central issue is the question of encounter, the "who question" about the person of Jesus Christ. "The question 'Who are you?' is the question of dethroned and distraught reason; but it is also the question of faith: 'Who are you? Are you God himself?' This is the question with which christology is concerned. Christ is the Counter-Logos" (*CC*, 30). What is excluded from christological thinking, however, are the questions concerning the "whether" and "how" of revelation.

As it is, all "thought-forms of objectification" have been overcome in Christology by the counter-logos (*CC*, 102, T.a.). The mistake of those thought-forms lies in "that the nature of God and that of humans were spoken of in a theoretical, spectator-like way. In this way, the two natures were viewed like two distinguishable entities, separated from each other until they come together in Jesus Christ. The relationship between God and humans cannot be thought of as a relationship between entities, but only as between persons" (*CC*, 101, T.a.).

In this sense, Bonhoeffer seeks to understand the paradoxical and "contradictory statements that stand one over against another in the Chalcedonian Definition" (*CC*, 102, T.a.). Against the liberal critique of the two-nature doctrine, which held that "the understanding of Jesus Christ of the Gospels" had been "Hellenized and thereby corrupted" here, Bonhoeffer maintains that "there is no more 'un-Greek' product of thought than the Chalcedonian Definition" (*CC*, 101). According to that definition, God and the human encounter each other "without confusion and without change, without separation and without division." "What remains are simple negations. No positive thought-form remains to say what happens in the God-human Jesus Christ. . . . Entry is open to faith alone. All thought-forms are broken off" (*CC*, 87-88). Thus, the Chalcedonian Definition did not at all establish an "objectifying" two-nature doctrine; rather "it . . . superseded the doctrine of the two natures." "This critical sense of the Chalcedonian Definition is to be taken further" (*CC*, 97-98). And so the Definition ultimately shows itself to be the question: Who is the person of Jesus Christ (*CC*, 102)?

Does the intensification of the christological dogma in the doctrine of the virgin birth mean that reason oversteps its bounds and seeks to enter into the mystery rather than to protect and glorify it? Is the question about the person of Jesus Christ displaced by an illegitimate "how" question? Bonhoeffer depicted both the *"extra Calvinisticum"* of Reformed Christology and the Lutheran counterargument of the *"genus maiestaticum"* as "the result of asking the question, 'How?'" (*CC*, 55), and indicated the problems with that. According to him, both these teachings are founded in "unbiblical" abstractions (*CC*, 93). All attempts to get beyond the "negative formulations" of the Chalcedonian Definition have proven themselves, in the light of the history of theology, to fall short of Chalcedon itself.

There are indications that Bonhoeffer detected also in the doctrine of the virgin birth traces of theological inquisitiveness that cannot contain itself within the conceptual tension of Chalcedon's negative formulations but attempts instead to overcome the critical sense of Chalcedon by means of positive assertions in the thought-forms of "objectification" (*CC*, 102). In the context of developing a "positive christology," Bonhoeffer rejects the doctrine of the virgin birth because it is based in the illegitimate "how question." Instead of "the incarnation," we should talk of the one who became human (*CC*, 104). The "hypothesis of the virgin birth" is questionable "both historically and dogmatically. . . . The biblical witness is ambiguous." The doctrine of the virgin birth expresses "the incarnation of God . . . and not the fact of the one who became human" (*CC*, 105, T.a.).

In contrast, how does Barth address Christology and, in particular, the ancient church's teaching of the "virgin birth" in the second part-volume of the "prolegomena" of the *Church Dogmatics* (*CD* I/2 [1938])? In section 15, "The Mystery of Revelation," Barth takes up the problem of Christology because "christology deals with the revelation of God as a mystery." The answer to the question "Who is Jesus Christ?" is at first "true God and true human" as a paraphrase of John 1:14 ("The Word was made flesh") (*CD* I/2, 131-32). Barth emphasizes that this is "an equalising of the *un*equal." The sovereignty of God's Word is maintained in this irreversible equation (*CD* I/2, 136).

In contrast to Bonhoeffer's Christology lectures, Barth wants to understand "the event of the incarnation," as a result, not only as "a *completed* event" but at the same time also as "a completed *event*" (*CD* I/2, 165). In face of the Lutheran emphasis on the "accomplished fact" (*CD*

I/2, 165), Barth wonders whether "the *freedom,* majesty and glory of the Word of God" do not become absorbed by and submerged in God's "becoming flesh" (*CD* I/2, 166-67). A synthesis of Lutheran and Reformed Christology, such as Bonhoeffer obviously tried to achieve, seemed quite realistic to Barth on the basis of the *"extra Calvinisticum."* However, he thinks it more advisable to keep the matter open, since it is precisely in the duplication of the theological schools that the one mystery is reflected (*CD* I/2, 171).

The problematic of the "virgin birth" is addressed in the section entitled "The Miracle of Christmas." First, Barth looks back and sums up. "God's revelation in its objective reality is the incarnation of His Word, in that He, the one true and eternal God, is at the same time true human being like us. God's revelation in its objective reality is the person of Jesus Christ." Very much in the spirit of Bonhoeffer, Barth emphasizes that revelation is in no way "brought . . . into the series of other objects of our knowledge" in this description; rather, it is depicted precisely as *"mystery"* and "not only *a* mystery but *the* mystery" (*CD* I/2, 172, T.a.). But it is precisely the mystery of the incarnation which, as such, "is *indicated* in Scripture and in church dogma by reference to the *miracle* of Christmas. This miracle is the conception of Jesus Christ by the Holy Spirit or His birth of the Virgin Mary" (*CD* I/2, 173). Thus, in contrast to Bonhoeffer, the double statement of the Apostles' Creed about the conception and birth of Jesus Christ is obviously unavoidable for Barth as a reference to the mystery of faith.

But then Barth immediately admits that, in relation to the "necessity" of this doctrine, "both in extent and form the grounds for the dogma in the *statements of Holy Scripture* are not at first sight so strong or so clear as one might wish for such a dogma in the strict sense of the term" (*CD* I/2, 174). Nonetheless, Barth wants to hold on to the doctrine of the virgin birth on account of its "certain inward, essential rightness and importance in [its] connexion with the person of Jesus Christ." The dogma "denotes not so much the christological reality of revelation as the *mystery* of that reality. . . . The dogma of the Virgin Birth is thus the confession of the boundless hiddenness of the *vere Deus vere homo* and of the boundless amazement of awe and thankfulness called forth in us by this *vere Deus vere homo*" (*CD* I/2, 177).

Thus Barth, like Bonhoeffer, knows of a "doxological" structure of dogma, of an irreducible character of mystery. But unlike Bonhoeffer, he seeks to make that structure clear with the help of this doctrine.[72] For the question is whether a theologian who believes that the birth by a virgin can be denied as a mere "externality" still understands by "the mystery of Christmas" the same as one who "acknowledges and confesses the Virgin Birth to be the sign of the mystery. . . . May it not be the case that the only one who hears the witness of the thing is the one who keeps to the sign by which the witness has actually signified it? Among those who dispute the sign we must first discover [those] concerning whom we can at the same time unhesitatingly admit that [they] show a reliable acquaintance with the thing signified by this sign" (CD I/2, 179-80).

Might Bonhoeffer have been the one who contested the birth by a virgin while acknowledging very well the mystery signified by this sign? What is certain is that Barth, like Bonhoeffer, was concerned here with the glorification of the mystery of faith. Barth thinks he can correspond appropriately only by speaking of it in terms of dogmatic tradition. Bonhoeffer thinks the "how question" has to be left open — for the sake of that very same mystery. Still, in his answer to "the question of popular theology, whether in order to believe in a really Christian way 'one' would have to believe fully in the Virgin birth," Barth allows that "there is certainly nothing to prevent anyone, without affirming the doctrine of the Virgin birth, from recognising the mystery of the person of Jesus Christ or from believing in a perfectly Christian way. . . . But this does not imply that the Church is at liberty to convert the doctrine of the Virgin birth into an option for specially strong or for specially weak souls." To "affirm the doctrine of the Virgin birth is a part of real Christian faith." Those who seek to forge a "private road" around this dogma need at least to be warned against making their doubts "an object of their proclamation." They are expected to "at least pay the dogma the respect of keeping si-

---

72. In this context, the "how question" is not a matter of taboo, as it was for Bonhoeffer. In explicit contrast to Bonhoeffer's *Doktorvater* R. Seeberg, Barth rather turns the answer to that question into the criterion for whether the "who question" has been appropriately answered. "To describe this How?, i.e. to describe this mystery of revelation, is the aim of the doctrine of the Virgin Birth. . . . [The] doctrine of the Virgin Birth is merely the description" and not the matter itself, form and not content. But in spite of this distinction, one has to begin with the acknowledgment that in the Bible "[s]ign and thing signified, the outward and the inward . . . are never separated in such a ('liberal') way that according to preference the one may be easily retained without the other" (CD I/2, 178f.).

lence about it" (*CD* I/2, 181). It might seem as if in these words Barth had wanted to propose to Bonhoeffer the alternative of the "arcane discipline."

And yet, Barth does not rest with this simple affirmation of the doctrine as a kind of "watch" outside "the door to the mystery of Christmas." Rather, he clearly strives so to interpret the doctrine that it obtains a contemporary meaning that may also be actually received. In so doing he unexpectedly enters upon paths that take him beyond the repetition of the ancient church's doctrine to theologically new territory. "'Born of the Virgin Mary' means born as no one else was born, in a way which can as little be made clear biologically as the resurrection of a dead man, i.e., born not because of male generation but solely because of female conception" (*CD* I/2, 185). But that means that "In the *ex virgine* there is contained a judgment upon humans." This in turn means that "human nature possesses no capacity for becoming the human nature of Jesus Christ, the place of divine revelation. . . . The virginity of Mary in the birth of the Lord is the denial, not of humans in the presence of God, but of any power, attribute or capacity in them for God." It is the issue of "the recollection of the so-called *inherited sin,* or original sin as it is better expressed" (*CD* I/2, 188-89).

But what does this "original sin" consist of that is broken down by the *natus ex virgine,* this "born of the virgin"? The ancient church tended to embrace "the quite unbiblical view that sexual life as such is to be regarded as an evil to be removed." Indeed, "Virgin birth means birth without previous sexual union between man and woman" (*CD* I/2, 190).[73] Still,

> if the actual sinfulness of sexual life as such constituted the problem . . . why could not . . . the new beginning be achieved just as well . . . in the form of an extraordinary sanctification of a sexual event unsanctified in itself because of the Fall? Instead of the *natus ex virgine,* why do not Scripture and Creed speak of the natural fruit of an elect and specially blessed human couple? . . . How much simpler it would all have been,

---

73. Barth states that "it is not the natural but the sinful element in sexual life which caused it to be excluded here as the origin of the human existence of Jesus Christ." But this makes no difference to the fact that — given that humans are altogether sinners from birth — "all sexual life (not only it, but it too!) is involved in sin as well, and is itself sin" (*CD* I/2, 190, T.a.).

and how valuable it might have been for Christian ethics, especially for the Christian doctrine of marriage and the family, if Scripture and Creed had said this at this point! But this is just what they do not say. (*CD* I/2, 190-91)

Hence, the problem must lie elsewhere.

Apparently, the doctrine of the virgin birth makes good sense only when it is noted that God's judgment on human sin is a *"gracious judgment,"* so that "the human is involved in the form of Mary, but involved *only* in the form of the *virgo Maria,* i.e. only in the form of non-willing, non-achieving, non-creative, non-sovereign human, only in the form of the human who can merely receive, merely be ready, merely let something be done to and with the human self. This human being, the *virgo,* becomes the possibility, becomes the mother of God's Son in the flesh." But if it is "only the *virgo*" whom God's grace wants to use to be "the mother of the Lord," it means conversely that, "as such[,] willing, achieving, creative, sovereign human is not considered. . . . This is the mystery of grace to which the *natus ex virgine* points. . . . [N]ot because of the nature of sexual life nor because of its sinfulness, but because every natural generation is the work of willing, achieving, creative, sovereign human" must sexual life be "excluded as the source of the human existence of Christ" (*CD* I/2, 191-92, T.a.). In other words, it is "particularly the function of the *male*" that is excluded (*CD* I/2, 192).[74]

Thus, the point of this doctrine consists in critiquing "patriarchy," which gave and still gives shape to world history.[75] In light of this, "the sign of the mystery of Christmas, the sign of the lack of a human father of Jesus," becomes understandable as a "countersign": the "willing, achieving, creative, sovereign human . . . cannot be considered as a participator in God's work. . . . So it is the male who must be set aside here, if a countersign is to be set up as a sign of the incarnation of God. . . . And as the

74. ". . . that willing, achieving, creative, sovereign human, the human as an independent co-worker with God, the human in the impulse of his *eros,* who as such, where God's grace is concerned, simply cannot be a participator in God's work, is *a parte potiori* the male human being and the father of humans in the sexual act which humans have to thank for their earthly existence" (*CD* I/2, 193, T.a.).

75. Correspondingly, Barth accuses Schleiermacher of having missed the decisive issue in that even though he had wished to keep "the general idea of a supernatural conception" of the Redeemer, he declared "the more precise definition of this . . . conception as one in which there is no male activity" to be superfluous (*CD* I/2, 180).

sign of this fact . . . the *genesis Iesou Christou* in contradiction to the becoming of all other human beings, is in no sense a history of males." But this includes that "In token of that the woman is adopted apart from the male and her relation to him, and in spite of the sin of which she is guilty along with him, to be the conceiver of the eternal God . . . on earth, to be the *theotokos*" (*CD* I/2, 194 and 196, T.a.).[76]

Is it conceivable that Bonhoeffer experienced the manner in which Barth dealt with "virgin birth" and "Trinity" in the *Church Dogmatics* as "positivism of revelation"? On first glance this seems unlikely, since Bonhoeffer could speak of the "mysteries of the Christian faith" no less positively than Barth. Even his mention of "virgin birth, Trinity or anything else" in the prison letters is in no way intended to be depreciative, but is meant to highlight precisely the dignity of dogma within the context of the arcane discipline that was called for.

And yet, one cannot help noticing already in Bonhoeffer's Christology lectures that he has hesitations concerning the doctrine of the virgin birth as a subject of dogmatics. The summary of his christological thinking in his circular letter for Christmas 1939 is also void of any reference to the "virgin birth." He writes there: " 'God revealed in the flesh,' the God-human Jesus Christ, is the holy mystery which theology is appointed to guard and to preserve. What senselessness to think that it is the task of theology to unravel God's mystery, to drag it down to the flat, ordinary human wisdom of experience and reason! This alone is its task: to preserve, defend and glorify God's wonder as wonder" (*TP,* 28, T.a.). Again, we meet the "doxological" structure of dogma which arcane discipline is to serve. Right at the beginning of this letter, Bonhoeffer wrote, "*Theologia sacra* arises from those on bended knee who do homage to the mystery of the divine child in the stable" (*TP,* 28, T.a.). It appears, therefore, that veneration is the position which alone is appropriate to the mystery.

The Chalcedonian Creed may be respected as an appropriate reference to the christological mystery, but only under this presupposition. "Nowhere else but in and through the person of Jesus Christ are Godhead

76. Unfortunately, Barth decided to treat the antipatriarchal dimension of the doctrine of the virgin birth only as a "secondary" issue (*CD* I/2, 192). In the *Christian Dogmatics* of 1927, this was still the dominant aspect of the parallel section entitled "The Miracle of the Birth of Christ" (cf. 365ff. in the new edition). How much "relevant" truth there is in the ancient church's teaching could have become apparent exactly at this point.

and humanity united, 'without confusion, without change, without division, without separation,' as the Chalcedonian definition put it in supreme paradox, and at the same time in a most reverent preservation of the mystery of the person of the Mediator. Rarely in later ages has reason been so ready to humble and surrender itself before the miracle of God as it does in these words. But precisely because of that has reason been made a better instrument for the glorification of the divine revelation than at that time" (*TP*, 31-32, T.a.). But still no mention of virgin birth, although this is precisely where its place in dogmatics would be according to Barth.

In his lectures on the church, delivered in the summer of 1932, Bonhoeffer expressed general doubts about the adequacy of the Apostles' Creed. "The confession [of faith] must *be utterly true*. (It is) response to the true Word of God. Confessing is a matter of immediate presence! . . . Confessing [faith] is a dimension of our truly standing in God's presence!" (*DBW*, 11:283). In this connection he makes this objection against that creed: "The *word* itself must be true! Not only what is meant!" From this perspective "the questions of liberalism (and Harnack) remain open." Bonhoeffer thinks in particular of the statement "he descended into hell" and the "virgin birth" (*DBW*, 11:283-84). Mere conformity with tradition is not sufficient for the *"truthfulness of the confession."* For at issue here is not "general truth" but the "specific cognition of the truth of faith." Thus, "the Apostles' Creed is not appropriate to the evangelical confession of faith." Ordaining ministers on the Apostles' Creed is "indefensible." The "question of the creed" is by no means "settled" (*DBW*, 11:284-85).

Recalling unsettled questions of liberal theology, Bonhoeffer clearly alludes to the so-called "Apostles' Creed controversy" of 1892 in which his teacher Adolf von Harnack argued the liberal case against the dogma of the virgin birth in particular. And as late as his "Outline for a Book," written in Tegel Prison — in which he wanted to lift up anew not least the legitimate legacy of liberal theology on the theological territory that Barth's reorientation had created (*LPP*, 378) — Bonhoeffer recalls that problem area by asking in the second chapter of the "Outline": "What do we really believe? I mean, believe in such a way that we stake our lives on it? The problem of the Apostles' Creed?" At the same time, he rejects "What *must* I believe?" as a "false" question, and brands the controversies between the Lutherans and the Reformed (and to some extent the Roman Catholics and the Protestants) as unreal now (*LPP*, 382-83).

What is significant in comparison to Barth is that, in Bonhoeffer's eyes, treating the ancient church's dogma of the virgin birth as a matter of dogmatic instruction represents a danger to the mystery of faith. Accordingly, he recommends that the mystery be subjected to a discipline that protects it against profanization, that is, against ill-timed propagation. The doctrine of the virgin birth may point to the "mystery of the faith," the veneration of which is to continue in the arcane discipline. But it obviously is no longer for him an element of Christian faith on which we "stake our lives" and, consequently, not a matter of dogmatic instruction. According to Bonhoeffer, there are "degrees of knowledge and degrees of significance" (*LPP*, 286) which bring it about that not everything in doctrinal studies is treated in the same way.

Did Bonhoeffer want to call Barth's attention to the danger of saying too much in dogmatics when he depicted Barth's position in the declaration "*Friss Vogel oder stirb!* — Take it or leave it!" — and then charged him with "positivism of revelation"? It would appear so. In consciously leaving open the question of the virgin birth instead of proclaiming it as church teaching, it would seem that Bonhoeffer decidedly sides with Philipp Melanchthon, who, in relation to this piece of ancient church doctrine, declared, "we would rather venerate the mysteries of the divine than investigate it. *(Mysteria divinitatis rectius adoraverimus quam vestigaverimus)*" (introduction to his *Loci communes* of 1521).

Melanchthon had himself already repudiated "scholastic" speculation in Christology and endeavored to understand Christ entirely on the basis of his *"beneficia,"* his redeeming work, instead of exploring his natures and the manner of his incarnation.[77] In the Christology lectures of 1933, Bonhoeffer still rejected this classic injunction of Melanchthon's because here "the christological question is referred back to the soteriological one and disposed of in it" (*CC*, 37, T.a.). This understanding of Christ made Melanchthon the spiritual father of theological liberalism.[78]

It would seem that in the prison letters Bonhoeffer's own liberal inheritance emerged once again more clearly than he thought it affordable

77. The classic phrase in Melanchthon's *Loci communes* of 1521 is "Nam ex his proprie Christus cognoscitur, siquidem hoc est Christum cognoscere beneficia eius cognoscere, non . . . eius naturas, modos incarnationis contueri."

78. Cf. *CC*, 37: "This was an epoch-making point of view and was followed through by Schleiermacher and Ritschl."

at the beginning of the church struggle. He still wants to overcome "liberal theology . . . (and even if Barth is still influenced by it, though negatively)," but feels this can be seriously accomplished only when "its question [is] genuinely taken up and answered (as is *not* the case in the Confessing Church's positivism of revelation)" (*LPP,* 328).

In light of the foregoing, we formulate this *thesis:* in his charge of "positivism of revelation," Bonhoeffer wanted above all to warn against the danger of saying too much in dogmatics and of becoming "loquacious." It is likely that Barth's holding on to the doctrine of the virgin birth, more than anything else, caused him to utter the charge. But the question remains whether Bonhoeffer responded adequately to that danger in charging Barth this way. Is the charge against Barth justified? Did Karl Barth, in the relative completeness of his dogmatics and in the endeavor to stay in touch with tradition, step across a boundary imposed by the mystery on theology? Or is Bonhoeffer's charge more an expression of his having misunderstood Barth's intention in principle? In what is to follow now, we turn to these questions, aware that on occasion we shall think beyond Barth and Bonhoeffer.

CHAPTER IV

Proceeding on Barth's and Bonhoeffer's Way

1. Merely a Misunderstanding?

Does the relative "completeness" of the conception of Barth's dogmatics necessarily imply that it has to be "swallowed whole"? If Bonhoeffer had understood Barth that way, he would rank with a crowd of "Barthians" and "anti-Barthians" who "assume that every subsequent volume of the *Dogmatics* is *based* on the preceding one in the sense that the later derives the substance of its truth and the form of its concepts from the earlier, preceding volume."[1] Kornelis Heiko Miskotte counters this view, saying that "it is *not* so, or only in a very relative way. It is, rather, that every individual point contains the *whole* of dogmatics, each under a specific aspect. . . . What we encounter here is the utterly *modern* feature of the *Church Dogmatics;* it is a clear break with a systematics that was handed on to us by scholasticism and the fathers of orthodoxy. . . ."[2] It is the uniqueness of Barth's dogmatics, "its

---

1. Kornelis Heiko Miskotte, *Über Karl Barths Kirchliche Dogmatik. Kleine Präludien und Phantasien,* Theologische Existenz heute, n.s., vol. 89 (Munich: Chr. Kaiser Verlag, 1961), 17f.

2. Miskotte, *Über Karl Barths Kirchliche Dogmatik,* 18. Cf. 18: "It is an attempt not to engage the wide range of interpreting concepts in terms of a polyvalent consistency but, rather, to relativize them in relation to, and placing them at the service of, the never 'posited' multidimensional truth."

fugue-like repetition," which makes it possible to consume it "piece by piece" rather than swallowing it as a whole.[3] Every individual piece stands for the whole: *"pars pro toto."*[4] The virgin birth may well be about the most beautiful "mystery" of dogmatics, but that does not mean that this mystery now has to be turned into a "law of faith." What should be considered instead is this: if what is to be seen here can also be seen elsewhere in the *Dogmatics* — even though perhaps not in the same beauty and clarity — then there are indeed "stages of understanding" and freedom of faith, liberation for faith, is what reigns here.

Hence, Barth's early insight, according to which "[b]iblical dogmatics are fundamentally the suspension of all dogmatics" (*WGWM*, 73), still stands behind the *Church Dogmatics*. In that work's first part-volume, Barth expresses a self-critical "word of caution" precisely in the context of a section entitled "The Speech of God as the Mystery of God." "[I]t may be feared that we are all on the point of becoming much too positive. I am thinking . . . of a certain assurance of voice, speech and attitude with which, it seems, we can work on the new or older field, a certain confidence with which we think we can take those great concepts on our lips and analyse them and interrelate them constructively or in other ways, a certain sprightliness with which we speak about the things denoted by them as though we were speaking *of* them because we know how to speak *about* them with such comparative freedom from restriction" (*CD* I/1, 162f., *185*, T.a.).

There is no doubt: Barth too recognized the threat of "positivism of revelation." That he fell victim to it in the *Church Dogmatics* can be asserted only by those who read this work "from above," from the "abstractions," the "most formidable of which [is] . . . talk about 'God'": "God in general." For "if God is not Emmanuel, God-with-us, then we talk about an abstract construction of God." But "one of the most general characteristics of the *Church Dogmatics*" is precisely "the fight against abstractions."[5] It does not want to be understood "from above, from the height of philosophizing theology," but "from below," from "the small-print excursuses on biblical interpretation."[6]

3. Miskotte, *Über Karl Barths Kirchliche Dogmatik*, 12ff.

4. Miskotte, *Über Karl Barths Kirchliche Dogmatik*, 19ff.

5. Miskotte, *Über Karl Barths Kirchliche Dogmatik*, 29.

6. Kornelis Heiko Miskotte, "Die Erlaubnis zum schriftgemässen Denken," in *Antwort* (Festschrift for Karl Barth's seventieth birthday) (Zürich: EVZ, 1956), 33f. On

Might Bonhoeffer have overlooked this return "to the biblical movement . . . from specific to general"[7] that had taken place in Barth's dogmatics? Should the charge of "positivism of revelation" against Barth be, therefore, no more than a profound misunderstanding of the *Church Dogmatics* on Bonhoeffer's part? This is how Friedrich-Wilhelm Marquardt seems to understand it; he sees in "Bonhoeffer's charge of 'positivism of revelation' an expression of the misunderstanding, now spread throughout the whole world," that in his "great defensive move against every form of 'natural theology'" Barth had also rejected every kind of "theology of history." "An a-historical and therefore necessarily a-political reading of Barth's dogmatics misses its meaning. Particularly in Germany, such a reading is the highly equivocal mystery of the success that Barth enjoyed in the church [there] for a time. The history of how Barth was received has yet to be written; its German chapter is likely to be its most intimate and, yet, most devastating: positivism of revelation and neo-orthodoxy were products of the essentially un-political 'Barthianism,' a movement that was born in Germany."[8] In Hans Asmussen we have come to know one of the most notable representatives of such a "Barthianism" against whom Bonhoeffer's charge is laid with justification. But what of Barth himself: Did he not at least give cause to "Barthianism"?

In a different way, Hans-Joachim Kraus has judged "Bonhoeffer's reminder of the 'arcane discipline'" within the context of his charge of "positivism of revelation" to be a misunderstanding. That reminder is "based in a distorted juxtaposition and a misreading of the self-understanding of the *Church Dogmatics*. Where and how is any one topic of the Christian faith 'profaned' in this work of dogmatics?"[9] Be-

---

the Karl Barth reception "from below" practiced in the Netherlands, cf. Anke M. Wolff-Steger, "Frans Breukelman: Ein Meister des Wortes," in *Texte und Kontexte,* no. 31/32 (Stuttgart: Alektor Verlag, 1986), 8ff.

7. Miskotte, "Erlaubnis zum schriftgemässen Denken," 37; cf. 37: "Here scholastic speculation comes to grief; here the Israelite idiom is discerned as the Prophets and Apostles used it and with which their language is nourished." This is where "deduction from the concept has to make room for *induction from the name.*"

8. Friedrich-Wilhelm Marquardt, *Theologie und Sozialismus. Das Beispiel Karl Barths,* 3rd enlarged ed. (Munich: Chr. Kaiser Verlag, 1985), 245f. It remains to be seen whether a historical and political understanding of Barth's *Dogmatics* necessarily also includes a form of "theology of history," as Marquardt asserts.

9. Hans-Joachim Kraus, *Theologische Religionskritik* (Neukirchen-Vluyn: Neukirchener Verlag, 1982), 35. References which follow in the text are to this work.

sides, Bonhoeffer "did not understand what Barth's critique of religion was aiming at. In the final analysis, he did not grasp the theological acumen and clarity, the import of the expositions in the *Church Dogmatics*" (30). Bonhoeffer misreads Barth's discussion of "true religion" as a "supra-naturalistic solution of the enigma of 'religion' by the Christian theologian who knows what is to be known about revelation, and who is anxious to help his 'positivism of revelation' win the day" (29).

But we do not wish simply to settle for knowing that Bonhoeffer may have misunderstood Barth when he charged him with "positivism of revelation" and go on by just taking something of "the best from . . . the postulate of un-religious speech . . . in the way . . . indicated or in some other way — without searching for a deeper meaning which he himself did not offer us, and perhaps had not even thought through himself . . ." (*WCA*, 90f.). That would be altogether too smooth. Of course, Bonhoeffer did not think everything to its conclusion while in prison. He knew he was saying things that were "controversial," but he had to risk it if it meant that this would "get down to the serious problems of life" (*LPP*, 378). It is for this reason that we turn to a study of Barth's "doctrine of election," a doctrine that Bonhoeffer was still able to read in prison. Our question is whether Bonhoeffer's last opportunity to read Barth could confirm the image he had formed in his memory from the study of Barth's "Prolegomena" which had provoked the indeed ambiguous charge of "positivism of revelation." Unfortunately, there exist no direct communications about how the study of Barth's doctrine of election affected Bonhoeffer in prison. Therefore, what follows must of necessity be hypothetical and, for that reason, "controversial." But the attempt is to be made because it "gets down to the serious problems of life."

2. "Arcane Discipline" and "Double Predestination"

Karl Barth was mistaken in tracing Bonhoeffer's charge, among other things, to a possibly unclear recollection of Barth's books which Bonhoeffer "certainly did not have with him in his prison cell" (*WCA*, 90). Bonhoeffer knew the *Church Dogmatics* up to volume II/2, having obtained page proofs of that volume in 1942 while on his third visit to

Switzerland.[10] His wish, expressed in the letter from prison dated on the fourth Sunday in Advent 1943, to get "something good to read over Christmas," perhaps "Barth's *Doctrine of Predestination* (in sheets)" (*LPP,* 171), could be fulfilled. Thus, Bonhoeffer was able to refresh his "recollection" of Barth by reading his doctrine of election (*CD* II/2) after having obviously read only the ethical section of that same volume in May 1942.[11]

This gives rise to the question whether Bonhoeffer's charge of "positivism of revelation" against Barth and the concurrent call for reinstituting the arcane discipline was possibly strengthened by the form Barth gave the doctrine of election as "the sum of the Gospel" (*CD* II/2, 3).[12] Heinz Eduard Tödt suspects that "the most important basis" for Bonhoeffer's critique of Barth in the prison correspondence was quite likely volume II/2 of the *Church Dogmatics.* "Barth treats predestination and God's commandment in the sense of the foundation for the objective side of ethics. Over against religious subjectivism, Barth here radically stresses the sovereignty of God. . . . But could Barth also depict God's preeminent sovereignty in such a way that human beings did not become puppets but emerged with spontaneity, as self-acting agents being of age in the condition of the world that God had made possible?"[13] We have already seen that the impetus of the critique of religion, which Barth maintains fully also in his doctrine of election, could not possibly have been the matter that had provoked Bonhoeffer's critique. He, too, wanted in no way to take away from God's sovereignty. But how was that sovereignty to be thought of in its relation to human beings?

In comparison to traditional presentations of the doctrine of predestination, which frequently appear to disfigure and constrain the biblical

---

10. *MBBC,* 5 and 9; Kraus, 34, raises the question whether the volumes of Barth's *Church Dogmatics* to which Bonhoeffer had access at the time could indeed have been the cause of the "positivism of revelation" charge which was addressed and corrected in later volumes of the *CD,* corrections Bonhoeffer would not have been able to take cognizance of.

11. Cf. Eberhard Bethge, ed., *Schweizer Korrespondenz,* Theologische Existenz heute, n.s., vol. 124 (1982), 28.

12. Cf. also *CD* II/2, 13f.: "[T]he election of grace is the whole of the Gospel, the Gospel *in nuce.*"

13. Heinz Eduard Tödt, "Glauben in einer religionslosen Welt. Muss man zwischen Barth und Bonhoeffer wählen?" in *Genf '76. Ein Bonhoeffer-Symposion,* ed. Hans Pfeifer, Internationales Bonhoeffer Forum 1 (Munich: Chr. Kaiser Verlag, 1976), 100f.

language of God's electing grace, the first thing one notices in Barth's presentation is how antispeculative it is. "[There is] no question [then] of arbitrary speculation concerning an arbitrarily conceived highest being, but rather an obedient reckoning with the One whom Jesus Christ called his Father, and who called Jesus Christ His Son." God's "freedom of choice" ought not be confused with "caprice"; God's "mystery" is not dark but bright since what is at issue is God's "election of grace" (CD II/2, 24f.). It is the Bible that prohibits every form of formal speculation: "When Holy Scripture speaks of God, it does not permit us to let our attention or thoughts wander at random . . . it concentrates our attention and thoughts upon one single point . . ." (CD II/2, 52). This one point, on which alone we are to focus "away from all others, and excluding all sideglances or secondary thoughts" (CD II/2, 58f.), is the name of Jesus Christ "as the substance of all the preceding history of Israel and the hope of all the succeeding history of the Church" (CD II/2, 53). But if Jesus becomes so much "the mirror of election,"[14] then this history between God and human beings can be called "a triumph only for God's grace and therefore for God's sovereignty" (CD II/2, 194).[15]

Evidently, Bonhoeffer clearly perceived this eminently joyful strain in Barth's dogmatics, particularly in the doctrine of election that he was reading in prison. It was quite likely this reading that caused him to refer to Barth in his letter of 9 March 1944 to Eberhard Bethge before he takes

14. Cf. John Calvin, *Institutio* III, 24, 5: *"Christus ergo speculum est, in quo electionem nostram contemplari convenit, et sine fraude licet"* [Christ, then, is the mirror wherein we must, and without self-deception may, contemplate our own election]. Cited in *CD* II/2, 62.

15. Barth's revision of the traditional doctrine of predestination was cause for K. H. Miskotte to speak of the "jubilation of reason" in Barth's dogmatics: "The *heart is not enough* to be the seat, the space, the resonating chamber for this jubilation. . . . We will, we may go forward (if it be given us) to a jubilation of reason" (*Über Karl Barths Kirchliche Dogmatik,* 59). Cf. 61: "One might say that the CD is better understood when one understands its forms, its logic, its eloquence, its expanse and its persistence as *reason exercising singing.* . . . Behold!, if Medusa is truly swallowed up in the victory of the mystical rose, that rose wherein, according to the final canto of Dante's *Paradiso,* light reflects itself in a threefold way, and if it becomes *clear* also and especially to reason that God is light and that there is no darkness in God (I Jn 1:5), then this knowledge, this clarity desires to be out in the open. It bursts forth into *speech* — speech that comes from reason; it bursts forth into *song* — song that comes from reason; it bursts forth into *jubilation* — jubilation that comes from reason *and* goes beyond it."

up his theological train of thought and his critique of Barth. In line with Luther, Lessing, and others, he cites Barth as an example of "*hilaritas*, which I might describe as confidence in one's own work, boldness and defiance of the world and of popular opinion, a steadfast certainty that in one's own work one is showing the world something *good* (even if the world doesn't like it), and a high-spirited self-confidence" (*LPP*, 229, T.a.).[16]

Why is it that, in spite of this barely concealed affirmation of the "triumph of grace" in Barth's revision of the doctrine of predestination, Bonhoeffer comes to the conclusion a few weeks later that Barth has set up a "law of faith" which has turned his doctrine of revelation into a "positivism"? Why does he instead wish to subject the "mysteries" of the Christian faith to an "arcane discipline" in order to protect them "against profanation"?

One cannot help but notice that, in the context of the doctrine of predestination in its traditional form, Barth was also preoccupied with the question whether certain aspects of it, especially the teaching of "double predestination" as election *and* rejection, should not "be reserved as a kind of arcane wisdom [!] of theologians . . . and not published abroad amongst the people" (*CD* II/2, 18, T.a.). But, following Calvin, he rejects that idea, for "true discretion cannot consist in burying away a truth to which all true servants of God testify, but only in the sober and reverent yet quite open confession of what is learned in the school of the heavenly Teacher" (*CD* II/2, 18). In any event, Barth wants to formulate the doctrine of predestination in a manner "less speculative and more in accordance with the biblical testimony" in comparison to theological tradition. If it is understood strictly in terms of the gospel, the mystery of election does not need to be kept quiet but can "lay claim to . . . full publicity within the Church" (*CD* II/2, 18).[17]

16. On the absence of *hilaritas* in recent literature, cf. *LPP*, 189: "[O]n the whole all the newest productions seem to me to be lacking in the *hilaritas* — 'cheerfulness' — which is to be found in any really great and free intellectual achievement. One has always the impression of a somewhat tortured and strained manufacture instead of a free delight in creativity" (T.a.).

17. Cf. also *CD* II/2, ixf.: "The specific subject-matter of this half-volume made it necessary for me to set out more fully than in previous sections the exegetical background to the dogmatic exposition." The content is special in that "I had to let go of the handrails of theological tradition to a far greater extent than in the first part on the

Now, Bonhoeffer also has no desire to establish a secret knowledge of theologians over against ignorant "lay people," yet he calls for an arcane discipline for the mysteries of the faith as he explicitly sets himself apart from Barth. There may indeed be a misunderstanding on Bonhoeffer's part, for Barth certainly does not talk of an unqualified "publicity" into which those "mysteries" are being "profaned." Rather, when he speaks of "full publicity within the church," he focuses on theology as it is used within the church and its service and not on the world far removed from the church. Yet, Bonhoeffer seems to think of just that world when, in connection with Barth's *"hilaritas,"* he speaks of the possibility of "showing the world something *good* (even if the world doesn't like it)" (*LPP,* 229). Indeed, the danger of positivism of revelation that turns the mysteries of faith into a "law" for the religionless world would seem to be close at hand here.[18]

In his rejection of "positivism of revelation," Bonhoeffer is concerned not only with the renewal of arcane discipline but also with recapturing biblical "worldliness" in which "Christ [can] become the Lord of the religionless as well" (*LPP,* 280). In other words, Bonhoeffer seeks to discern how God's sovereignty, God's free and gracious election impinge on the "religionless world." This is where Barth's depiction of the doctrine of election appears to become "positivistic" in his view that the world "is left to its own devices" (*LPP,* 286). For that reason, the doctrine falls short of doing justice to the biblical witness. But one may well ask at this point whether it is one of the essential tasks of a "church dogmatics" to be concerned with an explicit interest in the world "come of age," or in a world that thinks it has come of age and is outside the church. This is a proper question to ask. It is the objection that Hans-Joachim Kraus, calling upon Barth's description of the tasks of dogmatics, brought against Bonhoeffer's call for an arcane discipline that repre-

---

doctrine of God. I would have preferred to follow Calvin's doctrine of predestination much more closely, instead of departing from it so extensively. . . . The more I let the Bible itself speak to me on these matters and the more I reflected upon what I seemed to hear, reconstruction imposed itself irresistibly" (T.a.).

18. Kraus, 35, refers to a possible misunderstanding on Bonhoeffer's part at this point. "What is really the point and aim of dogmatics? . . . What is decisive about dogmatics is that it is *a conversation of dogmaticians among themselves.* . . . Did Bonhoeffer not heed these guiding principles in the *Church Dogmatics?*"

sented a presupposition of a "religionless-worldly" Christianity according to Bonhoeffer.[19]

Yet, in light of this objection, it must not be forgotten that it was not the reality outside the church "as such," or even its "self-understanding," that interested Bonhoeffer. For then he would not have been allowed to ignore as blatantly as he did that this reality was ever so religious and not at all come of age.[20] What *he* was interested in was its being "in Christ" from the perspective of the promise according to which Christ shall be "really the Lord of the world" (*LPP,* 281).[21] And so, Bonhoeffer's question is: "Christ and the world that has come of age" (*LPP,* 327), irrespective of what it appears to be in fact. Thus, the question becomes more precisely: "the claim of a world that has come of age by Jesus Christ" (*LPP,* 342). On that basis, "the world *must* be understood better than it understands itself, but not 'religiously' as the religious socialists wanted" (*LPP,* 328); it must be understood, rather, "on the basis of the gospel and in the light of Christ" in its "coming of age" (*LPP,* 329).

Only from this christological perspective is it possible together with Bonhoeffer to reckon with a "godlessness which is full of promise" that, precisely in its stance "against religion and against the church," is closer to Christ than the "hopeless godlessness" that is "in religious and Christian clothing" (*E,* 103). So it is that in his final theological letter from prison before the failed insurrection — it is dated 18 July 1944 — he writes these seemingly paradoxical words: "The world that has come of age is more godless, and perhaps for that very reason nearer to God, than the world not of age" (*LPP,* 362, T.a.).

In his doctrine of election Barth by necessity also encountered the question as to the meaning of God's sovereign, gracious election for the

---

19. Cf. Kraus, 35: "Even though the task of dogmatics is not fenced off by the walls of the church, dogmatics must address itself in the first instance to its regular task rather than to *the proclamation that goes on outside the church.*"

20. Cf. *LPP,* 279: "Even those who honestly describe themselves as 'religious' do not in the least act up to it, and so they presumably mean something quite different by 'religious.'"

21. Cf. Barth, *CD* II/2, 571: "The kingdom of Christ is greater than the sphere of Israel and the Church. But it is in this sphere, and in it alone, that it is believed and known that the kingdom of this world is His, and not the devil's. From this sphere all human beings may and must be told who it is to whom they and their activity are properly subject, whom alone they and their activity can serve."

godless world outside the church. "The election of each individual involves, and his [her] calling completes, an opening up and enlargement of the (in itself) closed circle of the election of Jesus Christ and His community in relation to the world . . ." (*CD* II/2, 417, T.a.). Thus, according to Barth, the meaning of the church resides particularly in that it becomes "serviceable to the Lord . . . and therefore, in the omnipotent lovingkindness of God . . . to the rest of the world" (*CD* II/2, 428f.). Here an important motif of Bonhoeffer's formula of "the church for others" is found in the continuation of Barth's thought. "But as God Himself is glorious in His power to proclaim Himself and in the act in which He does this . . . , so the exaltation, honouring and quickening which he communicates to His only-begotten Son, and therefore to His brothers elected in and with Him, will inevitably become a proclamation to others" (*CD* II/2, 429, T.a.). However, it is clear that in Bonhoeffer the voicing is different than in Barth; this is an important symptom. In Barth the "triumph of grace" appears to work itself out in a missionary consciousness in the elect that is not far removed from ecclesiastical triumphalism[22] and the eagerness to convert the "godless" world. For Bonhoeffer, the church's service for the world consists simply in "being for others." Just as Jesus "is there for others," so "the church is the church only when it exists for others" (*LPP*, 381f.). In fact, the christological motive for Bonhoeffer's "being for others" is not the exaltation of the crucified one, as it is for Barth. It is the crucifixion itself: "God in human form! . . . 'the man for others' and therefore the Crucified" (*LPP*, 381f.).[23]

Here we approach the neuralgic point in Barth's doctrine of election. The world outside the church is present in more ways than only in the "god-

---

22. Gerrit C. Berkouwer has voiced this suspicion in his work *The Triumph of Grace in the Theology of Karl Barth,* trans. Henry R. Boer (Grand Rapids: Eerdmans, 1956); Berkouwer wants to distinguish radically "between a *true* proclamation of triumph of grace and that of a *false* triumphalism which expresses itself in the form of "manifest pride and elevation of self" on the part of the church toward the world (356).

23. But here the question arises whether in concentrating almost entirely on the "cross" and the corresponding ideas of impotence and suffering, Bonhoeffer does not constrict Christology, contrasted to which Barth's emphasis on the exaltation of Christ is completely legitimate. The issue then is, of course, how to speak theologically of resurrection and the power and glory of Jesus Christ without falling victim to ecclesial triumphalism. This is where the understanding of "ascension" would likely take on decisive significance as a counterpoint to "the missionary commandment" (Luke 24:44-53). (The author owes this consideration to a conversation with Hanfried Müller.)

less"; it is present within the congregation itself in its "double form" as Israel and church. Barth does say of it that "the bow of the *one* covenant arches over the *whole*" (*CD* II/2, 200), but he still comes to a surprisingly unambiguous allotment within this whole that corresponds to the traditional doctrine of double predestination. Israel has to "reflect the judgment" (*CD* II/2, 206) in relation to the church, which is the "reflection of . . . mercy" (*CD* II/2, 210). This does not resonate well with "the essentially christological approach" of Barth's doctrine of election,[24] the intention of which was to show "that in some way or other the Word of the free grace of God is spoken of and heard as the dominating theme and the specific meaning of the whole utterance" (*CD* II/2, 18, T.a.). Barth knowingly avoids the theological tradition of the rejection of Israel; still, the old scheme of "law and gospel" and its concern with the substitution of Israel by the church sneaks up again from behind when, in his section entitled "The Determination of the Rejected," he allows himself to be dragged into an assertion that disputes Israel's right to exist. "This Judas must die, as he did die; and this Jerusalem must go down, as it did go down. Israel's right to existence is extinguished, and therefore its existence can only be extinguished" (*CD* II/2, 505, T.a.).[25] This corresponds only too much to the church's traditional sense of having been chosen as the "new" people of God over against Israel as the allegedly rejected "old" one. In no way whatsoever should that sense have been stated in that form, especially in 1942, when the destruction of European Jewry was at its high point. But in light of Barth's own christological approach to the doctrine of election, that sentence is not only superfluous but also plainly false. For, "if we would know what rejection is as determined in God's eternal counsel . . . [w]e must look to what God elected for Himself in His Son . . ." (*CD* II/2, 165). But if that is where we fix

24. Cf. Bertold Klappert, *Israel und die Kirche. Erwägungen zur Israellehre Karl Barths,* Theologische Existenz heute, n.s., vol. 207 (Munich: Chr. Kaiser Verlag, 1980), 51: "Contrary to the actual christological approach, . . . Karl Barth addresses the relationship of Israel and the church in CD II/2, section 34, essentially in terms of the relation between 'law and gospel' or judgment and grace, a relation that is oriented by the sequence of cross and resurrection, rather than primarily in terms of the systematically foundational perspective of the covenant with Israel and through it with the gentile world fulfilled in cross and resurrection."

25. Certainly, Barth does not wish to deny the Jewish people their right to physical existence. And yet, he disqualifies it as an "unreal life." Ecclesial triumphalism manifests itself exactly in that Israel is taken note of finally only as an object of the church's missionary zeal: "the future of the Synagogue [lies] in the Church"; "it lives on" in it (*CD* II/2, 301 and 201).

our gaze, we see that "they who have Jesus Christ in faith cannot wish *not* to have the Jews. They must have them along with Jesus Christ as His ancestors and kinsfolk. . . . Otherwise with the Jews they reject Jesus Himself" (*CD* II/ 2, 289, T.a.). In that God has chosen rejection in the Son as God's own burden, mirroring that rejection in the congregation can no longer take the form of the congregation calling Israel's right to existence into question. Rather, it can only be the conversion and renewal of the old existence of the congregation itself.

Nonetheless, it is unmistakable that in his doctrine of election, Barth had much trouble taking Jewish existence after Christ's crucifixion seriously theologically. Nor could he readily see anything positive in the Jewish "No!" to Jesus. In the Jewish denial of Jesus as the Messiah, he was unable to hear a signal of Israel's "faithfulness to the Torah."[26] What he heard, instead, was only "a carnal loyalty to itself."[27] For that reason, the life and "continuing existence" (*CD* II/2, 265) of Israel next to and outside of the church appeared to him as a woeful "unreal life,"[28] when instead Israel could "live in the Church . . . [and] believe in its Messiah" (*CD* II/2, 265). Then, according to Barth, Israel's unbelief would hardly differ — setting aside the perspective of Israel's "living on" in the church[29] — from the gruesome "godlessness of *others*,"[30] a godlessness in which Barth cannot find even a trace of promise.

Here we see the core relationship between an understanding of the

---

26. Cf. F.-W. Marquardt, " 'Feinde um unsretwillen.' Das jüdische Nein und die christliche Theologie," in *Verwegenheiten. Theologische Stücke aus Berlin* (Munich: Chr. Kaiser Verlag, 1981), 315: "In Jewish self-understanding, saying No to Jesus Christ is an act of faithfulness to the Torah."

27. *CD* II/2, 261f.: "That Israel should come to faith and into the Church . . . is God's purpose for it, the promise given to it with its election. . . . It takes a rigid stand on a carnal loyalty to itself and on a carnal hope corresponding to this loyalty." Cf. also 204f.

28. Cf. *CD* II/2, 263: "It must be the personification of a half-venerable, half-gruesome relic, of a wondrously preserved antique, of human whimsicality" (T.a.).

29. *CD* II/2, 201: "Where Israel apprehends and believes its own election in Jesus Christ it lives on in the Church and is maintained in it. . . ."

30. *CD* II/2, 452: the elect "will recognize the rejected in the godlessness of others: in all the blatant and refined examples of dreadful corruption; in the brutality and sophistry, the stupidity and lack of character, the self-will and frivolity, the superstition, heresy and unbelief by which they see themselves surrounded on every hand in ever widening circles." On this, see F.-W. Marquardt, *Die Entdeckung des Judentums für die christliche Theologie. Israel im Denken Karl Barths* (Munich: Chr. Kaiser Verlag, 1967), 300f.

significance of Israel's "No!" to Jesus being the Messiah, and the theological assessment of the world outside the church "being of age," also and especially in its "godlessness." Friedrich-Wilhelm Marquardt sees "the dignity of the Jewish No" in that "with its No, Israel has made itself an advocate of every human No to the God revealed in Jesus Christ." "If one regards the deepest secret of serious atheism as an intellectual, spiritual and practical way of keeping open the wound of the imperfect, the as yet incomplete world, the human being not yet human, the still to be experienced 'Behold, the tabernacle of God is among the people' and 'God with us,' then every serious atheism has its biblical justification in the Jewish No. More precisely, in the Jewish No, it can become serious."[31]

Even in his later self-correction, Barth could no longer bring himself to such a serious contemplation of both the Jewish "No!" and the "godlessness" of a "world come of age." "[T]hinking in terms of the humanity of God, we cannot at all reckon in a serious way with *real* 'outsiders,' with a 'world come of age,' but only with a world which *regards* itself of age (and proves daily that it is precisely not that). Thus, the so-called 'outsiders' are really only 'insiders' who have not yet understood and apprehended themselves as such."[32] We may, therefore, concur in Heinz Eduard Tödt's comment that "in the assessment of the world's secularization and of its being of age, there remain contrasts between Barth and Bonhoeffer. Karl Barth cannot regard what has come about through that world as something earthshakingly new. Bonhoeffer, on the contrary, is deeply impressed by the fact that the world is becoming religionless."[33]

31. Marquardt, "'Feinde um unsretwillen,'" 336. Cf. his "Solidarität mit den Gottlosen. Zur Geschichte und Bedeutung eines Theologumenon," in *Verwegenheiten*, 139: "The Apostle Paul's solidarity with Israel, which is conveyed to us most strongly in Rm 9:1-5, is the foundation for the central biblical-reformatory meaning of the term 'solidarity with the godless.'"

32. Karl Barth, *The Humanity of God*, trans. Thomas Wieser and John Newton Thomas (Richmond: John Knox, 1960), 58f.; what has to be kept in mind here is that in this implicit critique of Bonhoeffer, Barth is not primarily addressing Bonhoeffer but — as the context indicates — much more a certain interpretation of him (such as that of G. Ebeling, G. Krause, and H. Ott) that perceives Bonhoeffer's concern to be above all the "problem of language."

33. Tödt, 107; cf. 107: "Bonhoeffer's prognosis of the approaching religionlessness is not refuted by the mere fact that, after a progressivistic emancipatory phase, we find ourselves perhaps again in a boom of new 'religiosity.'" Bonhoeffer's point actually is less a prognosis than it is a biblical-theological insight: it is God who desires the human being come of age.

In a sketch for his *Ethics* entitled "Inheritance and Decay," Bonhoeffer not only spoke of the atheists' "godlessness which is full of promise" in contrast to the "hopeless godlessness" of the religious (*E,* 103). In the course of 1941, Bonhoeffer adds: "The Jew keeps open the question of Christ" (*E,* 89). In what is likely the secret presupposition of his discovery, he thus spoke of a positive significance of the Jewish "No!" for church and theology in the sense of Marquardt's "keeping open the wound of the imperfect." When Bonhoeffer bases himself in that context on Israel being not only "the sign of the free mercy-choice" but also the sign of "the repudiating wrath of God," then his statement about the open question of Christ clearly sounds the free *grace* of God within the dialectics of election and rejection as "the dominant factor" (Barth). For Bonhoeffer, Israel evidently "testifies with its confession of God's transcendence *in spite* of Christ . . . to the eschatological proviso in the self of God that is not annulled even in the sending of Jesus Christ."[34]

In light of this, Marquardt diagnosed the weakness of Barth's doctrine of Israel to be its "lack of eschatological content," since "even though he [holds] Israel to be an ongoing witness to God, he does so in the perduringly negative form of a witness to unbelief and divine wrath."[35] For Bonhoeffer, on the other hand, the dialectics of election and rejection yields also a perduringly positive role of Israel in history, namely, "in a genuine uninterrupted encounter."[36] With this terminology of the "encounter" between "Western history" and "the people of Israel," Bonhoeffer has conclusively renounced the idea of "the conversion" of Israel that secretly still governs Barth's doctrine of Israel. Therefore, it may

---

34. Marquardt, " 'Feinde um unsretwillen,' " 335; cf. 335: "Christians need this testimony so that they may become aware of their 'unbelieving' sisters and brothers in the world."

35. Marquardt, " 'Feinde um unsretwillen,' " 335.

36. *E,* 89f.: "Western history is, by God's will, indissolubly linked with the people of Israel, not only genetically but also in a genuine uninterrupted encounter. . . . An expulsion of the Jews from the West must necessarily bring with it the expulsion of Christ. For Jesus Christ was a Jew." The words from "not only genetically but also in a genuine uninterrupted encounter" to "For Jesus Christ was a Jew" were added later in 1941. This addition was probably caused by the dangerous escalation of the Nazis' policy regarding Jews: on 19 September 1941, Jews were ordered to wear the yellow star, and during the night of 16 and 17 October that same year, the mass deportations from Berlin began. (Cf. *DBW,* 6:95 n. 9.)

be assumed on the basis of this that the weakness of Barth's position on Israel provoked Bonhoeffer's opposition at this point.

But this raises a new problem. According to Bertold Klappert, had Barth remained true to his actually christological approach to the doctrine of Israel, he would have had to say that "the crucified and risen Christ, who as such is the future of Israel, is also the reconciler and Lord of the world and the church," so that "as the witness to the promise received and heard, Israel [would receive] at the same time a positive qualification from the raising of Jesus Christ."[37] But if Israel is "witness to the resurrection from the dead" already on account of its seeking "'first' the kingdom of God and its righteousness" and not only "in the Jewish 'living on' in the church,"[38] then "double predestination" and its unambiguous ascription of election and rejection to church and Israel would have to be replaced by "dialectical predestination" in a manner prefigured by Bonhoeffer.[39] In the latter view, the judgment of election and rejection would have to be applied to "one and the same person," namely, Jesus Christ, just as it would to one and the same people, namely, Israel,[40] but

---

37. Klappert, 64f.

38. Marquardt, *Die Entdeckung des Judentums für die christliche Theologie,* 352; cf. 352: "Does not Israel, even in its bruised form, already attest to this mercy even now? As a witness to judgment, is it not already now also a witness to God's condescending goodness? Hence, as a witness to the death of Jesus Christ, is it not also a witness to his resurrection? . . . Does not coming forth long actualize itself in and through Israel as much as fading away, rising again as much as dying? . . . Of course, it does not testify to the empty tomb of Jesus Christ 'voluntarily,' but God lets it testify to the resurrection of the 'flesh' 'involuntarily.' . . . If God keeps to them — and God does keep to them! — then [the Jews] are as a result already witnesses to the resurrection." On this whole topic, see Marquardt, *Die Gegenwart des Auferstandenen bei seinem Volk Israel. Ein dogmatisches Experiment* (Munich: Chr. Kaiser Verlag, 1983).

39. Cf. Marquardt, *Die Entdeckung des Judentums für die christliche Theologie,* 260: "According to Barth, next to the particular elect in Israel, the whole people of Israel also remains elect. . . . Thus, in relation to Israel we are not to speak of a *praedestinatio gemina,* but of a *praedestinatio dialectica:* not of *electio* and *reprobatio,* but of a double election." On the concept of *praedestinatio dialectica,* see Heinrich Vogel, "Praedestinatio gemina. Die Lehre von der ewigen Gnadenwahl," in *Theologische Aufsätze. Karl Barth zum 50. Geburtstag* (Munich: Chr. Kaiser Verlag, 1936), 231: "The election in Christ of those who are themselves guilty of their rejection would have to be described as the *praedestinatio dialectica* in relation to the judgment of election and rejection of one and the same person."

40. Cf. Vogel, 231: "*Praedestinatio dialectica* is at one with the justification of the godless in that the election of the rejected, as based in God's eternal decree, occurs again

---

— we note — always with *grace* as the "dominant factor" in election, in other words, ultimately as "double election" (Marquardt). And that means that the doctrine of "the recapitulation of all things" *(apokatastasis panton)* is inescapable. According to Marquardt, "when applied to the Jewish-Christian relation (as the basic ecclesiological relation per se), the *apokatastasis* doctrine is [indeed] the only possible eschatological teaching supported by both the witness of Scripture and their effective christo-logical relation one to the other. But as such a teaching, it functions highly critically in relation to the theological abandonment of Israel, thereby showing that it is no mere speculation. . . . If *apokatastasis* had been taken a little more seriously in the past, it would have had beneficial consequence, at least for the theological view of Israel."[41] In actual fact, Barth was attacked precisely in connection with his doctrine of election and charged by neo-Calvinists with being taken by his language of "the triumph of grace" at least "to the verge of the apokatastasis."[42]

In his doctrine of election and in relation to the "determination of the rejected," Barth leaves this question open.[43] However, it cannot es-cape our attention that in fact Bonhoeffer already wanted to talk earlier of an "inner necessity of the idea of apokatastasis" instead of a "double issue" of judgment since the judgment was, after all, a *judgment of grace* (*SC,* 286). He did not want to make "this final word of eschatological think-ing" into "a self-evident point of departure for a dogmatic train of

---

and again but in such a way that God's faithfulness can in no way be abrogated by human unfaithfulness. It is this victory of God's promise which the apostle praises in face of Is-rael's rejection."

41. Marquardt, *Die Entdeckung des Judentums für die christliche Theologie,* 154. Per-haps it would be more correct to say the converse: if what *apokatastasis* means for the Christian-Jewish relationship had been recognized in the past, it could not have been de-famed so easily as a frivolous speculation. We may leave open the question whether the chances of an official approbation of the special teaching on the part of the church would have been greater as a result of such recognition.

42. Berkouwer, 295. Berkouwer finds a problem here in relation to "the meaningfulness of the hortatory kerugma and of the human decision" (296). Cf. his dis-cussion of the "church and Israel," 107-22, which includes the question of *apokatastasis.*

43. Cf. *CD* II/2, 477: "The Church will then not preach an *apokatastasis,* nor will it preach a powerless grace of Jesus Christ or a human wickedness which is too powerful for it. But without any weakening of the contrast, and also without any arbitrary dualism, it will preach the overwhelming power of grace and the weakness of human wickedness in face of it."

thought" (*SC,* 171 n. 29).[44] Instead, he wanted to keep this perspective "open" as "the sigh of theology whenever it has to speak of faith and unfaith, election and rejection" (*AB,* 161). Next to the tradition of pietism,[45] Bonhoeffer here called on Luther's saying that "the curses of the godless sometimes sound better in God's ear than the hallelujahs of the pious" (*AB,* 160). It is noteworthy that in his *Ethics,* at the very place where he speaks of the possibility of a "godlessness which is full of promise," Bonhoeffer cites just this saying of Luther's — with which he had "delighted" Barth during their first encounter in Bonn in 1931 (*DBE,* 132). This topic undergoes some variation in the prison letters where, now in historical perspective, Bonhoeffer discusses it under the heading of "the recapitulation of all things." "It means that nothing is lost, that everything is taken up in Christ, although it is transformed, made transparent, clear, made free from the anguish of selfish desire. Christ restores all this as God originally intended it to be" (*LPP,* 170, T.a.).

In light of the foregoing, our hypothesis in connection with Bonhoeffer's charge of "positivism of revelation" against Barth and the Confessing Church is this: in this word "positivism of revelation," Bonhoeffer's protest against the "Christian pathos of final time, truth and judgment" (Marquardt), as it still manifests itself also in Barth's doctrine of Israel, has found a preliminary expression that is quite open to misunderstanding. Bonhoeffer raises this protest in the name of the "world come of age" and its "religionlessness" in face of a "church on the defensive" that is no longer prepared for "taking risks for others" (*LPP,* 380f.) and has become "guilty of cowardly silence . . . when she should have cried out because the blood of the innocent was crying aloud to heaven" (*E,* 112f.).

44. Cf. *SC,* 287: "But all statements in this regard only express a hope; they cannot be made part of a system."

45. Cf. Erik Pontoppidan, *Heller Glaubensspiegel* (1726 and 1768): "Now there are many who have truly laid hold of Christ, even though they do not feel that they have done so; but they are no less justified"; cited by Bonhoeffer in *AB,* 160 n. 31. This sentence may well help correct the summary view of pietism as a "religion of feelings" with a legalistic character, if only pietists themselves were to take it more strongly to heart.

3. Barth's "Doctrine of Lights"
as a Correction of "Positivism of Revelation"?

It is to be noted that Bonhoeffer's notion of "positivism of revelation," coined in its orientation even more for the Confessing Church than for Barth, was *his* last word on this matter. However, this preliminary statement of his correspondence should never have been turned into a *final judgment* on Barth's theology as a whole. That is not how Bonhoeffer meant it, nor does it do justice to Barth. As the example of the first edition of *The Epistle to the Romans* and some early essays has shown, Barth himself did not only set out from a "religionless-worldly" understanding of the Bible similar to the one Bonhoeffer presented later in the prison letters. Barth's earlier approach also forms the, albeit hidden, backdrop to the intensification of his understanding of revelation in the second edition of *Romans* and the *Church Dogmatics* that caused Bonhoeffer to get the sense of "positivism of revelation." After Bonhoeffer's violent death, Barth had ample opportunity to remove misunderstandings of his theology, clarify occasional statements that had the ring of such positivism, and — where necessary — make corrections. In so doing, the hidden "religionless-worldly" backdrop to his understanding of revelation had to move into the foreground again, but now clearly illuminated christologically.

We recall at the outset Barth's 1956 address "The Humanity of God," in which he was prepared to make "a *genuine* revision," much to the surprise particularly of his opponents.[46] Indeed, "the famous 'wholly other' breaking in upon us 'perpendicularly from above,' the not less famous 'infinitive qualitative difference' between God and humans" (42) with which Barth frightened theology and church in his "dialectical phase," "however well it may have been meant and however much it may have mattered, was nevertheless said somewhat severely and brutally" (43). Still, "those who may not have joined in that earlier change of direction, to whom it still may not have become quite clear that God is God, would certainly not see what is now to be said in addition as the true

---

46. Barth, *The Humanity of God,* 41f.: "A *genuine* revision in no way involves a subsequent retreat, but rather a new beginning and attack in which what previously has been said is to be said more than ever, but now even better." References which follow in the text are to Barth, *The Humanity of God.*

word concerning [God's] humanity" (42, T.a.).[47] For the "essential infirmity in our thinking and speaking at that time . . . consisted in the fact that we were wrong exactly where we were right, that at first we did not know how to carry through with sufficient care and thoroughness the new knowledge of the *deity* of God which was so exciting both to us and to others" (44). Properly understood, however, "the *deity* of the *living* God . . . [finds] its meaning and its power only in the context of His history and of His dialogue with *humans,* and thus in His *togetherness* with humans. . . . It is the deity which as such also has the character of humanity. . . . It is precisely God's *deity* which, rightly understood, includes His *humanity.*" In the final analysis, this "is a *Christological* statement, or rather one grounded in and to be unfolded from Christology" (45f.).[48] For "Jesus Christ is in His one Person, as true *God, humans'* loyal partner, and as true *human, God's* . . . both, without their being confused but also without their being divided . . . wholly the one and wholly the other" (46f.).[49]

The later volumes of the *Church Dogmatics* clearly manifest how Barth accommodated Bonhoeffer's concern. There is initially the explicit approving reference to Bonhoeffer's work *Discipleship (Nachfolge)* in section 66, entitled "The Sanctification of the Human Being," and to *Sanctorum Communio* in section 67, "The Holy Spirit and the Upbuilding of the Christian Community" (vol. IV/2, published in 1955; ET in 1958).[50] Barth's most substantive agreement with Bonhoeffer is

47. It is here where the decisive difference might be between Bonhoeffer's critique of Barth and the judgment on Barth that has since been made on the basis of that critique. In contradistinction to all those who found the scent of "positivism of revelation" everywhere in Barth, Bonhoeffer "joined" in Barth's "earlier change of direction" and still presupposed it in the prison correspondence.

48. Cf. *LPP,* 381f. ("Outline for a Book"): "God in human form — not . . . in the conceptual forms of the absolute, metaphysical, infinite, etc., . . . but 'the man for others,' and therefore the Crucified, the one who lives out of the transcendent" (T.a.).

49. Cf. how Bonhoeffer describes love for God and earthly love in Chalcedonian language: "undivided and yet distinct" (*LPP,* 303), for which reason the exposition of the Song of Songs as an "earthly love song" is also "the best 'Christological' exposition" (*LPP,* 315, T.a.). In contradistinction to Barth, Bonhoeffer's question appears to be more about the relation of "God to the whole world" (*LPP,* 310) and less about that between God and human beings.

50. Cf. *CD* IV/2, 505 ("cheap grace"); 540ff. ("simple obedience"); and above all 533, "Easily the best that has been written on this subject is to be found, it seems to me, in

found, however, in section 69, "The Glory of the Mediator" (*CD* IV/3, pt. 1, published in 1959; ET in 1961). Without directly referring to Bonhoeffer, Barth comes very close to Bonhoeffer's discussion of "the world come of age," the world that seeks to be taken seriously precisely in its "religionlessness" and possibly even in its "godlessness which is full of promise" in light of Christ, the Lord of the world. Here, within the context of his doctrine of the "true words" outside the church — often referred to in the simplified term "doctrine of lights" — Barth interpreted the *solus Christus* of the Reformation and did so according to the renewed emphasis by the Barmen Declaration.[51] He declared that also in the secular world outside the walls of the church, the community has to reckon with "true words, parables of the kingdom, [of a] very different kind. . . . the community which lives by the one Word of the one Prophet Jesus Christ, and is commissioned and empowered to proclaim this Word of His in the world, not only may but must accept the fact that there are such words and that it must hear them too, notwithstanding its life by this one Word and its commission to preach it. . . . Should it not be grateful to receive it also from without, in very different human words, in a secular parable?" (*CD* IV/3, pt. 1, 114f.).[52]

Barth stresses in this context that the acknowledgment of such "true words" outside the church and in the profane realm has "no need to appeal either for basis or content to the sorry hypothesis of a so-called 'natural theology'" (*CD* IV/3, pt. 1, 117). That is because "natural theology" has no interest whatever in words that are, in full accord with the testimony of Scripture, true as "parables of the reign of God." "We do not leave the sure ground of Christology, but with the prophets and apostles,

---

The Cost of Discipleship" (1937; abridged ET 1948, unabridged 1959). Barth's repudiation of the danger of "perfectionism" along the line of Kohlbrügge-Bonhoeffer (*CD* IV/2, 576f.) is significant insofar as it agrees in substance with Bonhoeffer's self-criticism in *LPP,* 369. In section 67, *CD* IV/2, 641, Barth writes: "I may again refer to a book by Dietrich Bonhoeffer. This is the dissertation he wrote. . . ." Nonetheless, Barth signals at the same time quite clearly (esp. 653ff.) that he can accept Bonhoeffer's notion of "Christ existing as community" only with reservation.

51. The heading for the entire sec. 69 is the first thesis of the Barmen Declaration: "Jesus Christ as attested to us in Holy Scripture is the one Word of God whom we must hear and whom we must trust and obey in life and in death" (*CD* IV/3, pt. 1, 3).

52. During his first visit with Karl Barth in Bonn in 1931, Bonhoeffer came to know Barth's "doctrine of lights" in an earlier version; on that occasion he strongly resisted it (*NRS,* 116).

and the Christian community established and living by the Gospel and making Christ the object of its faith and love and hope, we look to the sovereignty of Jesus Christ which is revealed in His resurrection and which we find to be attested by the Bible and the Church, but not restricted according to this testimony" (*CD* IV/3, pt. 1, 117f.).[53]

On account of the "radical investigation of this question," Barth does not want to give examples of such "true words" outside the church within the context of dogmatics (*CD* IV/3, pt. 1, 135). Nevertheless, he provides criteria for distinguishing them from untrue words and gives certain indications. He distinguishes in the "secular world" between a "more distant" and a "closer periphery" of the biblical-ecclesial sphere (*CD* IV/3, pt. 1, 118). The "mixed and relative secularism" on the closer periphery he describes as "a worldliness affected, coloured and embellished by Christianity," whereas the "secularism which approximates to a pure and absolute form" on the more distant periphery appears to him as "the express and unequivocal secularism of militant godlessness" (*CD* IV/3, pt. 1, 118f.). When he writes "we must continually ask ourselves whether this mixed and relative secularism might not be characterised by perhaps an even greater resistance to the Gospel for the very reason that it is used to being confronted by and having to come to terms with it, and is thus able the more strongly to consolidate itself against it, making certain concessions and accommodations no doubt, parading in large measure as a world of Christian culture, but closing its ears the more firmly against it, and under the sign of a horrified rejection of theoretical atheism cherishing the more radically and shamelessly a true atheism of practice," Barth is keeping to Bonhoeffer's line (and thereby once again also to that of the first edition of *Romans*) (*CD* IV/3, pt. 1, 120).[54]

53. Bonhoeffer would without doubt have been delighted with that formulation. For it appears that what is expressed and developed here with theological consistency — far removed from every kind of "positivism of revelation" — is what he sensed when in prison he asked: "How can Christ become the Lord of the religionless as well?" (*LPP*, 280). Here, the world is no longer "left to its own devices" (*LPP*, 286), but now Christ is "really the Lord of the world" (*LPP*, 281). Cf. what he writes already in *E*, 58: "The more exclusively we acknowledge and confess Christ as our Lord, the more fully the wide range of His dominion will be disclosed to us." For some strange reason, it is in Barth's "doctrine of lights," of all places, where Heinrich Ott detects "positivism of revelation" most clearly.

54. Cf. Bonhoeffer's distinction between "godlessness which is full of promise" and "hopeless godlessness" (*E*, 103). Barth's question seems to have been answered here already in the sense that atheism on principle is given preference to practical atheism.

According to Barth, on that more distant periphery, next to the "so-called heathen territories," are found the newer generations "in Eastern peoples now overrun by an avowedly atheistic culture, education, psychology and ethics," on the one hand. On the other, "in the greatest proximity to the Christian Churches," there is a whole world that still or once again considers itself "to be of age," and does so obstinately, a world that "boasts of its own sovereignty" (CD IV/3, pt. 1, 119). Barth maintains that, "while humans may deny God, that is, be without God, according to the Word of reconciliation God does not deny humans, that is, God is not without humans. . . . In the world reconciled by God in Jesus Christ there is no secular sphere left by Him to its own devices or withdrawn from His disposition, even where from the human standpoint it seems to approximate most dangerously to the pure and absolute form of utter godlessness. If we say that there is, we are not thinking and speaking in the light of the resurrection of Jesus Christ." The community can and may expect to hear "true words even from what seem to be the darkest places" (CD IV/3, pt. 1, 119, T.a.). Barth gives some indications of where such true words may be heard even in a sometimes "openly pagan" worldliness.

> We may think of the mystery of God, which we Christians so easily talk away in a proper concern for God's own cause. . . . We may think of the disquiet, not to be stilled by any compromise, at the various disorders both of personal life and of that of the state and of society, at those who are inevitably driven to the wall. We may think of the resolute determination, perhaps, to attack these evils. We may think of the lack of fear in face of death which Christians to their shame often display far less readily than non-Christians far and near. . . . Especially we may think of a humanity which does not ask or weigh too long with whom we are dealing in others, but in which we find a simple solidarity with them and unreservedly take up their case. (CD IV/3, pt. 1, 125)

Friedrich-Wilhelm Marquardt interprets that passage as follows: next to the great light Jesus Christ, there are "essentially . . . Judaism, . . . Socialism [and] the manifold forms of practical humanness without 'faith.'" These may be regarded as small lights radiating from him "in our generation." Among them, "given [Barth's] own development, . . . the prevalence of the Socialist option over the other examples is beyond doubt."[55] This interpretation of Barth's intimations can hardly be refuted; yet, one must ask why Barth himself shied away from explaining that point in his dogmatics. The same reluctance to be drawn into speculation that we have already observed in connection with the doctrine of "apokatastasis" seems to be at work here: If "utter godlessness" continues to comprise the extreme danger, what about claiming for himself an unambiguous identification particularly of godless "Socialism" (and not only of godless "social democracy") as a "light" next to Jesus Christ? Does that not appear to be reckless high-handedness? Would it not be more appropriate then neither to "canonize" nor to give "dogmatic status" to such "extraordinary" ways and "free communications" of Jesus Christ (*CD* IV/3, pt. 1, 133f.)?[56] Nonetheless, Barth provides criteria; next to correspondence with Scripture and confession and importance for the congregation, he names as a "supplementary and auxiliary" criterion "the fruits which such true words . . . seem to bear in the outside world . . ." (*CD* IV/3, pt. 1, 127f.).

Bonhoeffer was less circumspect at this point when, in an outline for his *Ethics* ("Church and World I"),[57] he named "all suffering for a just cause" as a criterion in which the community may discern the breadth of the lordship of Jesus Christ (*E*, 60).

> It was not metaphysical speculation, it was not a theologumenon of the *logos spermatikos,* but it was the concrete suffering of injustice, the organized lie, of hostility to humankind and of violence, it was the persecution of lawfulness, truth, humanity and freedom which impelled the people who held these values dear to seek the protection of Jesus Christ

55. Marquardt, *Theologie und Sozialismus,* 254.

56. Barth is obviously concerned that "giving dogmatic status" could result in the misunderstanding that in his doctrine of lights he sought to renew "natural theology." That is why it seems somewhat unfortunate that in face of the "structural change" of natural theology in Barth, Marquardt speaks of "establishing 'natural theology' by means of christology" (*Theologie und Sozialismus,* 264). Cf. against this view, Kraus, 50: "The so-called 'doctrine of lights' represents the positive pole of the negation of natural theology. . . . Barth presents a christologically founded counterproposal to the theory of religion that is based in the doctrine of the *logos spermatikos* and was developed within the domain of natural theology."

57. The editors of the new critical edition of *Ethics* believe that this section was written at the end of 1942 so that it may be assumed that Bonhoeffer had already read the ethical sections of Barth's *CD* II/2.

and therefore to become subject to his claim through which the community of Jesus Christ discerned the extent of its responsibility. . . . The relationship of the Church with the world today . . . [consists] solely in [the] recognition of the origin which has been awakened and vouchsafed to humans in this suffering, solely in the seeking of refuge from persecution in Christ. . . . It is with the Christ who is persecuted and who suffers in His Church that justice, truth, humanity and freedom seek refuge. (E, 58f., T.a.)

What one notices right away in this outline is how much more concrete than Barth's "doctrine of lights" this description is of the circle of disciples around Jesus Christ. Yet, the concreteness is paid for with a concealed clericalism inasmuch as it envisages those suffering from persecution fleeing to Jesus Christ and his community. It is the persecuted and suffering congregation of which Bonhoeffer speaks. Therefore, there can be no talk of an open claim on the part of the church to dominion over the world. The issue here is solidarity in persecution, so that (in connection with Matt. 5:10) Bonhoeffer immediately adds this clarification: this "does not refer to persecution for Jesus Christ's sake. . . . Jesus gives His support to those who suffer for the sake of a just cause, even if this just cause is not precisely the confession of His name. . . . [W]e in our time must say rather that before any can know and find Christ they must first become righteous like those who strive and must suffer for the sake of justice, truth and humanity" (E, 60f., T.a.). Conversely, Bonhoeffer obviously also reckons that those who are persecuted for a just cause are also moved subjectively to "profess themselves a Christian" (E, 60, T.a.) on account of Christ having taken them to heart.

There is something new and well-nigh revolutionary in Bonhoeffer's chapter on church and world in comparison to Barth's notion of "the fruits of true words" in the secular world. It is the fact that Bonhoeffer no longer thinks in the first instance of "undertakings and deeds" but of persecution and suffering, no longer of the actions but of the "passion" of the just. When he speaks of the "just," it is not only the active fighters of the resistance, the socialists, communists, and humanists of every stripe, that he wants to call to mind. Clearly, he speaks also and in particular of the "others" who are persecuted for no reason, who were discriminated against, persecuted, and destroyed as "non-Aryans," especially the Jews as the "weakest and most defenceless brothers [and sisters] of Christ" (E, 114, T.a.). They are just, not as a result of their actions, but simply on the basis of what they have to suffer. In their "pure" passion, they are in closest proximity to *the* suffering one who was crucified guilt-less.

This provides a criterion in terms of which one might avoid the danger of arbitrary identifications within the "doctrine of lights" or of a wildly speculative doctrine of "apokatastasis" without having to forgo concreteness. Thus, Bertold Klappert has a corresponding question: "Why is Barth's doctrine of the signs of Jesus Christ's prophecy in world history not to be understood first with a view to Jewish and only then to creaturely self-depiction? . . . What we ask is this: why does Barth not de-velop an Israelite contour of the doctrine of lights? Why is it that he is cognizant of a transformation of the prophecy of Jesus Christ into the form of a general, creaturely self-depiction but not into a specifically Jew-ish one?"[58] It would appear that Bonhoeffer was moving in the direction Klappert proposes.

When Bonhoeffer met Barth in Bonn in 1931, he was still strongly re-sistant to the early shape of the latter's "doctrine of lights," in that Bon-hoeffer would have liked to "kill" everything else "beside the one great light" (*NRS*, 116). But in the prison correspondence he accuses Barth of let-ting the "birds" in the world outside the church "die" if they refuse to "eat." [Bonhoeffer's German sentence *Friss, Vogel, oder stirb!* — eat, bird, or die! — is rendered as "take it or leave it!" in the letter of 5 May 1944. Transl.] Once again, the reversal of fronts is complete. Bonhoeffer would certainly have attacked Barth less harshly had he discerned more clearly Barth's lean-ing toward *apokatastasis* which already qualifies his "doctrine of Israel." Barth took up this tendency again in his address "The Humanity of God." With a view to the "danger" that surrounds the concept of the "reconcilia-tion of all things," he asks: "What of the 'danger' of the eternally skeptical-critical theologians who are ever and again suspiciously questioning, be-cause fundamentally always legalistic and therefore in the main morosely gloomy? Is not their presence among us currently more threatening than that of the unbecomingly cheerful indifferentism or even antinomianism, to which one with a certain understanding of universalism could in fact de-

58. Klappert, 58f.; yet by speaking of guarding "the mystery of God, which we Christians so easily talk away" (*CD* IV/3, pt. 1, 125), Barth included Israel in the doctrine of lights. Klappert is correct, nonetheless, insofar as for Barth this Jewish testimony is in essence on the same level as every other creaturely testimony (socialism, humanism, and the like).

liver oneself?"[59] Since even God's "No!" is always about "the affirmation of humans," it is certain that "we have no theological right to set any sort of limits to the loving-kindness of God which has appeared in Jesus Christ."[60]

To a certain extent, Barth here meets Bonhoeffer's affirmation of "apokatastasis" as the "sigh of theology" that ought not be systematized theologically. As long as *apokatastasis* was not anchored centrally in the "doctrine of Israel," that was all that could be said. Only in prison did Bonhoeffer say more, when he saw himself as one who suffered for a just cause (cf. *LPP,* 129). Now he was ready to engage without reserve the idea of the "restoration of all things" (*LPP,* 170). Only from "the 'view from below'" which he had come to know as a conspirator, "from the perspective of the outcast, the suspects, the maltreated, the powerless, the oppressed, the reviled — in short, from the perspective of those who suffer" (*LPP,* 17) — was he ready to accept the world outside the church, and specifically in its "godlessness," as full of promise and to acknowledge it as being of age in its "religionlessness."

Finally, in *Church Dogmatics* IV/3, part 2, section 72 ("The Holy Spirit and the Sending of the Christian Community"), there is an allusion to Bonhoeffer's conception of the church "for others." In a section entitled "The Community for the World," Barth identifies a gap in the traditional teaching on the church exactly at the place where Bonhoeffer, in his prison letters, proposed that "being for others" should be one of the *notae ecclesiae,* the marks of the church. The being of the community, "[w]onderful and glorious as [it] is, . . . is not an end in itself. . . . The true community of Jesus Christ is the community which God has sent out into the world in and with its foundation. As such it exists for the world" (*CD* IV/3, pt. 2, 764 and 768).[61] What had already been materially suggested in the christological basis of the "doctrine of Israel" in *Church Dogmatics* II/2, is now explicitly developed: the rejection of the "mission to Jews." "Jews, even unbelieving Jews, so miraculously preserved, as we must say, through the many calamities of their history, . . . as such are the natural historical monument to the love and faithfulness of God." In comparison to the service of witness the

---

59. Barth, *The Humanity of God,* 61f.

60. Barth, *The Humanity of God,* 60ff., T.a. Cf. also *CD* IV/1, 118f.

61. Cf. Bonhoeffer's "baptismal letter," *LPP,* 300: "Our church, which has been fighting in these years only for its self-preservation, as though that were an end in itself . . . ," and *LPP,* 382 (in "Outline for a Book"): "The church is the church only when it exists for others."

Christian community makes in relation to the world, the service of witness it offers to Israel can therefore consist only in "its own existence as the community of the King of the Jews manifested to it as the Saviour of the world" (*CD* IV/3, pt. 2, 877f., T.a.).[62]

Barth does not refer specifically to Bonhoeffer here, which may have to do with the fact that Bonhoeffer's language of "non-religious Christianity" in a "world come of age" — which would have its place in this context, according to Bonhoeffer — still made no sense to Barth. His rejection of a programmatic "non-religious interpretation" is clearly aimed at such Bonhoeffer interpreters who reduce the problematic of the "positivism of revelation" to a "problem of language." "The Christian community has its own message to impart but . . . it does not have its own language. . . . There has rarely been a conversation as lacking in substance as that about so-called religious and so-called non-religious language" (*CD* IV/3, pt. 2, 735, T.a.).[63] Barth's skepticism toward "a world said to have *come* of age" derives from the perfect tense "to have come," as if something had already occurred that for the Christian community is always a matter of hope.[64] But still:

---

62. In the relevant "failure" of the church, Barth sees "one of the darkest chapters in the whole history of Christianity and one of the most serious of all wounds in the body of Christ" (*CD* IV/3, pt. 2, 878). As Bonhoeffer perceives a similar failure also in relation to the "godless" world, he wants to present the service of the community to that world not so much in speaking as in the "doing of what is righteous." Barth still ranks speaking ahead of doing. (Cf. *CD* IV/2, pt. 2, 863.)

63. Cf. Barth, *The Humanity of God*, 59: "A little 'non-religious' language from the street, the newspaper, literature, and, if one is ambitious, from the philosopher may thus, for the sake of communication, occasionally indeed be in order. However, we should not let it become an object of particular concern. A little of the language of Canaan, a little 'positivism of revelation,' can also be a good thing in addressing us all. . . ." The fact that Bonhoeffer's name is not mentioned at all in all these polemical comments of Barth's against "non-religious language" is so apparent that it requires an explanation. The intent is obviously to remove Bonhoeffer from the line of fire, since Barth was convinced that *such* had not been Bonhoeffer's intent. There is one place in the "baptismal letter" where Bonhoeffer actually does speak of a "new language," but his concern is not at all the *form* of language but, instead, its revolutionary content: God's "righteousness and truth" that will "change and renew" the world (*LPP*, 300). Truly more than a "problem of language"!

64. In his prison letters, Bonhoeffer speaks now of "the world being of age" and "the world having come of age." For him, the perfect tense serves to point out that this is a historical "development" in progress and one that has already shown certain results that should not be denigrated but taken seriously (*LPP*, 359-61). What he does not want to propose is that this is a "perfect" stage of the world's being of age in the full, eschatological sense of the word.

a matter of *hope* and not fear! Certainly, Barth is substantively close to Bonhoeffer here, as his late "doctrine of baptism" in *Church Dogmatics* IV/4 *Fragment* demonstrates. There Barth stresses his interest in "the human being who ought to have come of age" (*CD* IV/4, x). Like Bonhoeffer, he is concerned with the development that takes the human being from not being of age to being of age. That is why Barth calls for a certain "*instruction* in the faith" prior to baptism on the model of the ancient church's catechumenate (*CD* IV/4, 151).[65] Hence his "opposition to the custom, or abuse, of infant baptism" (*CD* IV/4, x).[66]

The same question that Klappert put to Barth's "doctrine of lights" is to be put to Bonhoeffer's language of the "world come of age." Why did Bonhoeffer do that without providing that language with an explicitly Israelite contour? Would the language of the world *having come* of age not have lost its ambiguity and its speculative dimension had it been understood that the world attained to its nonreligious being of age in Israel, in the Jewish "No!" to the Messiah Jesus? Unlike the Christian church, Israel has understood itself always as God's *come-of-age* partner and, precisely in

65. The congruence of interests cannot be overlooked even if Lutherans, like Regin Prenter, locate the decisive "point of difference" between Barth and Bonhoeffer precisely at this point. Bonhoeffer himself had pointed to the importance of the ancient church's "catechumenate" — see, among others, *CoD,* 45f. Barth explicitly rejects an "arcane discipline" in this context (*CD* IV/4, 152) because changing the function of "instruction" into an "initiation . . . into deeper and higher mysteries" would only once again deny the baptismal candidate's being of age. I have tried to show in my dissertation "Dietrich Bonhoeffer's Call for an Arcane Discipline" (*Dietrich Bonhoeffers Forderung einer Arkandisziplin — eine unerledigte Anfrage an Kirche und Theologie* [Cologne: Pahl Rugenstein, 1988]) that, together with his call in the prison letters for such a discipline, Bonhoeffer also undertook to provide a new interpretation of "arcane discipline" that seeks precisely to overcome the character of mystery that marked the ancient church's catechumenate and that denied the candidates' being of age.

66. Contrary to widespread misconception, Bonhoeffer shared more of Barth's skepticism toward the institution of infant baptism than was to be expected of a Lutheran. In an assessment of "the question of baptism" for the Council of Brethren of the Church of the Old Prussian Union, prepared by him in 1942, he warned — with an eye on the end of the existing conditions of the popular church *(Volkskirche)* — against the "misuse of infant baptism," recommending instead a "new evaluation of adult baptism." He did not want to go quite as far as to call for the "abolition of infant baptism" but did call for "an authentic evangelical baptismal discipline." It would, "if need be, refuse to baptize infants when it has come to the firm conclusion that baptism is not desired in faith" (*TP,* 159ff.).

that, as God's people.[67] Thus, Franz Rosenzweig understands "revelation" explicitly as follows: "Under the love of God, the mute self [comes] of age as eloquent soul." And it is surely no coincidence that, long before Bonhoeffer, Rosenzweig interpreted this "coming of age" in relation to the Song of Songs. "The Song of Songs was an 'authentic,' that is, a 'worldly' love lyric; precisely for this reason, not in spite of it, it was a genuinely 'spiritual' song of the love of God for [humans]. [Humans love] because God loves. [Their] human soul is the soul awakened and loved by God" (T.a.).[68] In his letter to Eberhard Bethge dated 2 June 1944, Bonhoeffer writes similarly: "I should prefer to read it as an earthly love song" because "that is probably the best 'Christological' exposition" (*LPP,* 315, T.a.). If he had discerned the Israelite character of such "worldly-spiritual" interpretation of the Song of Songs, he could have spoken in a manner less open to misreading of the "world having come of age." Nevertheless, he was on the way there, as his repeated reference to the "Old Testament" as a criterion and motive of "religionless Christianity" would indicate (*LPP,* 282, 286, 303 — where he refers to the Song of Songs — and 337). But once the legitimacy of the Jewish "No!" to Jesus being the Messiah has been recognized as a consequence and presupposition of Israel's "being of age" in relation to its God, the "religionless world's being of age," that is to say, above all the humanistic claim of atheistic communism, can no longer be defamed theologically as "haughtiness" or "pride." It must be acknowledged as a wholesome challenge to the community of Jesus Christ.

Conclusion: Theological Liberalism Recycled?

The question needs to be raised once again at the end: Does the charge of "positivism of revelation" and the related questions to a Karl Barth who, in light of the Confessing Church's "Barthianism," is misunderstood as being "neo-orthodox" mean that Bonhoeffer is again treading the paths of theo-

67. See, for example, Emmanuel Lévinas, "Eine Religion für Erwachsene," in his *Schwierige Freiheit. Versuch über das Judentum* (Frankfurt am Main, 1992), 27: "For Judaism, the *ethical relation* is a very special relation: in it human sovereignty is not endangered by the contact with an external being but, on the contrary, is given and made operative by it."

68. Franz Rosenzweig, *The Star of Redemption,* trans. Wm. H. Hallo (Boston: Beacon Press, 1964), 198f.

logical liberalism? As indicated earlier, this question is not without substance inasmuch as "liberal inheritance" unquestionably breaks through in Bonhoeffer's prison period, an inheritance he had suppressed in himself during the hot phases of the church struggle. Thus, he refers to himself, in a letter to Eberhard Bethge dated 3 August 1944, as a "modern" theologian, that is, someone shaped by dialectical theology, who "is still aware of the debt he owes to liberal theology" (*LPP,* 378).[69] Also, the strong emphasis Bonhoeffer puts on the historical aspect of "religion" as a historically formed and transitory shape of Christianity may well reflect the understanding of Adolf von Harnack. According to him, "*dogmatic* Christianity is . . . a definite stage in the history of the development of Christianity" that "corresponds to the antique mode of thought" from which the gospel has been working itself free ever since the Reformation.[70]

But Bonhoeffer wants not simply to think as a "liberal (i.e. abridging the gospel)," but rather "theologically" (*LPP,* 285). The question of liberal theology must truly be taken up and answered, not in order to restore liberalism (as Bultmann was doing) but to overcome "liberal theology (even Barth is still influenced by it, though negatively) . . ." (*LPP,* 329). When we speak of a rehabilitation of theological liberalism in Bonhoeffer in connection with the charge of "positivism of revelation," we are speaking of a revised liberalism. This is fundamentally different from that of Bultmann and Bonhoeffer's liberal teachers. It is one that presupposes Barth's basic decision, which is antibourgeois and critical of religion. It does not, like Harnack, repudiate that decision or, like Bultmann, revise it.[71] Contrary to

69. Cf. Bonhoeffer's letter to W. Krause (July 1942) in which he, in reference to the debate about Bultmann's essay on "demythologization," confesses that, in a certain sense, he "had perhaps remained a pupil of Harnack" (*DBW,* 16:344).

70. Adolf von Harnack, *The History of Dogma,* vol. 1, trans. Neil Buchanan (New York: Dover, 1961), 15 and 20; cf. also 20: "Dogma, that is to say, that type of Christianity which was formed in ecclesiastical antiquity, has not been suppressed even in Protestant Churches, has really not been modified or replaced by a new conception of the Gospel. But, on the other hand, who could deny that the Reformation began to disclose such a perception . . . ? Who could further call in question that, in consequence of the reforming impulse in Protestantism, a way was opened up for a conception which does not identify Gospel and dogma . . . ?"

71. John D. Godsey, "Barth and Bonhoeffer," *Quarterly Review* (spring 1987): 25: "Thus Bonhoeffer is driven theologically — in this sense similar to liberalism — to take seriously the questions of the modern world, although unlike liberalism he wants to answer them in nonreligious terms."

Harnack's "docetism" (cf. *CC*, 84), it is a liberalism that undoubtedly has a certain "Ebionite" flavor, inasmuch as Jesus, rather than being evaporated into an "ideal humanity," is taken seriously as a "concrete human being," that is, as the Jew Jesus of Nazareth. Finally, it is a liberalism that holds fast to the "God of the Old Testament" and protects that God's mystery (cf. *CC*, 82). In this liberalism "dogma" is exactly what does not get eliminated. It is subjected to an "arcane discipline" in which it can be protected against profanation and liberal reduction and, at the same time, be biblically grounded and corrected. In that the difference between gospel and law is perceived here as a "surplus" of the Old Testament over the New,[72] human beings can be taken seriously precisely in their "religionlessness" and the world need no longer be "run down" for its being of age (*LPP*, 346).

Does this revised liberalism make for a contrast between Bonhoeffer and Barth? The term "positivism of revelation" is a clear symptom that Bonhoeffer surely felt a certain difference here. But he felt an even stronger difference in relation to "younger men" that were being shaped by Barth's theology without knowing the opponent the latter was attacking. According to Bonhoeffer, there would not be many among the younger "Barthians" who can combine liberalism and theology of revelation (*LPP*, 378). But it was the older one, namely, Barth himself, who in this respect showed himself to be far more flexible in his subsequent years than many a "Barthian." When Barth turned against his liberal teachers Harnack and Herrmann, their opposition to "positive" orthodoxy was in fact always presupposed. Therefore, in stressing the break between dialectical theology and liberalism, one must not overlook that there was at the same time an actual subterranean continuity.[73] So, it is not all that astonishing that in his older age Barth could indeed contemplate the possibility of a renewed liberal theology within which it was particularly a connection to Martin Buber and Leonhard Ragaz that seemed biblically legitimate to him.

To be anthropocentric need not mean to be egocentric. . . . At this point, taking as his starting point the unequivocal I-Thou theology of

---

72. On the "surplus" of the Old Testament, see Kornelis Heiko Miskotte, *When the Gods Are Silent,* trans. John Doberstein (New York: Harper & Row, 1967), esp. 173ff.

73. On this, see H. Ruddies, "Karl Barth und Wilhelm Herrmann. Aspekte aus den Anfängen der dialektischen Theologie," *Zeitschrift für dialektische Theologie* (Kampen), no. 2 (1985): 52ff. In a somewhat undialectical fashion, the subterranean continuity is played out against the quite apparent break.

the Old Testament prophets, Martin Buber made his breakthrough. . . . Liberal theology might well find new possibilities within the framework of such a pre-Messianic Judaism. . . . Surely Swiss liberalism missed a great opportunity some fifty years ago, when it failed to stand uncompromisingly behind . . . Leonhard Ragaz. I couple him with Martin Buber because he, too, was concerned . . . with the problem of the solidarity of God and my neighbour, my neighbour and God, and in this sense with the Kingdom of God. . . .[74]

We maintain, finally, that Barth and Bonhoeffer evidently had to misunderstand and talk past each other as long as they were not prepared to admit openly to each other their respective liberal substratum. This is a "liberalism" that can be regarded as biblically legitimate only when its roots in Israel are laid open and acknowledged. The great precursor of such a legitimate liberalism among the Reformers would have been Huldrych Zwingli. It is no coincidence that Barth cites him approvingly in the *Church Dogmatics* where he, full of admiration for Bonhoeffer's book *Discipleship (Nachfolge)*, interprets "the call to discipleship" on his part as a call "into the open, into the freedom of a definite decision and act" (*CD* IV/2, 539).[75] "For God's sake, do something courageous!" is what Zwingli urged certain of his contemporaries. Of course, it would have taken an incomparably greater effort for the Lutheran Bonhoeffer than the Reformed Barth to admit to himself the relationship to Zwingli that Barth registered in connection with *Nachfolge*.[76]

But must such urging not first be tested for its "truth claim" if theology wishes to be appropriate to the scholarly method in the "postBarthian period"? Bonhoeffer clearly agreed with Barth at least in that

---

74. Karl Barth, "Liberal Theology: Some Alternatives," *Hibbert Journal* 59, no. 3 (April 1961): 217f.

75. Cf. *CD* IV/2, 540: "This Adam is denied in the new act demanded by the call of Jesus, and the brave thing demanded of His disciples consists in what D. Bonhoeffer calls 'simple obedience.'" On Barth's "Zwinglianism," see Peter Winzeler, "Der Gott Israels als Freund und Bundesgenosse des Menschen im Kampf gegen das Nichtige. Zum Verhältnis von Dogmatik und Ethik im Werk Karl Barths," *Zeitschrift für dialektische Theologie* (Kampen), no. 1 (1985): 57ff. See also his " 'Tut um Gottes Willen etwas Tapferes!' Die Vorsehungslehre bei Ulrich Zwingli und Karl Barth" (unpublished manuscript, Berlin, 1985).

76. Still, Bonhoeffer draws quite a decisive line connecting Wycliffe, Hus, and Zwingli in his dissertation *Sanctorum Communio* (*SC*, 164 n. 22).

theology had to address "serious problems of life" (*LPP*, 378). But then one must "risk saying controversial things" (*LPP*, 378), even, one is tempted to say, if that means falling victim to "Judaism," "liberalism," or — if it has to be — "positivism of revelation" and therewith to what scholarship will judge to be "untenable." In that sense, Barth's and Bonhoeffer's questions are certainly not behind but still before us.

Bibliography

1. Dietrich Bonhoeffer

Dietrich Bonhoeffer Works. Wayne Whitson Floyd, Jr., general editor.
Volumes published to date:
- 1: *Sanctorum Communio.* Edited by Clifford J. Green. Translated by Reinhard Krauss and Nancy Lukens. Minneapolis: Fortress, 1998.
- 2: *Act and Being: Transcendental Philosophy and Ontology in Systematic Theology.* Edited by Wayne Whitson Floyd, Jr. Translated by H. Martin Rumscheidt. Minneapolis: Fortress, 1996.
- 3: *Creation and Fall: A Theological Exposition of Genesis 1–3.* Edited by John de Gruchy. Translated by Douglas Stephen Bax. Minneapolis: Fortress, 1997.
- 5: *Life Together: Prayerbook of the Bible.* Edited by Geffrey B. Kelly. Translated by Daniel W. Bloesch and James H. Burtness. Minneapolis: Fortress, 1996.

"Dietrich Bonhoeffers Abschied von der Berliner 'Wintertheologie' — Neue Funde aus seiner Spanienkorrespondenz 1928." Edited by R. Staats and M. Wünsche. *Zeitschrift für Neuere Theologiegeschichte / Journal for the History of Modern Thought* 1 (1994).

Ethics. Edited by Eberhard Bethge. Translated by Neville Horton Smith. New York: Macmillan, 1955.

The Cost of Discipleship. Translated by Reginald H. Fuller et al. London: SCM, 1959.

Gesammelte Schriften. 6 vols. Edited by Eberhard Bethge. Munich: Chr. Kaiser Verlag, 1960-74.

Die Mündige Welt. Vol. 5, *Dokumente zur Bonhoeffer-Forschung 1928-1945.*
Edited by J. Glenthøj. Munich: Chr. Kaiser Verlag, 1969.

Letters and Papers from Prison. Edited by Eberhard Bethge. Translated by
Reginald H. Fuller, Frank Clarke, John Bowden, et al. New York:
Macmillan, 1972.

Schweizer Korrespondenz 1941/42. Im Gespräch mit Karl Barth. Edited by
Eberhard Bethge. Munich: Chr. Kaiser Verlag, 1982. See also *Newsletter —
International Bonhoeffer Society for Archive and Research,* English Language
Section, no. 22 (June 1982); six letters from May 1941 to May 1942.

Predigten — Auslegungen — Meditationen 1925-1945. 2 vols. Edited by Otto
Dudzus. Munich: Chr. Kaiser Verlag, 1984/85.

Dietrich Bonhoeffer Werke. Complete in 16 vols. Munich and Gütersloh:
Gütersloher Verlagshaus/Chr. Kaiser Verlag, 1986-98.

Christ the Center. Translated by Edwin H. Robertson. San Francisco: Harper &
Row, 1978.

No Rusty Swords: Letters, Lectures and Notes 1928-1936 from the Collected Works.
Translated by Edwin H. Robertson and John Bowden. London: William
Collins Sons & Co. Ltd., 1965.

*The Way to Freedom: Letters, Lectures and Notes 1935-1939 from the Collected
Works.* Translated by Edwin H. Robertson and John Bowden. London:
William Collins Sons & Co. Ltd., 1966.

True Patriotism: Letters, Lectures and Notes 1939-1945 from the Collected Works.
Translated by Edwin H. Robertson and John Bowden. New York: Harper
& Row, 1973.

A Testament to Freedom: The Essential Writings of Dietrich Bonhoeffer. Edited by
Geffrey B. Kelly and Burton F. Nelson. San Francisco: HarperSanFran-
cisco, 1990.

2. Karl Barth

Der Römerbrief. 1st ed. Bern: G. A. Bäschlin, 1919. New edition: ed. Hermann
Schmidt (Zürich: Theologischer Verlag, 1985).

Die christliche Dogmatik im Entwurf. Vol. 1, *Die Lehre vom Worte Gottes. Prolegomena zur christlichen Dogmatik.* Munich: Chr. Kaiser Verlag, 1927. New
critical edition: ed. Gerhard Sauter (Zürich: Theologischer Verlag, 1982).

The Holy Ghost and the Christian Life. Translated by Richard Birch Hoyle. London: Hodder & Stoughton, 1929.

The Epistle to the Romans. Second revised German edition of 1922 translated by
Edwyn C. Hoskyns. London: Oxford University Press, 1933.

Theological Existence Today! A Plea for Theological Freedom. Translated by Richard Birch Hoyle. London: Hodder & Stoughton, 1933.

Church Dogmatics I/1-IV/4 (Fragment). Translated by Geoffrey W. Bromiley and G. T. Thomson. Edinburgh: T. & T. Clark, 1936-69.

The Knowledge of God and the Service of God: According to the Teaching of the Reformation. Translated by J. L. M. Haire and Ian Henderson. London: Hodder & Stoughton, 1938.

"No! Answer to Emil Brunner." In Emil Brunner and Karl Barth, *Natural Theology*, translated by Peter Fraenkel. London: Centenary Press, 1946.

The Teaching of the Church Regarding Baptism. Translated by Ernest A. Payne. London: SCM, 1948.

Theologische Fragen und Antworten (essays 1931-42). Zürich: Evangelischer Verlag, 1957.

The Word of God and the Word of Man. (Essays: 1916-1923). Translated by Douglas Horton. New York: Harper Brothers, 1957.

"Gospel and Law" and "Church and State." In Karl Barth, *Community, State, and Church: Three Essays,* translated by A. M. Hall et al. Garden City, N.J.: Anchor Books, 1960.

The Humanity of God. Translated by Thomas Wieser and John Newton Thomas. Richmond: John Knox, 1960.

Der Götze wackelt (essays from 1930 to 1960). Edited by Karl Kupisch. Berlin: Käthe Vogt Verlag, 1961.

"Liberal Theology: Some Alternatives." Translated by L. A. Garrard. *Hibbert Journal* 59, no. 3 (April 1961).

"Rudolf Bultmann — an Attempt to Understand Him." In *Kerygma and Myth: A Theological Debate,* edited by Hans-Werner Bartsch, translated by Reginald H. Fuller. London: SPCK, 1962.

Theology and Church: Shorter Writings, 1920-1928. Translated by Louise Pettibone Smith. London: SCM, 1962.

"Abschied von 'Zwischen den Zeiten.'" In *Anfänge der dialektischen Theologie,* vol. 2, edited by Jürgen Moltmann. Munich: Chr. Kaiser Verlag, 1963.

Briefwechsel mit Dietrich Bonhoeffer. In Dietrich Bonhoeffer, *Gesammelte Schriften,* vol. 2, edited by Eberhard Bethge. Munich: Chr. Kaiser Verlag, 1965. ET in *No Rusty Swords: Letters, Lectures, and Notes from the Collected Works,* edited by Edwin H. Robertson, translated by John Bowden, and *Newsletter — International Dietrich Bonhoeffer Society for Archive and Research,* English Language Section, no. 22 (June 1982).

"A Thank You and a Bow: Kierkegaard's Reveille." Translated by H. Martin Rumscheidt. *Canadian Journal of Theology* 11, no. 1 (1965). Also found in Karl Barth, *Fragments Grave and Gay,* ed. H. Martin Rumscheidt, trans. Eric Mosbacher (London: Collins, 1971).

"From a Letter of Karl Barth to Landessuperintendent P. W. Herrenbrück, 21. December 1952." In *World Come of Age,* edited and translated by Ronald Gregor Smith. London: Collins, 1967.

"Letter to Eberhard Bethge." Translated by H. Martin Rumscheidt. *Canadian Journal of Theology* 15, nos. 3-4 (1969). Also found in Karl Barth, *Fragments Grave and Gay,* ed. H. Martin Rumscheidt, trans. Eric Mosbacher (London: Collins, 1971).

"The Correspondence of 1923 between Adolf von Harnack and Karl Barth." Translated by H. Martin Rumscheidt. In H. Martin Rumscheidt, *Revelation and Theology: An Analysis of the Barth-Harnack Correspondence of 1923.* Cambridge: Cambridge University Press, 1972.

Briefwechsel Karl Barth–Eduard Thurneysen. Vol. 1, *1913-1921.* Edited by Eduard Thurneysen. Zürich: Theologischer Verlag, 1973. Selections in English: *Revolutionary Theology in the Making,* ed. and trans. James D. Smart (Richmond: John Knox, 1964).

Ethik. 2 vols. 1928/29. Edited by Dieter Braun. Zürich: Theologischer Verlag, 1973/78. Abridged translation: *Ethics,* trans. Geoffrey W. Bromiley (New York: Seabury Press, 1981).

Protestant Theology in the Nineteenth Century: Its Background and History. Translated by Brian Cozens and John Bowden. Valley Forge, Pa.: Judson Press, 1973.

Fides Quaerens Intellectum: Anselm's Proof of the Existence of God in the Context of His Theological Scheme. Translated by Ian W. Robertson. Allison Park, Pa.: Pickwick, 1975.

Das christliche Leben. Die Kirchliche Dogmatik IV/4, Fragmente aus dem Nachlass. Vorlesungen 1959-1961. Edited by H.-A. Drewes and E. Jüngel. Zürich: Theologischer Verlag, 1976.

Unterricht in der christlichen Religion. Vol. 1, *Prolegomena.* 1924. Edited by Hannelotte Reiffen. Zürich: Theologischer Verlag, 1985.

"Fate and Idea in Theology." In *The Way of Theology in Karl Barth: Essays and Comments,* edited by H. Martin Rumscheidt, translated by George Hunsinger. Allison Park, Pa.: Pickwick, 1986.

3. Others

Asmussen, Hans. "Vortrag über die Theologische Erklärung zur gegenwärtigen Lage der Deutschen Evangelischen Kirche." In *Die Barmer Theologische Erklärung,* edited by H. Burgsmüller and G. Weth. Neukirchen-Vluyn: Neukirchener Verlag, 1983.

Bartsch, Hans-Werner, ed. *Kerygma and Myth: A Theological Debate.* Translated by Reginald H. Fuller. London: SPCK, 1962.

Benktson, Benkt Erik. *Christus und die Religion. Der Religionsbegriff bei Barth, Bonhoeffer und Tillich.* Stuttgart: Calwer Verlag, 1967.

Berkhof, Hendrikus. *Two Hundred Years of Theology: Report of a Personal Journey.* Translated by John Vriend. Grand Rapids: Eerdmans, 1989.

Berkhof, Hendrikus, and Hans-Joachim Kraus. *Karl Barths Lichterlehre.* Theologische Studien 123. Zürich: Theologischer Verlag, 1985.

Berkouwer, Gerrit C. *The Triumph of Grace in the Theology of Karl Barth.* Translated by Henry R. Boer. Grand Rapids: Eerdmans, 1956.

Bethge, Eberhard. "The Challenge of Dietrich Bonhoeffer's Life and Theology." 1961. In *World Come of Age,* edited by Ronald Gregor Smith. London: Collins, 1967.

———. *Ohnmacht und Mündigkeit. Beiträge zur Zeitgeschichte und Theologie nach Dietrich Bonhoeffer.* Munich: Chr. Kaiser Verlag, 1969.

———. *Dietrich Bonhoeffer: Man of Vision, Man of Courage.* Translated by Eric Mosbacher et al. New York: Harper & Row, 1970.

———. *Dietrich Bonhoeffer in Selbstzeugnissen und Bilddokumenten.* Reinbek bei Hamburg, 1976.

———. *Am gegebenen Ort. Aufsätze und Reden 1970-1979.* Munich: Chr. Kaiser Verlag, 1979.

———. *Bekennen und Widerstehen. Aufsätze, Reden, Gespräche.* Munich: Chr. Kaiser Verlag, 1984.

———. "Bemerkungen." In Dietrich Bonhoeffer, *Schweizer Korrespondenz 1941/42.* Theologische Existenz heute, n.s., vol. 214. Munich: Chr. Kaiser Verlag, 1982.

Bloch, Emil. *Atheism in Christianity: The Religion of the Exodus and the Kingdom.* Translated by J. T. Swann. New York: Herder & Herder, 1972.

Brunner, Emil. "Nature and Grace." In *Natural Theology,* translated by Peter Fraenkel. London: Centenary Press, 1946.

Bultmann, Rudolf. "New Testament and Mythology: The Problem of Demythologizing the New Testament Proclamation." In *New Testament and Mythology,* edited and translated by Schubert M. Ogden. Philadelphia: Fortress, 1984.

Burgsmüller, H., and R. Weth, eds. *Die Barmer Theologische Erklärung. Einführung und Dokumentation.* Neukirchen-Vluyn: Neukirchener Verlag, 1983.

Burtness, James H. "As though God Were Not Given: Barth, Bonhoeffer and the *Finitum Capax Infiniti.*" *Dialog. A Journal of Theology* 19, no. 4 (fall 1980).

Busch, Eberhard. *Karl Barth: His Life from Letters and Autobiographical Texts.* Translated by John Bowden. Grand Rapids: Eerdmans, 1994.

Dibelius, Otto. *Das Jahrhundert der Kirche. Geschichte, Betrachtung, Umschau und Ziele.* Berlin, 1928.

———. *Friede auf Erden? Frage, Erwägungen, Antwort.* Berlin, 1930.

Feil, Ernst. *The Theology of Dietrich Bonhoeffer.* Translated by H. Martin Rumscheidt. Philadelphia: Fortress, 1985.

———, ed. *Verspieltes Erbe? Dietrich Bonhoeffer und der deutsche Nachkriegsprotestantismus.* Internationales Bonhoeffer Forum 2. Munich: Chr. Kaiser Verlag, 1979.

Feil, Ernst, and Ilse Tödt, eds. *Konsequenzen. Dietrich Bonhoeffers Kirchenverständnis heute.* Internationales Bonhoeffer Forum 3. Munich: Chr. Kaiser Verlag, 1980.

Fürst, W., ed. *"Dialektische Theologie" in Scheidung und Bewährung 1933-36.* Munich: Chr. Kaiser Verlag, 1966.

Godsey, John D. *The Theology of Dietrich Bonhoeffer.* Philadelphia: Westminster, 1960.

———. "Barth and Bonhoeffer: The Basic Difference." *Quarterly Review: A Scholarly Journal for Reflection of Ministry* 7, no. 1 (Spring 1987).

Goes, Helmut. "Der Sichere und der Suchende." In *Begegnungen mit Dietrich Bonhoeffer,* edited by Wolf-Dieter Zimmermann. 4th enlarged ed. Munich: Chr. Kaiser Verlag, 1969.

Gollwitzer, Helmut. "Comments on Bonhoeffer's Article" ["The Question of the Boundaries of the Church and Church Union"]. Translated by Edwin H. Robertson and John Bowden. In Dietrich Bonhoeffer, *The Way to Freedom: Letters, Lectures, and Notes, 1935-1939.* London: Collins, 1966.

———. "The Way of Obedience." In *I Knew Dietrich Bonhoeffer,* edited by Wolf-Dieter Zimmermann and Ronald Gregor Smith, translated by Käthe Smith. London: Collins, 1966.

———. "Martin Bubers Bedeutung für die protestantische Theologie." In *Leben als Begegnung,* edited by Peter von den Osten-Sacken. Berlin, 1978.

———. "Das eine Wort für alle. Zur I. und VI. These der Barmer Theologischen Erklärung." In *Junge Kirche,* 1984.

Gremmels, Christian, ed. *Bonhoeffer und Luther. Zur Sozialgestalt des Luthertums in der Moderne.* Internationales Bonhoeffer Forum 6. Munich: Chr. Kaiser Verlag, 1983.

Hammelsbeck, Oskar. *Der kirchliche Unterricht. Aufgabe — Umfang — Einheit.* 2nd ed. Munich: Chr. Kaiser Verlag, 1947.

Harnack, Adolf von. *The History of Dogma.* Vol. 1. Translated by N. Buchanan. New York: Dover, 1961.

Heim, Karl. *Glaube und Denken. Philosophische Grundlegung einer christlichen Lebensanschauung.* 5th ed. Hamburg, 1957.

Herlyn, O. *Religion oder Gebet? Karl Barths Bedeutung für ein "religionsloses Christentum."* Neukirchen-Vluyn: Neukirchener Verlag, 1979.

Hildebrandt, Franz. "Zehn Thesen für die Freikirche." 1934. In Dietrich Bonhoeffer, *Gesammelte Schriften,* vol. 2.

Holl, Karl. *Gesammelte Aufsätze zur Kirchengeschichte.* 1: Luther. 4th/5th ed. Tübingen: J. C. B. Mohr, 1927.

Huber, Wolfgang, and Ilse Tödt, eds. *Ethik im Ernstfall. Dietrich Bonhoeffers Stellung zu den Juden und ihre Aktualität.* Internationales Bonhoeffer Forum 4. Munich: Chr. Kaiser Verlag, 1982.

Kierkegaard, Søren. *Der Einzelne und die Kirche. Über Luther und den Protestantismus.* Edited by W. Kütemeyer. Berlin, 1934.

———. *Kierkegaard's Attack upon "Christendom."* Translated by Walter Lowrie. Princeton: Princeton University Press, 1944.

———. *Fear and Trembling.* Translated by Walter Lowrie. Garden City, N.J.: Doubleday, 1954.

Kirschbaum, Charlotte von. "Brief an D. Bonhoeffer vom 17.5.1942." In Dietrich Bonhoeffer, *Schweizer Korrespondenz 1941/42. Im Gespräch mit Karl Barth,* edited by Eberhard Bethge. Theologische Existenz heute, n.s., vol. 124. Munich: Chr. Kaiser Verlag, 1982.

Klappert, Bertold. *Israel und die Kirche. Erwägungen zur Israellehre Karl Barths.* Theologische Existenz heute, n.s., vol. 207. Munich: Chr. Kaiser Verlag, 1980.

———. "Weg und Wende Dietrich Bonhoeffers in der Israelfrage — Bonhoeffer und die theologischen Grundentscheidungen des Rheinischen Synodalbeschlusses." In *Ethik im Ernstfall. Dietrich Bonhoeffers Stellung zu den Juden und ihre Aktualität,* edited by Wolfgang Huber and Ilse Tödt. Internationales Bonhoeffer Forum 4. Munich: Chr. Kaiser Verlag, 1982.

Köbler, Renate. *In the Shadow of Karl Barth: Charlotte von Kirschbaum.* Translated by Keith Crim. Louisville: Westminster/John Knox, 1989.

Konukiewitz, Enno. *Hans Asmussen. Ein lutherischer Theologe im Kirchenkampf.* Gütersloh: Gütersloher Verlagshaus, 1984.

Kraus, Hans-Joachim. *Theologische Religionskritik.* Neukirchen-Vluyn: Neukirchener Verlag, 1982.

Krause, Gerhard. "Dietrich Bonhoeffer und Rudolf Bultmann." In *Zeit und Geschichte. Dankesgabe an Rudolf Bultmann zum 80. Geburtstag.* Tübingen: J. C. B. Mohr, 1964.

———. "Dietrich Bonhoeffer." In *Theologische Realenzyklopädie,* vol. 7. Berlin and New York: Walter de Gruyter, 1981.

Lenin, W. I. "Die nächsten Aufgaben der Sowjetmacht." *Ausgewählte Werke.* Moscow: Verlag Progress, 1981.

Lévinas, Emmanuel. *Difficult Freedom: Essays on Judaism.* Translated by Sean Hand. Baltimore: Johns Hopkins University Press, 1990.

Luther, Martin. "Dass diese Wort Christi 'Dies ist mein Leib' noch feststehen wider die Schwarmgeister." 1527. In *Luthers Werke,* Weimar edition, vol. 23.

Marquardt, Friedrich-Wilhelm. "Solidarität mit den Gottlosen. Zur Geschichte und Bedeutung eines Theologumenon." 1960. In *Verwegenheiten. Theologische Stücke aus Berlin.* Munich: Chr. Kaiser Verlag, 1981.

————. *Die Entdeckung des Judentums für die christliche Theologie. Israel im Denken Karl Barths.* Munich: Chr. Kaiser Verlag, 1967.

————. *Theologie und Sozialismus. Das Beispiel Karl Barths.* Munich: Chr. Kaiser Verlag, 1972. 3rd enlarged edition, 1985.

————. *"Der Christ in der Gesellschaft" 1919-1979. Geschichte, Analyse und aktuelle Bedeutung von Karl Barths Tambacher Vortrag.* Theologische Existenz heute, n.s., vol. 206. Munich: Chr. Kaiser Verlag, 1980.

————. "'Feinde um unsretwillen'. Das jüdische Nein und die christliche Theologie." In *Verwegenheiten. Theologische Stücke aus Berlin.* Munich: Chr. Kaiser Verlag, 1981.

————. *Verwegenheiten. Theologische Stücke aus Berlin.* Munich: Chr. Kaiser Verlag, 1981.

————. *Die Gegenwart des Auferstandenen bei seinem Volk Israel. Ein dogmatisches Experiment.* Munich: Chr. Kaiser Verlag, 1983.

————. "Gott *oder* Mammon aber: Theologie *und* Ökonomie bei Martin Luther." In *Einwürfe I.* Munich: Chr. Kaiser Verlag, 1983.

————. "Karl Barth: Der Störenfried?" In *Einwürfe III.* Munich: Chr. Kaiser Verlag, 1986.

————. "Der Aktuar. Aus Barths Pfarramt." In *Einwürfe III.* Munich: Chr. Kaiser Verlag, 1986.

Melanchthon, Philipp. *Loci communes.* 1521. In *Melanchthon and Bucer,* edited by Wilhelm Pauck, translated by Lowell J. Satre. Library of Christian Classics, vol. 19. London: SCM, 1969.

Meyer, Winfried. *Unternehmen Sieben. Eine Rettungsaktion für vom Holocaust Bedrohte aus dem Amt Ausland/Abwehr im Oberkommando der Wehrmacht.* Frankfurt am Main: Anton Hain, 1993.

Miskotte, Kornelis Heiko. *Biblisches ABC. Wider das unbiblische Bibellesen.* 1941. Neukirchen-Vluyn: Neukirchener Verlag, 1976.

————. "Die Erlaubnis zu schriftgemässem Denken." In *Antwort. Karl Barth zum 70. Geburtstag.* Zürich: Evangelischer Verlag, 1956.

————. *Über Karl Barths Kirchliche Dogmatik. Kleine Präludien und Phantasien.* Theologische Existenz heute, n.s., vol. 89. Munich: Chr. Kaiser Verlag, 1961.

————. *When the Gods Are Silent.* Translated by John W. Doberstein. New York: Harper & Row, 1967.

Moltmann, Jürgen. "Die Wirklichkeit der Welt und Gottes konkretes Gebot nach Dietrich Bonhoeffer." In *Die Mündige Welt III.* Munich: Chr. Kaiser Verlag, 1960.

————, ed. *Anfänge der dialektischen Theologie I.* Munich: Chr. Kaiser Verlag, 1963.

Müller, Hanfried. *Von der Kirche zur Welt. Ein Beitrag zu der Beziehung des Wortes Gottes auf die societas in Dietrich Bonhoeffers theologischer Entwicklung.* Leipzig: Koehler & Amelang, 1961.

————. "Das 'Evangelium vom Gott der Gottlosen' und die 'Religion an sich.'" *Weissenseer Blätter* (Berlin), no. 4 (1986).

Mündige Welt, Die. 4 vols. Munich: Chr. Kaiser Verlag, 1955-63.

Osten-Sacken, Peter von der, ed. *Leben als Begegnung. Ein Jahrhundert Martin Buber (1878-1978). Vorträge und Aufsätze.* Berlin, 1978.

Ott, Heinrich. *Reality and Faith: The Theological Legacy of Dietrich Bonhoeffer.* Translated by Alex. A. Morrison. Philadelphia: Fortress, 1971.

Pangritz, Andreas. "Bonhoeffer und das Barmer Bekenntnis." *Neue Stimme* (Cologne), no. 12 (1984).

————. "Dietrich Bonhoeffer — wissenschaftlich verharmlost. Anmerkungen zu Gerhard Krauses Bonhoeffer-Artikel in der Theologischen Realenzyklopädie." In *Bonhoeffer-Rundbrief. Mitteilungen des Internationalen Bonhoeffer-Komitees, Sektion Bundesrepublik Deutschland,* no. 17. Düsseldorf, 1984.

————. "Eine Entdeckung — und eine verpasste Chance." *Weissenseer Blätter* (Berlin), no. 3 (1986).

————. "'Dialektik der Aufklärung' in Bonhoeffers 'Ethik'?" *Neue Stimme* (Cologne), no. 8 (1988).

————. *Dietrich Bonhoeffers Forderung einer Arkandisziplin — eine unerledigte Anfrage an Kirche und Theologie.* Cologne: Pahl-Rugenstein, 1988.

————. "Aspekte der 'Arkandisziplin' bei Dietrich Bonhoeffer." *Theologische Literaturzeitung* 119 (1994).

————. "Dietrich Bonhoeffers theologische Begründung der Beteiligung am Widerstand." *Evangelische Theologie* 55 (1995).

Pannenberg, Wolfhart. *Theology and the Philosophy of Science.* Translated by Francis McDonagh. Philadelphia: Westminster, 1976.

Peters, T. R. "Der andere ist unendlich wichtig. — Impulse aus Bonhoeffers Ekklesiologie für die Gegenwart." *Weissenseer Blätter,* no. 1 (1986).

Pfeifer, Hans. "Das Kirchenverständnis Dietrich Bonhoeffers." Unpublished diss., Heidelberg, 1963.

————, ed. *Genf '76. Ein Bonhoeffer-Symposion.* Internationales Bonhoeffer Forum 1. Munich: Chr. Kaiser Verlag, 1976.

————, ed. *Frieden — das unumgängliche Wagnis. Die Gegenwartsbedeutung der Friedensethik Dietrich Bonhoeffers.* Internationales Bonhoeffer Forum 5. Munich: Chr. Kaiser Verlag, 1982.

Phillips, John A. *Christ for Us in the Theology of Dietrich Bonhoeffer.* New York: Harper & Row, 1967.

Powell, Douglas. "Arkandisziplin." In *Theologische Realenzyklopädie,* vol. 4. 1979.

Prenter, Regin. "Dietrich Bonhoeffer and Karl Barth's Positivism of Revelation." Translated by H. Martin Rumscheidt. In *World Come of Age,* edited by Ronald Gregor Smith. London: Collins, 1967.

Prolingheuer, Hans. *Der Fall Karl Barth. Chronographie einer Vertreibung 1934-1935.* Neukirchen-Vluyn: Neukirchener Verlag, 1977; 2nd ed. 1984.

Rasmussen, Larry. *Dietrich Bonhoeffer: Reality and Resistance.* Nashville: Abingdon, 1972.

Rendtorff, Heinrich. "Buchman." In *Religion in Geschichte und Gegenwart.* 3rd ed. Tübingen: J. C. B. Mohr, 1957.

Rosenzweig, Franz. *The Star of Redemption.* Translated by William W. Hallo. Boston: Beacon Press, 1964.

Ruddies, H. "Karl Barth und Wilhelm Herrmann. Aspekte aus den Anfängen der dialektischen Theologie." *Zeitschrift für dialektische Theologie* (Kampen), no. 2 (1985).

Seeberg, Erich. *Luthers Theologie. Motive und Ideen.* Vol. 1, *Die Gottesanschauung.* Göttingen: Vandenhoeck & Ruprecht, 1929.

Seeberg, Reinhold. *Die religiösen Grundgedanken des jungen Luther und ihr Verhältnis zum Ockamismus und der deutschen Mystik.* Berlin, 1931.

————. *Dogmengeschichte.* Vol. 3. 5th ed. Darmstadt: Wissenschaftliche Buchgesellschaft, 1959.

Smith, Ronald Gregor, ed. *World Come of Age.* London: Collins, 1967.

Staats, Reinhart. "Adolf von Harnack im Leben Dietrich Bonhoeffers." *Theologische Zeitschrift* (Basel) 37 (1981): 94ff.

————. "Das patristische Erbe in der Theologie Dietrich Bonhoeffers." *Berliner Theologische Zeitschrift,* no. 2 (1988).

Tertullian, Quintus Septimus Florens. "On the Flesh of Christ." In *The Ante-Nicene Fathers,* vol. 3. New York: Christian Literature Company, 1896.

Tödt, Heinz Eduard. "Glauben in einer religionslosen Welt. Muss man zwischen Barth und Bonhoeffer wählen?" In *Genf '76. Ein Bonhoeffer-Symposion,* edited by Hans Pfeifer. Internationales Bonhoeffer Forum 1. Munich: Chr. Kaiser Verlag, 1976.

Troeltsch, Ernst. *Richard Rothe. Gedächtnisrede, gehalten zur Feier des hundertsten Geburtstages.* Freiburg i. Br., Leipzig, and Tübingen, 1899.

Vogel, Heinrich. "Praedestinatio gemina. Die Lehre von der ewigen Gnaden-wahl." In *Theologische Aufsätze. Karl Barth zum 50. Geburtstag.* Munich: Chr. Kaiser Verlag, 1936.

————. *Das Nichaenische Glaubensbekenntnis. Eine Doxologie.* Berlin and Stutt-gart, 1963.

Weber, Otto. *Karl Barth's Church Dogmatics: An Introductory Report.* Translated by Arthur C. Cochrane. London: Lutterworth, 1953.

Winzeler, Peter. "Der Gott Israels als Freund und Bundesgenosse des Menschen im Kampf gegen das Nichtige. Zum Verhältnis von Dogmatik und Ethik im Werk Karl Barths." *Zeitschrift für dialektische Theologie,* no. 1 (1985).

————. " 'Tut um Gottes Willen etwas Tapferes!' Die Vorsehungslehre bei Ulrich Zwingli und Karl Barth." Unpublished manuscript, Berlin, 1985.

Wolf, Ernst, ed. *Offenbarung und Heilsgeschehen.* Munich: Chr. Kaiser Verlag, 1941.

Wolff-Steger, Anke M. "Frans Breukelman: ein Meister des Wortes." In *Texte und Kontexte,* no. 31/32. Stuttgart: Alektor Verlag, 1986.

Zimmermann, Wolf-Dieter. "Years in Berlin." in *Begegnungen mit Dietrich Bonhoeffer,* edited by Wolf-Dieter Zimmermann. 4th enlarged ed. Munich: Chr. Kaiser Verlag, 1969.

————, ed. *Begegnungen mit Dietrich Bonhoeffer.* 4th enlarged ed. Munich: Chr. Kaiser Verlag, 1969.

Index

Apokatastasis pantōn. See "Recapitulation of all things"

Apostles' Creed, 107, 112. *See also* Faith

Arcane discipline, 5-7, 30, 86, 94, 98-99, 104, 109, 111, 113, 117, 118-19, 121-22, 142n.65, 145; arcane wisdom, 121; *arcanum,* 100. *See also* Mystery

Althaus, Paul, 77

Asmussen, Hans, 77-82, 100, 117

Baptism, 9, 85, 142

Barmen, Synod of, 51-52, 55, 59, 69, 77, 103; Barmen and Dahlem, 58-59; Declaration, 3, 51n.85, 59, 77, 134

Barth, Karl, works of: *Anselm: Fides Quaerens Intellectum: Faith in Search of Understanding,* 38, 57, 76, 85; "Biblical Questions, Insights and Vistas," 91, 95; *Christian Dogmatics,* 22n.22, 24, 29n.40, 38, 41n.62, 70, 94, 100, 101; *Das christliche Leben* (ethical fragment), 95-96; *Church Dogmatics,* 8, 13, 35, 38, 61, 63, 70, 76, 86, 94, 97-98, 100-102, 106-11, 115-18, 122, 132, 137, 146; vol. I/1 and 2 (Prolegomena: doctrine of the Word of God), 35, 41n.62, 69-70, 89, 94, 100-102, 106-11, 116, 118; vol. II/1 (doctrine of God), 51n.48, 61; vol. II/2 (doctrine of election), 8, 61-62, 67-69, 118-21, 123-26, 128, 130-31, 139-40; vol. III/4, 67; vol. IV (doctrine of reconciliation), 60n.108, 133-37, 140-42, 146; *Church and State* (Rechtfertigung und Recht), 63-70; "Ethics II" (lectures), 35; "The Holy Spirit and Christian Life," 42; "The Humanity of God," 132-33, 139-41; "Instruction in the Christian Religion" (lectures), 15-18, 93-94; *Knowledge of God and the Service of God according to the Teaching of the Reformation,* 63; "The Problem of

I would like to thank Antje Menn for her work on the index.

Ethics Today," 42; *The Epistle to the Romans,* 1st edition, 41, 65n.114, 82, 87n.36, 88, 90, 93, 98, 132, 135; 2nd edition, 8, 15-17, 23, 24n.27, 41-42, 45, 54-55, 82-84, 87-89, 92-94, 98, 132; Tambach address ("The Christians' Place in Society"), 28, 44-45, 65, 83, 95; *The Word of God and the Word of Man,* 15, 36n.55

Barthianism, 11, 15, 22, 25, 31, 34, 59, 60, 76, 77, 115, 117, 143, 145. *See also* Dialectical theology

Basil the Great, 19

Bell, George, 66

Berkhof, Hendrikus, 1-2

Berkouwer, Gerrit C., 124n.22, 130n.42

Berlin, 48, 50, 61, 78; eastern section, 40; University of (theological faculty), 2, 18, 21n.20, 29-32, 34-36, 46-47, 51-52, 60n.106, 69, 71-73, 75-76, 80, 82, 104. *See also* Confessing Church

Bethge, Eberhard, 2, 7, 9-11, 13, 15-17, 26, 32, 36, 38-39, 49, 51, 53, 57, 62-64, 70, 84n.31, 89-90

Bible, 31, 35, 36, 47, 67, 91, 93n.51, 101-2, 107, 108n.72, 120, 130, 132, 134-35, 137; biblical dogmatics, 116-17, 119; biblical theology, 98; Scripture and creed, 109-10. *See also* New Testament; Old Testament

Bonhoeffer, Dietrich, works of: *Act and Being,* 10, 18, 25-26, 27-29, 33-34, 36-37, 47n.81, 75-76, 101, 131; *Christ the Center* (Christology lectures), 11, 47, 54n.92, 104-6, 111, 113, 144-45; *Creation and Fall,* 45n.76; *The Cost of Discipleship (Nachfolge),* 52-57, 60, 64, 133, 146; *Ethics,* 60-62, 65-67, 72, 128, 131, 137-38; "Is There a Christian Ethics?"

(seminar), 41-42, 51n.87; "The History of Systematic Theology in the Twentieth Century" (lectures), 36-37, 40; *Letters and Papers from Prison* (prison correspondence), 3, 5-7, 10-13, 17-18, 68-69, 72, 76-77, 81-82, 85-86, 88, 90-92, 94, 97-99, 111-14, 118-19, 122-23, 131-33, 135n.53, 139-41, 142n.64, 143-45, 147; "Baptismal letter," 84, 94-96, 141n.63; "Outline for a Book," 77, 79, 112, 131; "New Publications in Systematic Theology" (lectures), 45; "The Nature of the Church" (lectures), 37, 112; *Sanctorum Communio,* 18, 22-24, 28, 54-55, 59n.103, 130-31, 133

Bonn, 34-35, 39, 46, 131, 134n.52, 139

Brunner, Emil, 72

Buber, Martin, 145-46

Bultmann, Rudolf, 62, 78-82, 144

Burtness, James H., 9-10

Calvin, John, 121

Calvinism. *See* Reformed

Capax, incapax, 9-11, 15-16, 22, 26-27, 30, 47, 60, 69, 76, 83

Chalcedonian definition (Creed), 12, 16, 105-6, 111-12. *See also* Christology

Child (and theology), 9, 25, 28-29

Christ, 1, 6, 8, 25, 26-27, 40, 43-45, 64, 72-74, 78, 87, 91, 103-5, 107-11, 113, 120, 123-24, 126-29, 131, 134-40; existing as community, 27-28, 59n.103; the lord of the world, 3; the mediator of creation, 72; present, 37. *See also* Christology

Christology, 21, 22, 47, 91, 104-7, 134; christological approach (concentration), 3, 12, 64n.113, 65n.114, 72, 97-98, 105, 123-25, 129, 132-33; the two natures (divinity and humanity)

of Christ, 12, 105, 107, 109-11, 113, 132-33. *See also* Chalcedonian definition; Cross; Incarnation; Resurrection; Virgin birth

Church, 8, 10, 19-21, 22, 27-29, 31, 36-38, 48-49, 53-56, 59, 75-76, 85, 89-91, 94-95, 104, 143; *Bekenntniskirche* (confessional church), 20; ecumenical, 44; *Frei(willigkeits)kirche,* 20, 48-49, 51; German, 40, 50; for others, 124, 131, 140; and politics (state), 50, 52, 58, 63; question of, 46; servant, 69; union, 58, 69; United Church of Prussia, 11, 47-49, 142n.66; *Volkskirche,* 20, 50, 142n.66; and world, 12, 72, 83, 94, 124, 129, 135, 137-38. *See also* Confessing Church; Ecclesiology; Israel: and the church

Church struggle, 29, 48-49, 51-53, 55n.96, 60, 69, 82, 114, 144. *See also* Confessing Church

Commandment (of God), 20, 41, 45-46, 52, 119; as permission, 67-68. *See also* Concreteness; Ethics; Mandate(s)

Community of faith, 23, 27-29, 37-38, 87, 134-38, 140-41, 143; with God, 28, 88-89

Concreteness: ethical, of the commandment(s), 13, 38, 39-46, 47, 51, 62, 68, 69; earthly, ecclesial, of revelation, 10, 15, 22, 34, 85. *See also* Revelation

Confessing Church, 12, 50, 51-53, 58-59, 60n.106, 63, 68, 76-82, 85, 114, 131-32, 143; Council of Brethren *(Bruderrat),* 78, 80, 142n.66. *See also* Barmen; Church struggle

Confession of faith, 48-49, 100, 107, 112, 128, 137; Altona, 100; Lutheran, 59; Scottish, 63. *See also* Barmen,

Synod of: Declaration; Confessing Church; Guilt

Conspiracy, 13, 61-64, 67-68, 91, 140; coup d'état, 67; Operation Seven, 68. *See also* Resistance

Critique: of the church, 88, 91, 94; of religion, 7, 17, 76-77, 82, 87-89, 91-94, 99, 118-19, 144

Cross, 13, 73, 103-4, 124, 126. *See also* Christology

Dehn, Günther, 47

Dialectical theology, 15, 23, 26, 30, 31-32, 36, 46, 69, 71-72, 92, 144-45

Dialectics, 23, 76; historical, 23; theological, 13, 36-37, 42, 82, 89-90, 132. *See also* Dialectical theology

Dibelius, Otto, 40

Discipleship, Christian, 52-53, 55, 69, 146

Dogmatics, 13, 35, 87-88, 98-99, 113-14, 115, 122. *See also* Barth: *Church Dogmatics*

Dohnanyi, Hans von, 68

Ecclesiology, 19, 23, 27, 47-48, 70; ecclesial concentration of theology, 86; *extra ecclesiam nulla salus* (outside the church, no salvation), 58. *See also* Church

Election. *See* Predestination

Eschatology, 40, 42; Christological-eschatological beginning, 57; lack of eschatological content in Barth's theology, 128, 130; eschatological proviso, 91, 128

Ethics, 23, 35, 39-46, 61-62, 69, 71, 119; of orders, 45, of principles, 40; of responsibility, 62; of revelation, 43. *See also* Bonhoeffer: *Ethics;* Commandment; Concreteness; Mandate(s)

Extra Calvinisticum, 10-11, 15-16, 26, 54n.88, 60n.107, 106-7

Faith, 77, 81, 83, 85, 131; law of, 81, 98, 116, 121-22; *sola fide,* 27n.36, 37. *See also* Mystery: of faith
Fascism. *See* National Socialism
Feil, Ernst, 90
Finkenwalde, 52, 57-58, 86. *See also* Life together
Freedom, 67-68, 116, 137-38; from religion, 88
Friedenthal, Charlotte, 68

German Christians (Nordic religion), 78-79, 100
Germany, 24, 66. *See also* National Socialism
God, 26-27, 29, 36, 87, 105; action of, 18, 26, 96; doctrine of, 62, 101, 116; freedom of, 26-27, 29, 36-37, 75-76, 107, 119-20, 122-23, 125; grace of, 12-13, 30, 35, 110, 120, 125, 128, 130; hidden *(deus absconditus),* 73-74; in history, 92; in human being, 92, 97, 103, 106; humanity of, 92, 124, 127, 132-33; knowledge of, 37, 73, 75; love of, 103-4, 140, 143; majesty of, 9-10, 15, 21, 22, 26, 120; peace of, 95; as reality, 33, 41; reign of, 95, 134; revolution of, 84; righteousness of, 96; time of, 94-96; will of, 41-42. *See also* Mystery: of God; Revelation of God, Trinity; Word: of God
Godlessness (atheism), 8, 91, 123, 126-27, 135-37, 143; full of promise, 123, 128, 131, 140
Godsey, John D., 11-13
Gogarten, Friedrich, 46
Gollwitzer, Helmut, 11-12, 58-59
Gospel. *See* Justification; New Testament

Grace: by grace alone *(sola gratia),* 18-19; costly grace, 56; mystery of, 110; triumph of, 121, 124, 130. *See also* God: grace of
Guilt, 61-62, 95, 131; confession of, 61, 131

Harnack, Adolf von, 15, 28, 30, 112, 144, 145
Heidegger, Martin, 26
Heim, Karl, 38-39, 77
Herrmann, Wilhelm, 145
Hildebrandt, Franz, 40, 48-50
History, 28, 90, 92-93, 139, 144; *Geistesgeschichte,* 90; of God, 92, 133; non-historical, 93; theology of, 117
Holl, Karl, 18-22, 30
Holy Spirit, 42, 74, 87, 89n.104, 104, 107

Incapax. See Capax
Incarnation, 74, 97, 106-7, 113; mystery of, 107-11
Individualism, 37, 53-55
Israel (the people of, the Jews), 120, 125-30, 138-39, 141-42, 146; Aryan Clause, 47-49; and the church, 15, 125-26, 129; doctrine of, 128-29, 131, 139-40; Jewish emigration, 68; the Jew Jesus, 145; mission to Jews, 140; persecution (destruction) of the Jews, 47-49, 79, 125, 128, 138n.36; question of the Jews, 51; the Jewish "No!", 127-28, 142-43

Judaism, 136, 143n.67, 146-47. *See also* Israel
Justice, 64-65, 137-38; social, *see* Socialism
Justification, 31, 34, 64n.113, 65, 88,

89; doctrine of, 18-21, 34; justification and sanctification, 56-57

Kierkegaard, Søren, 53-56, 83
Kirschbaum, Charlotte von, 66
Klappert, Bertold, 125n.24, 129, 139, 142
Kraus, Hans-Joachim, 117-18, 119n.10, 122, 123n.19, 137n. 56
Krause, Gerhard, 34, 71-72

Law. *See* Faith: law of; Justice
Lehmann, Paul, 10
Leibholz, Gerhard, 64
Liberal theology, 12, 16, 27-28, 30, 32, 77, 81-82, 94, 101, 112-14, 143-47
Life together (communal house), 52-53, 55, 57, 86. *See also* Finkenwalde
Lights, doctrine of, 35, 97, 132, 134-39, 142
Love, 23-24, 64, 143; of God, 103-4, 140, 143; mystery of, 103-4
Luther, Martin, 18-22, 41, 56, 73-76, 84, 131
Lutheranism, 7, 8-11, 16, 18, 22, 27, 30, 37, 41-43, 44-45, 47, 58-60, 69, 76-77, 82, 106-7, 112, 146; Luther renaissance, 18-21, 22, 30; Seeberg's view of Luther's theology, 71-75. *See also Capax, incapax*

Mandate(s), divine, 12n.21, 62, 67-68. *See also* Concreteness; Ethics
Marquardt, Friedrich-Wilhelm, 117, 126n.26, 127-31, 136-37
Melanchthon, Philipp, 19, 113
Miskotte, Kornelis Heiko, 115-17, 120n.15
Monastery, 19, 52, 55-57
Müller, Hanfried, 5n.2, 6n.4, 7n.6, 29n.41

Mystery, 93n.51, 103, 108; of Christian faith, 5-6, 99-100, 102, 104, 107-8, 111-14, 116, 121-22; of Christmas (incarnation), 107-11; of God, 103, 113, 116, 120, 136, 139n.58, 145; of grace, 110; of love, 103-4; of predestination, 36-37, 73, 121; of revelation, 106-7. *See also* Arcane discipline

National Socialism, 43-44, 46-48, 50, 66, 86n.35, 94, 100, 128n.36
Nature, natural life, 72; natural law, 72; natural reason, 84; natural science, 31-32; natural theology, 71-73, 75, 117, 134, 137n.56. *See also* Christology: the two natures of Christ
New Testament, 16, 40, 43, 58, 68, 72, 121, 135, 144n.70, 145; law and gospel, 125. *See also* Sermon on the Mount
Niebuhr, Reinhold, 63
Niemöller, Martin, 50
Non-religious interpretation, 6-7, 87, 98-99, 118, 141; religionless Christianity, 1n.1, 6, 8, 18, 76, 85-92, 94, 98-99, 122-23, 127, 131, 132, 134, 140-41, 143, 145

Ockham, William of, 75
Old Testament, 12, 89, 92, 93n.51, 143, 145-46
Opposition to the church, 49-50, 52-53, 55. *See also* Church struggle
Other(s), 23-24, 27, 126, 138. *See also* Church: for others
Ott, Heinrich, 97-99

Pannenberg, Wolfhart, 1-3
Peace: of God, 95; international, 40, 42-45, 47, 69
Penultimate, ultimate (the last things

and the things before the last things), 6, 65

Pfeifer, Hans, 16, 32-33

Politics, 3, 40, 42, 46, 58, 69; government, 66; political action, 95; political worship, 63, 66. *See also* Church: and politics; Conspiracy; Resistance

Positivism, ecclesial, 12, 13, 75-76, 85. *See also* Church

Positivism of revelation, 75-76, 114, 141, 147; in Barth, 1-4, 5-10, 12, 17, 38, 60, 69, 72, 81-86, 87, 94, 97-98, 99, 111, 113, 116-18, 119, 121-22, 131, 132, 143, 145; in Bonhoeffer, 11, 76; in the Confessing Church, 12-13, 76-77, 79-82, 114, 131, 132; in Luther, 71-75; Ockhamist, 74-75. *See also* Revelation: doctrine of; "Take it or leave it!"

Prayer, 6, 38, 66, 78, 96, 105; and righteous action, 94-96

Predestination (election): doctrine of, 8, 26, 41, 62-63, 118-26, 130; dialectical, 129; election and rejection (double [geminal] predestination), 118, 121, 125, 128-29, 131; double election, 130; mystery of, 36-37, 73, 121

Prenter, Regin, 7-9

Preservation, orders of, 43-45, 67

Ragaz, Leonhard, 57, 145-46

"Recapitulation of all things" (*apokatastasis pantōn*), 130-31, 137, 139-40

Reformation theology, 9, 21, 52n.88, 56, 64, 144n.70, 146

Reformed (Calvinism), 7, 9, 11, 30, 37, 47, 59-60, 64, 93, 106-7, 112, 146. *See also Extra Calvinisticum*

Religion: concept of, 3, 6, 31, 36, 81, 85, 88-90, 93-94, 144; death of, 91;

religious *a priori*, 89, 91n.46; true religion, 89, 93-94, 118. *See also* Critique of religion; German Christians

Religionlessness. *See* Non-religious interpretation; World

Resistance, 3, 52, 63, 66, 69, 138. *See also* Conspiracy

Responsibility, 62

Resurrection, 92-93, 129, 135-36; Easter message, 95

Revelation of God, 1, 3, 26-28, 30-34, 36, 38, 75-76, 101-2, 107, 112, 143, 145; continuity of, 27, 38, 42, 44; doctrine of, 8, 75, 77, 79, 84, 87, 99, 101, 118, 121, 132; mystery of, 106-7. *See also* Concreteness: of revelation; Ethics: of revelation; Positivism of revelation

Righteousness. *See* God: righteousness of; Prayer: and righteous action

Roman Catholicism, 25, 37, 93, 112

Rosenzweig, Franz, 143

Rott, Willi, 68

Sasse, Hermann, 11, 59

Scripture. *See* Bible

Secret discipline. *See* Arcane discipline

Seeberg, Erich, 71-75

Seeberg, Reinhold, 15, 16n.2

Sermon on the Mount, 20, 51-53, 55-56, 64.

Siegmund-Schultze, Friedrich, 40

Socialism, 3, 40, 42-45, 69, 136-38

Society, 3, 40, 44, 83, 95, 136

Song of Songs, 143

State. *See* Church: and state; Politics

Suffering, 86, 95, 138-40

Sutz, Erwin, 34-35, 43, 46, 51-53, 58, 64

Switzerland, 46, 60-64, 66-68, 118-19, 146

"Take it or leave it!", 1n.1, 6, 99, 113, 139. *See also* Positivism of revelation
Tertullian, Q.S.F., 75
Tillich, Paul, 77
Tödt, Heinz-Eduard, 119, 127
Trinity, 6, 8, 84, 99-104
Troeltsch, Ernst, 37
Two kingdoms, 20-21

Virgin birth, 6, 99-100, 104, 106-14, 116

Widmann, Richard, 17
Wittig, Joseph, 24-25
Wolf, Ernst, 78-80

Word(s): of God, 1, 3, 10, 12n.22, 20, 22, 26-27, 31, 34, 36, 46, 58-59, 73-74, 76, 83-84, 87, 93, 95, 104-7, 112, 125, 134; human, 3, 134, 136. *See also* Lights, doctrine of
World, 8, 41, 72, 121; biblical, 122; come of age (non-religious world), 6, 13, 85, 122-23, 127, 131, 134, 136, 140-43; godless (secular), 91, 123-24, 127, 134-35, 140; of the Old Testament, 89, 92, 99, 143; worldliness, 18, 88, 91-93, 135-36. *See also* Church: and world

Zwingli, Huldrych, 146